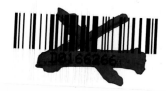

SKYSCRAPER

SKYSCRAPER

Karl Sabbagh

VIKING

VIKING
Published by the Penguin Group
Viking Penguin, a division of Penguin Books USA Inc.,
40 West 23rd Street, New York, New York 10010, U.S.A.
Penguin Books Ltd, 27 Wrights Lane,
London W8 5TZ, England
Penguin Books Australia Ltd, Ringwood,
Victoria, Australia
Penguin Books Canada Ltd, 2801 John Street,
Markham, Ontario, Canada L3R 1B4
Penguin Books (N.Z.) Ltd, 182–190 Wairau Road,
Auckland 10, New Zealand

Penguin Books Ltd, Registered Offices:
Harmondsworth, Middlesex, England

First American Edition
Published in 1990 by Viking Penguin,
a division of Penguin Books USA Inc.

10 9 8 7 6 5 4 3 2 1

The photographs are reproduced by permission of John W. Alexanders, John S. Harcourt, Skidmore, Owings and Merrill, and the author. The line drawings are by the author.

LIBRARY OF CONGRESS CATALOGING IN PUBLICATION DATA
Sabbagh, Karl.
Skyscraper/Karl Sabbagh
p. cm.
ISBN 0-670-83229-4
1. Skyscrapers—Design and construction.   I. Title.
TH846.S23   1990
690—dc20   89-40474

Printed in the United States of America
Set in Primer and Fairfield Medium
Designed by Beth Tondreau Design

ACKNOWLEDGMENTS

The first person to thank for making this book possible is John Ranelagh, who, as Commissioning Editor for Science Programs at Channel 4, U.K., had the temerity to commission a television series about a building that didn't exist, hadn't even been identified, and wouldn't be completed for over three years. Then, when she took over from John Ranelagh at Channel 4, Caroline Thomson was equally enthusiastic about the project.

A major contribution to the content of the series and the book came from Nicola Glücksmann, whose intelligent interviews helped in the task of unraveling the interlocking threads at each stage in

ACKNOWLEDGMENTS

the skyscraper's construction. As someone who claimed not to know the difference between shear and moment at the beginning of the project, she was almost a structural engineer by the end, as well as a real estate agent, an architect, a city planner, and a construction manager.

Then, many thanks are due to all the people who allowed themselves to be subjected to the scrutiny of a television team and a writer over the period of the building's construction. First, of course, Bill Zeckendorf, Jr., whose unwavering support in the face of occasoinal provocation made everybody else's cooperation possible. At the Zeckendorf Company and KG Land, Terry Soderberg, Edith Fisher, and Jack Schuster all gave the project their support and managed to find time in their busy lives to be interviewed and to explain patiently the nature of their jobs.

David Childs, the skyscraper's architect, was extremely helpful and encouraging during the writing of the book, and set the courteous tone for my relationship with Skidmore, Owings and Merrill. Leon Moed, Rob Schubert, Ed Narbutas, Suzanne Smith, Dick Rowe, and Gary Steficek all followed David's lead in providing encouragement, information, plans, and interviews for the series and the book.

At the construction managers, HRH, Artie Nusbaum was enthusiastic about the television series from the beginning and has provided very helpful comments on sections of the manuscript. Also at HRH, Dominic Fonti, who can't have known what he was letting himself in for, still managed, usually with good grace, to provide lengthy and illuminating accounts of the work of a project manager, while at the same time trying to build the skyscraper.

A host of people on the television production team have made the whole project enjoyable. Veronica Young shared the task of interviewing the participants and understanding the complexities of the whole project. Allan Palmer, Andy Cottom, Jane Clegg, Christin Cockerton, and Lucy Willis also played a part in building the television series while others were building the skyscraper. And

ACKNOWLEDGMENTS

thanks are due to my fellow directors at InCA, Chris Haws, David Kennard, André Singer, and William Woollard, who helped create the working conditions for such a complex television series and book to be produced.

At Macmillan, Kate Jones and Kyle Cathie have used their considerable editorial skills to try to make up for the defects in a book that was being written like a Victorian serial, with each chapter being completed in ignorance of what would happen next.

At Viking Penguin, Susan Moldow dealt with unfailing courtesy and tact with the task of persuading someone who writes English English that American readers might benefit by occasional changes in vocabulary, syntax, and style. She also produced great bursts of enthusiasm for the project at just the times when they were needed.

John Alexanders and John Harcourt have photographed many beautiful moments in the life of the skyscraper, and their results help to convey a little of what it was like to be on a floor where the concrete was being laid, or at the top of the building when the last steel was put in place.

Finally, my greatest thanks must go to my wife, Sue, and children, Isabella, Susanna, and Jonathan, who have lived patiently with Worldwide Plaza—the skyscraper, the television series, and the book—for more than three years, when they would rather have lived with me. I hope they will accept the dedication of this book to them.

CONTENTS

CONTENTS

Color illustrations appear between pages 180 and 181.

SKYSCRAPER

PROLOGUE

This book is about visions. It is about the faith that led thousands of people to work toward a goal that, for some of them, would not be realized for three, four, or five years from when they started. Each person working on Worldwide Plaza had a different goal: for a bricklayer, during 1987, to see the gleaming, soft beige-and-rose expanse of crisply laid brick reach up six hundred feet; for a steel fabricator in Houston, to see nineteen thousand tons of steel erected into a soaring stable framework of complex ellipses and sturdy rectangles; and for the developers, to see an investment that would

transform the West Side of New York, and bring profits for decades
to come.

The construction of a skyscraper starts with a hole in the
ground and ends high above the surface. Financing the building
is much the same: the owners start deeply in debt and, they hope,
end up substantially in profit. The main difference is in the depth
of the hole and the time it takes to rise above it. During the month
the first tenants moved into the completed building, the developers
took a major loan that would not be paid back for another twenty
years. In the course of the construction everybody from the architects to the construction workers felt the pressures transmitted from
the top to keep on budget and on schedule, for a month's delay
added a further $2–3 million to the hole in the developers' finances.
This interrelationship of money, time, and work made Worldwide
Plaza such an exciting, sometimes stressful, project to follow.

Many of us work in jobs that contribute in some small way to
a much larger enterprise, but we aren't always clear how we fit in
or how our own working methods compare with others', and not
just people in the same industry. In any job that involves working
with other people there are certain common factors—money, working hours, hierarchies, relationships, communications, risk, anger,
injustice, pleasure, tensions. Most of us could give examples of the
way these factors operate in our *own* jobs, but we rarely see how
they operate in other people's.

Every building is handmade. No one has yet devised a machine
to mass-produce a forty-five-story building and deliver it to the site,
ready assembled. Every element of a skyscraper has passed through
many human hands: even the crane that lifts a ten-ton concrete
slab merely magnifies the manual dexterity of the crane operator.
And you need an awful lot of hands to create a very large building.
Yet the public usually associates with a building not the people
who *make* the buildings but those who design them: the architects—as though the important work finishes when the architect
hands over a sheaf of rather neat if obsessively detailed drawings.

Yet, when you consider the transformation that took place in mid-Manhattan between 1986 and 1989, when an acre and a half of flat ground acquired a fully functioning 770-foot-high office building, the actual act of design—in the sense of specifying the public face of the building—was a comparatively small part of the whole enterprise.

Before every architect closes this book in disgust, let me explain. What a building will look like—flat-topped or pointed, glass or brick, Chrysler or Empire State in New York, Lloyd's or Centre Point in London—is a decision anyone could make. Five-year-old children draw perfectly buildable houses, if you don't mind one window lower than another, a front door with nonparallel sides, and permanently smoking chimneys. Turning a design into reality is a process that dominates the lives of thousands of people for many years and is every bit as interesting as the architect's transforming his brainchild into working drawings: a process that is all around us every day in every city in the world, but is rarely appreciated or understood. Linked to any major construction project are men and women with every type of personality, intellect, and qualification. Scientists and engineers, welders and electricians, artists and writers, salesmen and real-estate brokers, accountants and bankers, canteen managers and dynamite experts, seismologists and calligraphers—all feeling entitled to think of a building as "their" building in the same way as the architect or the principal developer. This possessiveness can be a driving force behind each craftsman and his task. It can lead to the excitement of competition, as the mason, the waterproofer, and the window installer will the steel erector to complete *his* stage in the building to make *their* work possible.

Some people were linked to the Worldwide Plaza project less willingly than those who built it. Local residents saw the project as either a hideous blot on a community with character or the savior of a declining slum; the directors and employees of companies in other areas of New York saw it as part of a major transformation of the West Side. But it would be a mistake to think that construction work began and ended in New York. The roll call of places that contributed to the project stretches from Luxembourg to Brazil, Verona to Tokyo. In North America itself, the building drew on resources from Miami to Quebec—including an Indian reservation near Montreal—and many other communities, each carrying out a task that provided essential components of the building.

When I started my three-year relationship with Worldwide Plaza,* I didn't realize how much time I would spend trying to understand the human factors that operate in a project of such size and complexity. As someone with a strong interest in science and technology, I expected to spend much of my time understanding and then explaining why a fillet weld was better or worse than a full-penetration weld, or why a skyscraper *has* to move several inches in the wind. What I didn't anticipate was how much time I would spend explaining what Arnie Kriegel does every day in his office, or why the brick manufacturer seemed to be playing games with the construction company, or how Artie Nusbaum lost seventy-seven pounds at the hands of a hypnotist and $30 at the hands of poker-playing friends, or how . . . But for the moment it's enough to say that these human factors can be as important as the physical and technological ones. In fact, my abiding impression as the project grew was of the people rather than the building: after a day on site I would remember one particular construction worker or superintendent; after a day at the steel fabrication plant I would recall particularly the plant manager's painstaking attempt to explain his job, something he seemed rarely to have been asked to do.

Of course, the physical facts of the building and the stages in its progress from an acre and a half of rock and rubble to a 770-

* At various stages during its development the project was called "World Wide Center," "World-Wide Center," "World Wide Plaza," and finally, "Worldwide Plaza." "Worldwide Plaza" is really the name for the whole site, but I often use it to identify the office tower, the skyscraper that is the focus of the book.

foot building provide the backbone of this major human enterprise. One thing that made my task easier was that none of these facts is difficult to understand or explain. If you take the back off a television set and peer inside, you're likely to be none the wiser without a degree in electronics. But if you look at the innards of a skyscraper, as any sidewalk superintendent will testify, you have a pretty good idea of how and why it fits together.

Many of the processes are like ordinary domestic engineering writ large. To take one small example: Like me, many people will have built bookshelves that are too long for the weight they must support, resulting in an unsightly, but liveable-with, sag in the shelf, a shallow curved dip. People building skyscrapers have the same problem. They like to use beams that are strong enough to span a large gap but that would have just such a dip in them when supporting their full load. The solution is simple—put a *reverse* sag, called a "camber," in the beam before it goes on site, so that it is curved upward, half an inch or so out of true. Now, the weight of the concrete will push the beam down to become approximately level. Of course, calculations and drawings are needed to calculate the exact camber, but the engineering solution to a construction problem can be as easy to understand as curved bookshelves. I feel that such wrinkles in the art of designing and constructing a build-ing are worth reporting, because they help to make such a huge project comprehensible.

Indeed, if the building of a skyscraper like Worldwide Plaza is made clearer by this book, it will be due partly to sleight of hand, because vast areas of the story have been left out. During the three-year planning, design, and construction period, subplots abounded which deserved a book in themselves. The renewal of the subway station, for example, presented a series of problems only hinted at here. Digging deeper into the Manhattan subsoil as they became more enmeshed in never-ending arguments with city bodies and transit authorities, the skyscraper builders began to wonder whether they would still be working on the station years after the

building was finished. The work involved in designing and installing a window-washing system kept many people busy for a couple
of years, but this is hardly mentioned. The connections to the various city supply systems, such as water, sewage, electricity, and
steam, led to hours of meetings with people who weren't quite sure
where they had last laid their pipes, and this task too has been
portrayed as though it were as simple as connecting a hose to a
garden faucet.

I have concentrated on a few key themes in order to tell a few
memorable stories rather than many confusing ones, so you will
read principally about the steel, the brick, the stone, and the roof
and how their stories unfolded over the years of the project. In
telling these stories, I have from time to time departed from chro-
nology to keep the narratives together, but I have also felt it worthwhile to give an occasional impression of how everything goes on
at once. In the middle of the project, every single part of the final
building is in a different place, being designed or manufactured or
installed, and certain members of the team responsible for building
it had to keep all these parts constantly in mind in case they were
made wrongly, were delivered to the wrong place or on the wrong
day, or were installed in the wrong place or the wrong orientation.

People often asked me, "Why pick this building?" It's simple:
I was looking for a large construction project to follow, and this
one had the right combination of factors, including a developer who
was sufficiently confident to allow me the access I needed to be
sure of understanding how such a project worked. As it has turned
out, in terms of floor space this project is one of the biggest to be
built in Manhattan for some years. The project's size has enabled
me to describe many development and construction processes that
apply wherever buildings are built. In addition, the project has
affected the community around it in ways that raise important questions about the role of development in any modern urban society.

When Jack Schuster, the owner's representative during most
of the design and construction, learned that there was to be a

television series and a book about Worldwide Plaza, he commented: "My mother said there are only two things you can be sure of— you can't bite your own ear and you can't kiss your own behind. But I was sure I'd never be on television or in a book." It's precisely because Jack and the thousands of other people who built the building are so rarely on television or in books that I found them so fascinating.

1
HOW IT
ALL BEGAN

"**L**et's all break ground before we break some bread."

Bill Zeckendorf had planned to say these words as he initiated construction of Worldwide Plaza at a ceremony in New York on November 12, 1986. Rather like Neil Armstrong's famous words about "one small step for a man . . ." they were chosen to draw attention to a moment of great significance. At noon bankers, company directors, construction managers, architects, New York City officials, and community representatives gathered in a parking lot to attend a ceremony organized by Dominic Fonti, an American-Sicilian project manager who for the next two and a half years was to have day-to-day responsibility for the construction of the sky-scraper.

For much of his time Dominic would be dealing with the control of multi-million-dollar contracts, but today's pressing problems were whether the chrome-plated shovels would arrive and whether there would be enough ceremonial hardhats to go around. He was also concerned about how to coordinate raising a banner saying "Worldwide Plaza," using a crane to hold up one end and a backhoe the other. Then there were the trucks. Like many ceremonies, this one was slightly out of touch with reality: while the dignitaries were assembling at one end of the site to listen to the speeches and watch the very first sod being turned, a huge hole was growing at the other end, as bulldozers and backhoes dug into the soil to reveal the walls of the old Madison Square Garden, which had originally stood on the site. Construction schedules could not wait for the social calendars of dignitaries to be synchronized, and the real groundbreaking had begun ten days before. Already, fifty trucks a day were carting the rubble away, and one of Dominic's worries was that those fifty trucks usually arrived, at about noon, through the entrance the guests for the ceremony would use—guests who thought they were to see a pristine site being penetrated for the first time.

But no one seemed to mind. The ceremony provided an opportunity for the dignitaries to catch up with people they rarely had time to see in the bustle of New York real estate and construction, and to bask in the attention of some of the other two hundred invitees. A city official put his arm around a developer; the chief executive of an advertising agency greeted a banker. And a short chubby woman with thick pebble-glass spectacles, Mary Dunn, mingled with the crowd. She lived in a brownstone overlooking the site and felt that she should have been invited. "But no invitation arrived," she said afterward, "so I said, 'I'm going anyway,' and I crashed their lovely champagne luncheon. They seemed very glad to see me and one of them said, 'I'm so glad you got your invitation. I'm glad you could make it.' I didn't say anything. I just smiled."

It was a cold day, but a hazy sun kept breaking through. Overcoats that year seemed to be either camel-colored cashmere or beige gabardine, and small knots of similarly coated men stood around discussing real estate or city politics. One man, wearing a cowboy hat and a loud check jacket, clashed somewhat with the overcoats and pinstripes. Then there were those who were not invited and had to be content to peer through the wire fence as the party preparations got under way. Near the lunch tent, a basketball court had been marked out for the occasion, and the asphalt cut back to reveal some earth. Here the groundbreaking ceremony was to take place, as twelve men with chrome-plated shovels put on their ceremonial hardhats and threw a symbolic shovel-load of earth onto the circle in the center. Zeckendorf announced that the Mayor was delayed but would be there soon, and then introduced Bill Phillips, chairman of Ogilvy and Mather, a future tenant of the skyscraper; a man from Kumagai Gumi, the Japanese equity partner; David Dinkins, then the Manhattan Borough President, and Edith Fisher, who had persuaded the community to accept the project. It was then time to utter the carefully chosen words that would lead into the ceremony itself.

"The Mayor sends his regrets he's not able to get here. He has a press conference downtown. We're all here together; there are refreshments in the big tent over here. If there are any people who would like to say a word, come up and say a word. If not, let's have something to eat. Thank you."

A minor ripple ran through the audience, and a voice from the front row said, "Bill," and murmured in his ear.

"Oh no, I'm sorry, we're here for a groundbreaking. I forgot we have a ceremonial part to this. We'll go over to the side."

So the carefully chosen ceremonial phrase remained unsaid, as the shovel wielders—all the important people on the project, from the architect to Zeckendorf—assembled around the basketball court, threw their loads of dirt, did it once or twice more for the cameras, and then headed for the food tent.

For another hour or so, the guests ate and talked about the transformation that would take place over the next two years. Terry Soderberg, one of Zeckendorf's key associates, an ex-architect who had the important role of securing tenants for the building, was asked whether he was optimistic about the construction schedule. "As we say down south," he said, "God willing the creek don't rise." Bill Phillips was describing how he had always wanted the new headquarters to be within walking distance of Grand Central Station. (Some of his employees were to dispute whether a mile was walkable or not.) And David Dinkins was heard to ask whether he could keep his chrome-plated shovel, engraved "Worldwide Plaza November 12, 1986."

At 2:00 P.M. Dominic heaved a sigh of relief that things had gone as planned—but this was the straightforward part, and he knew it. He and his wife, Elena, had a habit of starting children and buildings at the same time. Their son, Daniel, had been born at the beginning of Dominic's previous construction project, and Elena was now pregnant again. For Dominic and the others whose lives were linked to Worldwide Plaza, the next two and a half years were to engender the same mixture of fury and exhilaration, despair and pride, that parents experience with a growing and increasingly independent child.

Like many aspects of technology today, designing and constructing a large building are carried out in the same way all over the world. A new office building in the center of York, England, may well end up, inside and out, indistinguishable from a building in New York, U.S.A. What is likely to be different, however, is the time scale. If Worldwide Plaza had been built in London, it would have taken two or three times as long. This ability to build tall and fast in New York results from two factors.

First, in a city with a new multi-million-dollar construction project every month, the support structure of subcontractors and suppliers is immediately available as soon as the go-ahead is given. There is a labor force with all the necessary skills, and there are materials.

It has been suggested* that the pyramids of Egypt were built not as tombs but as a make-work program for the thousands of construction workers who built the first one and would have swamped the labor market unless quickly re-employed. The reverse is certainly true: the presence of a large labor force with specific manufacturing or construction skills makes possible a regular series of overlapping major construction projects at short notice and with tight and efficient costings.

The second factor is the need to borrow money for as short a time as possible. Once committed to a project, a developer borrows the money to pay for construction, and cannot repay until the property is leased. In New York this has led to a method of construction called "fast track," in which all the financing, design, and construction activities are condensed to an alarming degree, making life very difficult for the main participants in the project.

With Worldwide Plaza, there were three main groups of players: the developers, a group of financiers headed by Bill Zeckendorf; the architects, Skidmore, Owings and Merrill; and HRH, a company named after its three founders, Hymowitz, Ravitch, and Horowitz, whose job was to manage the construction by supervising and coordinating all the different subcontractors who would actually build the building. Having to adopt the fast-track method made life difficult for all three. This was because the need for speed meant that it was impossible for each participant to avoid making independent decisions that would affect the work of the others.

Activities often took place simultaneously that, in the past, would have happened sequentially. In earlier, more leisurely days,

---

* Kurt Mendelssohn, *The Riddle of the Pyramids*, Thames and Hudson, London, 1974.

skyscraper building would proceed roughly as follows: The financier would raise, or already have, the financing for the building. He would appoint an architect to draw up an initial design for the approval of the developer. The architect would then take each element of the building and break it down into a much more detailed series of drawings, containing the information a contractor would need to decide how to make an individual component. When completed, those drawings would be sent to potential subcontractors— steel manufacturers, brickmakers, window companies, and so on— who would bid for the work, specifying exactly how much they would charge. The owner could then decide among bids, add up

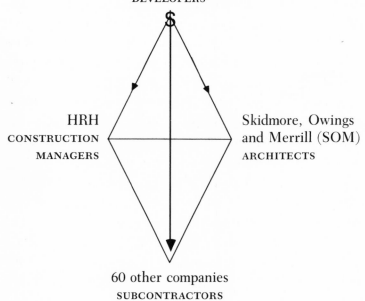

ZCWK
(The Zeckendorf Company,
World Wide Holding Corp., Kumagai Gumi,
Arthur Cohen Realty)
DEVELOPERS

HRH
CONSTRUCTION
MANAGERS

Skidmore, Owings
and Merrill (SOM)
ARCHITECTS

60 other companies
SUBCONTRACTORS

all the prices to ascertain how much the building would cost, and only then start to build it.

On a project the size of Worldwide Plaza the process could take a year or more. During that time the owner would have paid large amounts for the site, including interest costs, and for the legal and architectural work, yet would still be a long way from seeing any return.

The fast-track system can mean that major decisions about the roof, for example, have not been made while the foundations are already being dug and the steel cut to size. It is risky, because construction starts before the owner knows the total cost of the building, and before many of the subcontractors have devised and agreed on the way in which particular tasks will be undertaken. Problems can arise if a subcontractor decides to make minor changes in *his* component of the building—a window, say—and the person making the window openings doesn't receive the information in time. Such disparities can be expensive, but the fast-track method can lead to the building's being completed a year earlier, thus saving the developer interest charges amounting to perhaps $3 million a month, and hastening the start of rental receipts. The architect may have to accept some compromises in quality, owing to the fact that, as the building goes up, more of the developer's budget is spent than was anticipated, leaving less money for the later contracts, which tend to be the interior finishes, or other small details that convey the overall artistic qualities of the building.

To make the best use of his financing, Bill Zeckendorf planned to have his skyscraper built in about two years from groundbreaking. That in itself was a risk and imposed a fast pace on the designers and builders. But there was another risk: the site was not in a traditional area for prestigious and expensive office buildings, which might therefore deter the kind of high-class tenants Zeckendorf would need.

In 1985 the city block between 49th Street and 50th Street
and Eighth and Ninth Avenues was one large parking lot, with a
disused building in the northwest corner. The streets running the
length of the site were mainly residential, with some restaurants,
a nightclub called Better Days, and a row of apartment buildings.
Farther west is the Hudson River, creating the illusion that ocean
liners occasionally sail down the street. The area is called Clinton,
although visitors on forays west of Seventh Avenue could be forgiven for not discovering its name or even recognizing its identity.
Until the 1940s and 1950s the area took its identity from the water-
front, where shipping from around the world moored at the many
active piers. Called Hell's Kitchen until after World War II, the area
was the home of the longshoremen. When the shipping industry
died, the composition of the area changed, but it retained the character of a mixed-income residential neighborhood, a character the
city and the inhabitants felt worth preserving from the encroach-
ments of the type of commercial development taking place to the
east. In the mid-1960s the transformation of the Avenue of the
Americas (Sixth Avenue), only three blocks away, into a succession
of tall set-back monoliths was a warning to the residents of what
Clinton might one day become.

With a population of just over forty thousand, over half of them
white and the rest a mixture of Hispanics, blacks, and Asians, in
the early 1980s Clinton was a neighborhood that could develop in
one of three directions. It might preserve a careful balance of low-
and middle-income residents, together with a range of shops, restaurants, and other amenities to supply their needs; sink back into
the type of activities that gave it its original sobriquet—there were
still plenty of prostitutes and a self-sustaining drug market to help
it on its way; or become another soulless business district, efficient
and frenetic by day and deserted by night.

However careful the attempts to preserve what was good about
Clinton, there would inevitably be some transformation of the large
parking lot, once the site of Madison Square Garden. This had been

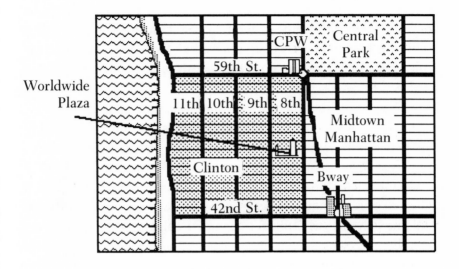

New York City's prime showbiz stadium, the scene of circuses, basketball, ice-skating, and boxing, before it was demolished in 1968. The owners of the site, Gulf and Western, had never quite sorted out what to do with it. Indeed, they had instructed Skidmore, Owings and Merrill to draw up plans for three million square feet of commercial space, twice as much as Worldwide Plaza, but the plans were soundly rejected by the community. It was clear that any straightforward attempt to build the maximum floor area on the site would be doomed to failure. Any successful scheme would require careful attention to the vision that the city and the community had for Clinton.

In 1975 Victor Elmaleh and Frank Stanton, two businessmen who owned a company called World Wide, looked at the site and thought it had potential. As Elmaleh remembers ruefully: "It was the depth of the New York financial crisis and it was virtually impossible to finance any kind of a building project. We had in mind to put in a square block of an indoor amusement park and we had it all designed. I think it would have been a terrific project for that area. The amusing thing about it is that we had an option for the property at a value of about $12 million at the time and just exactly ten years later we bought it for $100 million. Oddly enough, it's more usable now, at $100 million, than it was at that time at twelve."

Meanwhile, to the east, the Massif Central of midtown Manhattan grew taller, with new skyscrapers like Trump Tower, AT&T, and Citicorp. Whatever the financial climate, there still seemed an insatiable desire to build more office space, rentable or not. And the uniqueness of Manhattan as the location for a corporate headquarters seemed to justify yet more pressure for good sites for large buildings. In the early 1980s two major developments were planned for the unexploited airspaces of the West Side. To the north of Clinton was the Columbus Circle site and to the southeast the redevelopment of Times Square, both the subject of grand schemes for tall buildings, but both beset by continual changes of plan as one scheme fell out of favor and another came in. But what would strike anyone looking at a map was the fact that approximately halfway between those two major developments was the largest undeveloped plot of land in mid-Manhattan: the parking lot between Eighth and Ninth Avenues.

David Childs, the eventual architect of Worldwide Plaza, immediately saw the opportunities it presented:

> The first thing that struck me was the extraordinary nature of the site now that it is an empty full block. The original grid plan of the city of New York extends throughout the West Side in very long blocks, two hundred feet in the north-south dimension but eight hundred feet long, so the site is four acres of land, which was vacant. And in a city of the density and activity of Manhattan that is just unheard of. This clean palette to work with gave an extraordinary scale to the project. It was also of interest because the particular location was the center of a pinwheel of different

activities in terms of scale and people and building uses. In addition there was the opportunity to be a very strong presence on [Central Park West], which is the avenue that flanks the west side of Central Park, as Fifth Avenue does on the east, and [which, as Eighth Avenue,] descends through Manhattan.

So it was an extraordinary opportunity to do something new, and to set a tone, a pace for all the development that would happen around it. Here it was at the heart, at the locus of all of those different influences. It was almost a frightening opportunity.

The company that bought the site was called ZCWK Associates, a partnership of several different companies. Elmaleh's and Stanton's World Wide Holding Corporation was back in the picture, being joined by Arthur Cohen Realty and a large Japanese construction company, Kumagai Gumi, which was making major inroads in American development and construction.* But the driving force behind the partnership, and the man who set the pace throughout the project, was William Zeckendorf Jr.

The most puzzling thing about Bill Zeckendorf is that nobody has a bad word to say about him. As a person, that is. Of course, since he wears the badge "developer," to many people he's just the usual embodiment of the evil that one associates with people who buy land in big cities and put up large expensive buildings, displacing the poorer inhabitants in the process. Whether it is intrinsically evil to replace a parking lot with a complex of office and residential accommodations that will change the character of the area is not clear. The truth is probably more complex than that: it's a matter of how rather than whether you do it. But who can blame those living in low-rent apartments, soon to be affected by adjacent high-rent accommodations, and fearing the effects of changes in the neighborhood, for disliking the person they regard

---

* In fact, two linked companies were involved in running the project: ZCWK owned the residential accommodations and the theaters, while a company called NYCCA owned the tower and the plaza. For simplicity ZCWK is used throughout.

as the cause of the changes? Brad Baker, a Clinton resident, summed up the case against all developers:

> All the things that we've enjoyed here, are going to be gone. I have felt powerless to do anything about it. I still think, well, it's like tilting at windmills. What can you do, when the state of New York and the Mayor of New York all want this to go through? They've rolled out the red carpet for these developers, and any amount of squalling and yelling that the community can do is pretty much disregarded, no matter what they say. He's not allowing any of the community to live in the high rise. He's supposed to fix half a subway station, and for this we get a forty-five-story building on the corner of Eighth Avenue, and mid-block we get a thirty-eight-story building farther down. We lose. We get a lot more traffic in the area and we get highly increased rents all the way down the line and restaurants that no one who's been living here can really afford. The people who'll live in these buildings are going to be blocked off from the community. They're living in a little castle with a moat around it. They don't care about what this community was and is. They care about going down to Wall Street and working and they can afford $2,000 a month or whatever. This community was doing fine before Zeckendorf came in, and it's because it is doing fine that he came in. And now we're the victims of a community rape; it's nothing less than that.

Among the people who were to work with Zeckendorf over the time of the project, however, and among those who had worked with him in the past, he was a "good" developer. Here's how Bob Salomon, one of Zeckendorf's employees, sees people like Zeckendorf: "The people that build tall office buildings have great strength, they're gamblers, they have guts. Very few people can take the pressure that they go through when they build the building. Bill is unusual; everything about him is unusual. He's honest, he's decent, he's hardworking. He's a man who can work all day and all night and never stop. Every broker will say to me, 'You work for Bill; you're lucky; we trust him.' There are some developers that are tough, mostly honest; very few, probably, that are a little on the difficult side, but by and large I think that criticism is not founded in New York City. Developers I've known for the most part are honest and decent and hardworking and they have guts, more guts than most people ever thought they could have. But Bill stands out. I don't like to compare him with the others."

In the flesh, Zeckendorf is not a man to warm to immediately. Tall, bulky, somewhat shambling, he talks in clipped, blunt tones, with an occasional note of impatience. There are few conversational gambits in discussions or meetings. His abrupt style seems to represent a deliberate technique for saving time and avoiding confusion. He is said to make decisions very quickly—while the people who are talking to him still feel themselves to be making a case, he has made up his mind and is eager to move on to the next point. When you're halfway through a sentence, he'll interrupt if he's got the message, and you'd better move swiftly on.

Zeckendorf is a familiar name to citizens of many principal North American cities, including Washington, D.C., and Montreal. Zeckendorf's father, also William Zeckendorf, was a leading New York developer throughout the 1940s to the 1960s. In a style more colorful than accurate, Robert Moses, one of the most powerful figures in New York civic life, wrote of Zeckendorf Senior:

> Bill Zeckendorf's grandfather started his commercial career in the wigwams of the Indians in Arizona Territory. Bill is an Indian trader by inheritance, predilection and talent. Since the Dutch bought Manhattan Island from local Indians for $24 and a few beads, there has been no trader in real estate remotely comparable to Bill Zeckendorf. As a showman he makes P. T. Barnum look like a piker. He has sold coal in Newcastle and esquimeau pies at both Poles. His lively imagination, his knowledge of urban growth, steel skyscrapers, assembling, trading and developing

lots and lands, his endless acquaintance with tycoons and great names, are proverbial. Here is a talent not to be buried, but to be controlled. Incidentally, he is a hell of a nice fellow.

While Zeckendorf Senior was building up the fortunes of Webb and Knapp, a firm of real-estate brokers that had offered him a job as a partner, Zeckendorf Junior was learning some lessons from his father. He watched his father put together a series of larger and larger deals, until the company owned assets of $2 million. However, Zeckendorf Senior's personal finances failed to benefit from the same financial acumen. "The check for my son's first term at college was returned with the notation 'insufficient funds,' he later wrote, "and my tailor was waiting payment for my last two suits." But his business judgment seemed sound, and in a major maneuver he assembled various sites on the East Side of Manhattan, buying them under different names, until he owned a large parcel of land on the East River. It was the slaughterhouse district at the time, and apartment houses nearby were built without windows on the river side, so that tenants didn't overlook the ugliness or smell the stench. Zeckendorf Senior had intended to build a housing development on the site but, the story goes, when he discovered that the United Nations was looking for a site and had all but abandoned hope of obtaining one anywhere in Manhattan, he sold it at no profit to John D. Rockefeller Jr., who gave it to the United Nations. Nowadays, says Bill Junior, a twenty-five-foot frontage on the site is worth what the whole site cost Zeckendorf Senior.

By 1960 Webb and Knapp, with Bill Zeckendorf Jr. as a key figure in his father's company, had $500 million worth of construction. They had started the trend toward corporate offices on Park Avenue; they had assembled important sites on the Avenue of the Americas, such as the land where the Time-Life Building now stands. As development ate up more and more cash, the company took out first, second, and third mortgages on existing properties to pay for it. Meanwhile, a series of unrelated changes suddenly produced a glut of new property just as Webb and Knapp projects came on the market. Hoped-for rents never materialized, and a complex financial situation became even more difficult to control. Zeckendorf managed to fend off a series of creditors but one of them, Marine Midland, became more jittery than the others and called in a note for $8.5 million which Webb and Knapp were unable to pay, and so they were made bankrupt in May 1965.

Though Bill Zeckendorf Jr. was not directly involved in the bankruptcy, it must clearly have acted as a warning in the face of his own entrepreneurial ambitions. At thirty-five he was becoming a skilled and versatile developer in his own right but very different in character from his father. Sometime after the company went bankrupt, Zeckendorf Senior declared personal bankruptcy and became a consultant in a company set up by his son-in-law and Bill Junior.

Over the twenty years since his father's bankruptcy, Zeckendorf progressed from managing a series of renovation jobs on existing buildings to become Manhattan's most active real-estate developer. By the mid-1980s he had been senior partner or managing co-partner in twenty projects worth well over a billion dollars. He had become a key player in the New York real-estate game community, which is both tightly knit and secretive. There's a saying in New York, "Never talk real estate in men's rooms or elevators," and Zeckendorf himself would be the first to take advantage if anybody did: "I went up in an elevator with a group that wanted to sell us some fittings on one of the buildings we were building, and one turned to the others and said, 'I haven't seen the site—have you?' They said, 'No, we haven't seen it either.' And so they came up to make their presentation and I said, 'I understand none of you have seen the site.' They were quite surprised to see me, and that was the end of the relationship."

As he walks or drives through Manhattan, you get the feeling that Bill Zeckendorf is eyeing every vacant lot or building for sale, storing them up in his memory and ready to step in once they reach a critical mass that might lead to a large and viable site. He has a voracious appetite for knowledge about what is happening around every corner in New York City. He is like a man looking for pieces of a jigsaw that will fit neatly together, but he doesn't have the lid of the box to show what the final picture will be. An empty site here? But it's too small to do anything with. Check those apartment buildings next door—who owns them? This insurance company may be looking for a safe mortgage. This bank may want to put up some money for a construction loan. That last deal went well— there's some cash that could be used. Zeckendorf describes his own job as "a creative type of work for somebody who basically has little or no artistic talents of his own."

In the case of Worldwide Plaza, there was just one huge piece of land, although included in the purchase were sixty-six units of housing in six buildings near the site, a fact Zeckendorf would make use of later in his dealings with the community. When the land came on the market, a dozen or so serious purchasers put in bids. The two front runners each bid about $70 million for the site and a "gentlemen's auction" led to Zeckendorf and his partners' securing it for $100 million.

The partnership knew that the site was worth $100 million only if they could devise a project that conformed to city zoning regulations and was acceptable to the community. Also, most important of all, they needed to identify at least one major tenant for the building before they were too far into the project, so that banks would lend them the money they needed to start the construction on the best terms.

Within weeks of the partnership's buying the site, they heard that a major advertising agency, Ogilvy and Mather, had already expressed interest in the site when one of the competing purchasers was trying to acquire it. Ogilvy and Mather, known as O&M, was one of the world's largest and most successful advertising agencies, and this was an extraordinarily fortunate piece of news for the partnership. If there really were potential tenants for the space this early on, it would make everybody breathe easily, since financing would be easier to obtain and the whole design and construction process could be carried out much more effectively by involving the people who would actually live in the building. Furthermore, some tough negotiating led to O&M's becoming equity partners in the building so that they shared in its profits as well as leasing space.

Designing the project now became less a matter of what the Zeckendorf partnership thought would lease and more about what one major tenant actually wanted. Although they had sketches and initial ideas, O&M's presence really shaped the design process. O&M were eager to make a substantial contribution to their new corporate headquarters. At a press conference to announce their involvement, Bill Phillips, chairman of O&M Worldwide, declared: "Horace Greeley said 'Go West, young man!' We think four blocks west is just about right."

The pieces of the project were coming together in a remarkably smooth way. With a site that was looking more attractive by the month and a prime tenant, Bill Zeckendorf could begin to feel that the initial risk was justified: "When we put up the first $12 million all we had was a parking lot. We had no project, we had no financing, we had nothing. And that was a real gamble. The lease with Ogilvy made a lot of difference—if we had not been able to sign a pre-lease of the building for the six hundred thousand feet, we might not have ever been able to finance it. We would have found other equity partners, but certainly O&M was extremely helpful, coming in with $100 million of letters of credit. When we did this thing it was very hard to get financial groups to agree that we should build the whole project at once. And to finance a $550 million project on Eighth Avenue and 49th Street was loco, to say the least."

The $550 million Zeckendorf mentioned was the cost of the entire project, including design, construction, and financial fees.

The skyscraper was the largest element on the site, but there were also to be an apartment tower, eight movie houses, town houses, shops, and restaurants. The first key payment was a nonreturnable deposit on the land. This sum, a kind of option on the purchase, allowed time to obtain the approval of the city planning authorities for the development. The initial deposit of $12 million increased to $20 million as the time stretched out. During this initial period ZCWK had to pay the architects and the lawyers who would prepare the case for the development to be allowed to proceed: about $5 million. All this would have been wasted had the project not been approved. Once the project was approved, larger sums would be needed to complete the purchase of the site, pay for the construction of the buildings, and, a significant sum, pay the interest on the money borrowed for those purposes. The "hard" costs of construction (steel, concrete, bricks, labor, etc.) would be about $154 million, and the "soft" costs (site price, architects' fees, engineering, legal, and, most important, the cost of borrowing) would be about the same. (The office tower would cost $380 million out of the $550 million total.) Most of this money would have to be borrowed from banks and other financial institutions, on the strength of future repayments from rents.

"The hope of any developer," said Zeckendorf, "is that when he starts building he has no money of his own in it. In this case, it's not going to work that way. We might not have cash in but we're going to have very substantial guarantees." And those guarantees would be at risk until the project cleared two important hurdles: the approval of the City Planning Commission and of the Clinton community. Both groups would look very closely at the design of the project and at its effect on the neighborhood around it.

2

ARCHITECTS AND ENGINEERS

"**B**ill told me that he had just bought a piece of property with his partners and that he would love to talk to me about it. Although he thought they had already narrowed down their list of architects, they would be glad to have a conversation about it. So I went over to meet with Bill and his partners without any presentation material to see what they had decided and to get caught up to date on what he was doing. Lo and behold, the wonderful story is that he said, 'Well, we'd kind of like to have you do it.'"

The person Bill Zeckendorf "kind of liked to have do" his building was David Childs, a senior partner at Skidmore, Owings and Merrill, a leading firm of American architects.

Skidmore, Owings and Merrill, known universally as SOM, is a sedate company in what can be a flamboyant profession. There is a marked ecclesiastical feel to their office in the Daily News Building on 42nd Street, although it is a "with-it" church with leather pews, chrome-coated pillars, and a Henry Moore sculpture in the chancel. The "bishops" are the senior partners, gliding shirt-sleeved between one another's offices. Like all good modern churches, they have some female bishops; three in the New York office, among a total of eleven partners. There is a feeling that voices are never raised, but that is due mainly to good soundproofing and the muffling hum of the air conditioning. The firm is large: the New York office alone has about four hundred employees, and there are offices in Chicago, Washington, Los Angeles, San Francisco, and London. SOM are involved in many big international projects, including London's Canary Wharf, and display a contemporary ecumenical spirit by building mosques, synagogues, *and* Christian churches, in addition to their daily bread of office buildings, universities, and large municipal projects.

Over the years they have built a distinguished roll call of America's finest buildings, although they don't always make headlines in the same way as Philip Johnson, Helmut Jahn, or I. M. Pei. That's partly because the partners submerge their individual identities and personalities into the corporate structure of the company as a whole. "A building is built by an entire group of people," said Childs, "who come together to create something which not one of them can do on their own. The Gothic cathedrals were similarly designed in that sense. Nobody really knew who was the architect of Chartres: it was the bishop, it was the master sculptor and the stonemason who all came together, and then their names individually were lost but their work, as a collective example of their talent, is still there."

David Childs had worked for the last twelve years in SOM's

office in Washington, where no building is higher than 160 feet. In fact, the project he most enjoyed designing wasn't a building at all, but a space between buildings: the Mall in Washington, including a major park to commemorate the U.S. Bicentennial. His feeling for space was to stand him in good stead with Worldwide Plaza, a site where the maximum permitted floor-area ratio left a lot of space to play with between the buildings.

Childs's move to New York was seen by some in the company as a step up to taller and better things, a chance to stretch his wings on larger projects. His early training was in the sciences and he displays a cool rationality about what can be a rather impulsive profession. He is modest enough not to claim for himself the complete artistic freedom that has led to some of the most noticed skyscrapers of the last thirty years:

"When, in the sixties and seventies, all the rules were discarded, you could do anything you wanted. A great piece of art was painting yourself blue and running naked through the field; there were no rules anymore, no resistance that one could test oneself against; a piece of music was a man walking out to the stage, sitting down, and ripping apart a telephone book. Then you could do whatever you wanted to, and not benefit from the resistance of the pragmatism of structure and wind and water and financiers and tenants—all of those things that create an inner tension and produce a better product."

Childs shows none of the willful "artisms" of some architects. He always wears a tie, is polite and considerate to his guests, and only occasionally lets slip a comment about some minor irritation when things aren't going quite right. His office is a light, sparsely furnished room without a desk. One wall is covered with a Chinese painting of herons against a gilt background; another has burlap-covered boards for pinning up drawings. Daylight filters through perforated screens in front of the windows. Childs is a gentleman and, as you might expect, his approach is essentially collegial and pragmatic. To his colleagues he can sometimes seem unwilling to fight to the death for his artistic vision of a building in the face of other, more practical considerations:

> I believe that architecture is not the drawn elevation or the perspective, it's what's built. And if you're in the business of architecture, you must get your product built or you've done nothing, so one must compromise at certain times. You fight for things that are terribly important. And you virtually always win those things, because if you work for sensitive people they tend to listen—not only for the fact that they have some faith in you but that they're pragmatic. If you say it's important to have this lobby with a gilded ceiling, they'll think it might be important too because it'll enable them to lease the floor that the tenant is going to walk through that lobby to get to.
>
> So one has a certain respect for the other person's opinion, and by prioritizing those things that are critical you usually win the major battle. I also think, though, that a building should reflect an owner. If I had exactly the same program with exactly the same money on exactly the same site, it would be different if I were doing that design for another developer than Bill Zeckendorf. So it is a balancing act, trying to understand not only the desires of the several team members but "What does that building do for the city as a whole and for our society?" and "What do we want it to express in terms of the kind of concerns that we have at this moment?" That all comes together in the tremendously complicated process not only of getting the building built but reflecting the times and the people that are involved in it.

One of Childs's colleagues was Rob Schubert, the project manager for SOM, whose job was to run the regular in-house coordination meetings for Worldwide Plaza. He saw at close quarters the way in which Childs responded to the wishes and needs of the different participants in the project:

David Childs is very ambitious. This was the first major project David did in New York, and a lot of his actions had to do with establishing himself in New York as the design partner in charge. I'm learning how to deal with David—we had a few run-ins at the initial part of the project. Washington clearly dealt with project managers in a different way from New York, and when I went in with an expectation of things that *I* should handle, I found that he wanted much more involvement. I like David a lot and I watch his communication skills with clients and how he fosters their trust and I enjoy it. At first I really didn't like the uncertainty of dealing with him: now that I've gotten to know him better, I think I know what he's after, and what he wants out of me and my job. I think we're settling in, in terms of having a successful relationship.

Most people have some idea of what an architect does, perhaps from their experience of domestic extensions: he or she prepares remarkably neat drawings, using very sharp pencils, that make one's house look like something in *House and Garden*. When it comes to larger projects—fifty-story skyscrapers, for example—the neat drawings are done by computer, and there seem to be millions of them. But there is a stage, right at the beginning, where the client and the architect have that "sharpened-pencil" relationship, as the rolls of yellow paper come out and you feel that the architect, however senior, is back at school doing what he enjoys most: sketching his dreams, or perhaps somebody else's. Childs believes that SOM's best work is done for their most demanding clients, "because then we have a position to fight for in terms of the highest quality of the architecture. We're primarily designers, and although we care that the water stays out and that the building stands up and will last over time, we argue most for the design, for that's the unique point of view that we bring to the table. It's important that the contractor argue equally his concerns, and the owner the financial aspects. In that creative tension between individuals, something is added to the process. I have done buildings in the past when clients did not care, and that's very difficult. Having a client who has a strong point of view is usually an additive process to the design."

Bill Zeckendorf cares about both money *and* good architecture. And, like his father, for whom I. M. Pei had been an in-house architect, he believed that a developer could be a major force in architecture: "I think architects are to a great extent inspired by their clients. And I think it's very possible to take an architect who has not achieved great design up to that point and draw from him something that's much better than he has done in the past. But you have to spend more money on the design."

Whether or not Zeckendorf was thinking of Childs when he said that, during the early design process Childs was willing to pay a lot of attention to what Zeckendorf and his partners actually wanted out of the project. But Childs's openness to their wishes for the appearance of the building was sorely tried during the construction of Worldwide Plaza. It's fine when the owner is a financier—even if he has an amateur interest in architectural design, the architect can believe as a professional that, in the end, he'll win any battle about the appearance of the building. But what happens when one of the business partners is himself an architect, or has trained as one? In the case of Worldwide Plaza, Victor Elmaleh, one of the partners, took a close interest in the appearance of the building right from the beginning. Indeed, he almost spoke like the architect:

> I ought to stress something about the unique problems that this site offered that don't exist elsewhere. There isn't another site where architects had to design a commercial building and a residential complex and make them look like they were designed by one man. They both really have different elements and different criteria. If you designed the office building too much like an office

building and tried to make the rest of the complex look like it, it would have been totally out of kilter. So it was a really unique challenge. We went through many changes but I think the concept was always the same. I think it had to do with the color, particularly, and the choice of materials. It's going to be a very, very unique place.

All Childs's skills at handling personal relationships were to be tested during the coming months, as Elmaleh exerted an influence on the evolving design of the skyscraper. Initially, of course, it was entirely appropriate of Elmaleh and the other partners to let SOM know what they wanted done with the site—what architects call the "program" of the building. At the beginning of the design phase, in early 1985, SOM started sketching ideas for buildings that were entirely different from the final tower. This was because both Ogilvy and Mather and another advertising agency that had expressed interest were being wooed by tailor-made designs drawn up by Childs and his team. Childs described some of their early ideas: "The first program for the office block was enormously different from its eventual design. The two original major tenants needed large floor plates, large single-floor areas which would be side by side. So the first design was much longer into the block and much lower than the current plan. It had the proportions of a very large grand hotel such as the Plaza—very bulky and very low. When Ogilvy and Mather stayed in and the other tenant decided not to proceed, the building immediately lost a great deal of girth and became half its size in its floor plates. It was much more slender and became the tower that it now is."

A skyscraper would obviously be more distinctive than a low bulky design. But it would also be more expensive, as one of the construction managers explained: "The single most important thing that controls the cost of construction is the geometry of the building. 'Short fat' is a helluva lot cheaper than 'tall skinny' for a variety of reasons. 'Short fat' means fewer, slower elevators, fewer staircases, and so on. All the components that make up a building work better in a short fat building."

In the months of thinking about the shape and size of the project, the architects were given a working figure of $91 a square foot for construction: a reasonable but not generous figure. It would allow for a certain amount of architectural indulgence where it mattered, in the most visible parts of the building, but it would leave little leeway if some elements turned out to be more expensive than expected.

The site straddled the boundary between the central Manhattan area of tall buildings to the east and the low-rise housing and shops farther west. Childs started to think about ways of designing a development in which the layout and heights of the buildings would form a transition between the two areas. This meant rejecting designs that were symmetrical or that actually went against the downward flow of building height from east to west.

To decide in detail what would be appropriate for the site, the architects and the developers would have to pay close attention to what are known as "zoning regulations," embodied in a large book of rules, regulations, and resolutions of the city planning authorities. Most large cities have some mechanism for controlling or guiding the activities of developers so that their contributions to the environment fit an overall vision of what the city should be. But the history of New York development shows how haphazard such controls can be if there is *no* such clear vision. Obviously, in a free economy city planners cannot tell anyone what to build—only what *not* to build. When skyscrapers first started rising in downtown Manhattan, there were no controls. A developer who bought a piece of land could build as high as he wanted, and fill as much of his site as he wanted. This resulted in developments such as that at 120 Broadway in Lower Manhattan: the Equitable Building and two or three others built before the zoning regulations have created narrow, dark canyons. From the property line, walls rise sheer to the roof, so that little daylight reaches street level, or indeed the windows of the lower floors. Squeezing the maximum square footage of office space from a site requires building straight up, which is what the early developers did, until the city of New York stopped them with the first zoning resolution, passed in 1916. In fact, the people who had protested were not the local inhabitants—most of this development took place in the business district—but the other building owners, afraid that their lower buildings would lose "light and air." Their campaign for some form of control led to the introduction of zoning: the system by which the city tries to shape the types of buildings in different districts by passing regulations restricting height and floor area, and allowing exceptions, or bonuses, for certain preferred types of development.

The developers of Worldwide Plaza faced a zoning system infinitely more complex than the early regulations. By the 1980s the city had been divided into many different areas, each with its own subtle variations. Sometimes a site was part of two different zones, and a developer ended up with one building in two parts, obeying two different height or area requirements. The old Madison Square

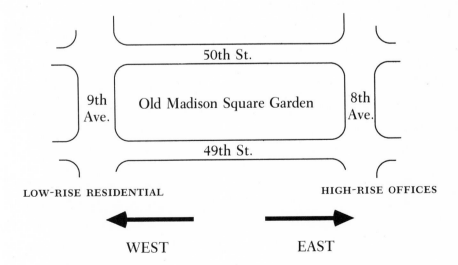

Garden site fell within three zoning areas, each with its own regulations for height and floor area.

The system of bonuses allowed give and take between a developer and the city planners, and the skill of a developer and his staff often lay in the ingenuity with which they could squeeze permission for an extra few square feet of floor space. A key acronym in the developer's vocabulary is FAR—floor-area ratio, the "usable"* floor area of a building expressed as a multiple of the area of the site. The bigger the FAR, the more space available to rent and, usually, the taller the building.

The city sets the FAR for particular districts. This figure, known as "as of right," fixes the amount of floor space a developer

---

* "Usable" is a contract term used by rental agents to define parts of a building deemed usable by the tenants. The figure for "usable" space excluded all floors below ground level and some other areas of the building used for essential equipment, such as cooling towers and elevator motors.

area of site $= 50 \times 50 = 2,500$

floor area of A $= 45 \times 45 + 40 \times 40 = 3,625$
so FAR $= 3,625/2,500 = 1.45$

floor area of B $= 8,000$
so FAR $= 3.2$

floor area of C $= 18,000$
so FAR $= 7.2$

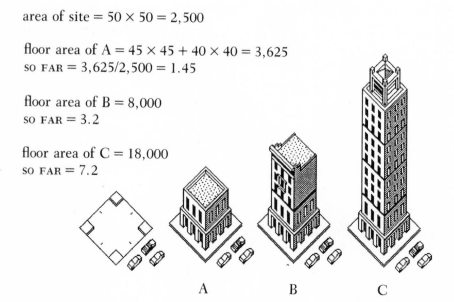

A B C

can build without needing to go through special procedures. The "as-of-right" FAR for the area around the Madison Square Garden site was 8.51. But the site itself straddled several zoning areas and, in a complex variation of the zoning procedure, ended up with an increased FAR of about 10. This meant that special planning permission was not required if the project's total usable floor area was about 1.6 million square feet—ten times the area of the site—provided it conformed with the variations in zoning across the site. However, the Worldwide partners required more floor area, spread about the site in a different way. Rob Schubert was involved in the early discussions:

> In March 1985 we began discussing the density of the project. When the old Madison Square Garden site was planned by Gulf and Western there was a 21 FAR talked about, an absurd amount of space. Bill and his partners came in and said, "Let's do a 14.4 FAR."* We tossed that around both internally and externally, talking to Con Howe in City Planning. Basically, the noise that was coming out was that 14.4 was not going to be favorably reviewed: "Look at a 12."† One of the interesting things about dealing with City Planning is that they will rarely say, "Yes, do this"—they'll always object to something or say, "Why don't you look at this?" or "Why don't you look at that?" They'd never say "I hate that, go do something else."

These discussions took place before any of the detailed design decisions had been made. Before a final design could emerge, the zoning regulations for the area of the site would have to be analyzed, and the developers ascertain how far they could push the city into allowing them as much square footage as possible. In terms of re-

---

* They decided to argue for a basic 12 FAR, plus a 20 percent bonus which they would be awarded if they could show that they would carry out extra work to benefit the community (see p. 38).

† I.e., 10 plus 20 percent bonus.

couping an investment, every extra square foot of usable office space is an additional $20, $30, or even, in the future, $40 a year in rent.

One of the ploys used by the developers and the architects of Worldwide Plaza was to show how the current confused zoning situation would allow them, *as of right*, to build a messy jumble of buildings, each maximizing what was allowed by the different zoning patterns within the site. They produced a drawing showing an office tower stretching a third of the way down the block at the Eighth Avenue end, a parking lot in the middle, and another tall thin residential tower at the Ninth Avenue end. As intended, in the words of one of the participants, it "scared the daylights out of the community" and led to discussions about what could be done with a more unified approach that respected the scale of the community.

Pushing the city to secure the maximum doesn't necessarily involve any undue pressure or illicit dealings. There is a well-tried way of giving developers more than "as of right," in return for services provided to the city. Here the creative impulses of the city planners can flourish, by granting what are called "bonuses," consisting of a greater FAR than "as of right."

Edith Fisher—"Bill once said I was his vice-president in charge of everything"—was Zeckendorf's main weapon in the negotiations with the community to justify the scale and design of the buildings and, in particular, the bonuses. Edith is a tough, energetic businesswoman who lives and breathes New York, and in the early stages of the project she exerted her personality on everyone from Mayor Edward I. Koch on down, in the service of Worldwide Plaza:

> There were actually two bonuses we related to. One was an improvement to the subway. Subways are very complicated animals, really, and very often they're old and they're delicate and they need a lot of "cozying," so to speak. When you're going in and developing a site, it's easy to do that work because you have the access. Once the building is built, there are some things that can never be done again. Therefore, the city of New York provided

that, when there is a subway on a site, if you would go in and make critical improvements to it which have nothing to do with cosmetics, but to the subway station's capacity and circulation, you would be entitled to add to your building. So we produced plans to enlarge the station, to bring in light, ventilation, escalators: better sight lines, safety, security—all those good things. The other bonus that we took advantage of was the plaza. We have close to one acre of open space on the site, which will have lots and lots of trees on it and a place for people on the site and in the neighborhood to use.

These two bonuses could each have given an extra 2 FAR but the partnership decided to ask for a more reasonable bonus of 2 overall, giving a total FAR of 12. The city planners granted this, which allowed up to 1.9 million usable square feet to be built on the site, divided between office and residential space, in buildings with almost 2.5 million square feet overall. But one condition was attached to this agreement. The city insisted on what are called "hostage floors" in the office tower, to ensure that the subway improvements and the plaza were completed properly. Terry Soderberg took a keen interest in these, since they could not be leased out until they were freed: "To make sure that the developer does what he says he's going to do, tenants are not allowed to occupy those floors until we get signed off by the Transit Authority for the subway and City Planning for the plaza. So I have ten floors in the middle part of the building which are held hostage until we can get the TA to sign off on their five floors and City Planning to sign off on their five floors."

One of Childs's colleagues described how their design ideas were dependent on this interplay between the zoning regulations and the size and shape of the site: "One of the major requests we put to the community for changes in the zoning of the site was to move portions of the height and bulk around to what we considered a more appropriate place on the site. This allowed us to maintain the low scale of the Ninth Avenue end and push the mass of the whole project toward Eighth Avenue, toward midtown, so that you'd have a clear diagonal stepping down. . . ."

Once they had settled into this stepped-down layout, the site fell naturally into three components. At the Eighth Avenue end, nearest to the commercial district, there would be an office tower of about forty-five stories. In the middle, separated by one of the bonus-generating plazas, would be a residential tower, just over half the height of the office building. And leading from the office tower to Ninth Avenue would be low-rise housing, reflecting the scale of building heights in the streets and avenues farther west.

To translate this pattern of buildings into the first architectural designs meant making certain decisions about the materials that would be used, both for the exteriors of the buildings and for the framework of the buildings, the structural support system. The first drawings of the office tower were derived from some firm decisions Childs had made about appearance, shape, and materials, but included many details that would be developed and changed during

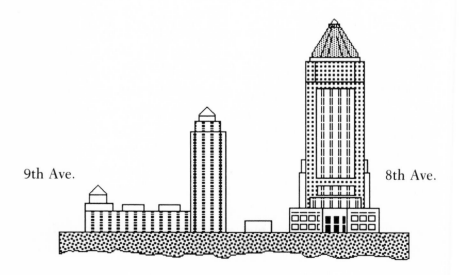

9th Ave.   8th Ave.

1985. The decision-making process about the sizes and shapes of the windows, for example, gives some idea of how many factors must be taken into account before arriving at a final design.

It had been decided that the exterior wall would be masonry—bricks laid layer upon layer all the way up the building. This meant that the structure of the building need not be "expressed," as architects term it. In other words, the outside surface would not necessarily reveal how the framework of the building was constructed. Exteriors made of glass, chrome, and aluminum often hang visibly around a framework of steel or concrete, effectively making the structural elements part of the exterior design. Indeed, in extreme cases, such as the Pompidou Centre in Paris or the Lloyd's Building in London, "expressing the structure" means that the main structural support system and the associated mechanical systems become the principal elements in the appearance of the building. With Worldwide Plaza, where the structure was not expressed, the windows were to be "punched in" to the brick wall, affording much more latitude in terms of size and position. The most important factor in the final window designs was the location of the building's columns.

The early designs had windows spaced every twelve feet, with columns slotting into that pattern at twelve- or twenty-four-foot intervals. This was a perfectly workable design, but an important factor intervened to change it. Even at this early design stage, Ogilvy and Mather had come into the project as equity partner and future tenant. They had appointed their own architect, José Lambert of Lambert Mancini Woods, to design the interior of their office floors. When he considered the twelve-foot window spacings, it became clear that individual office sizes would have to conform to this pattern. Bob McGarry, the O&M manager looking after the project, said: "When we looked at the original plans we realized that the windows, which are very important to people in the advertising business, didn't lend themselves to the square-footage requirements that we wanted. They were spaced at roughly twelve feet, which would have put us in a position in some cases of building people twenty-four-foot offices. José started playing with the plans and came up with a plan for our space that said the ten-foot window module was the ideal situation. We went back to Skidmore, and José found them most cooperative, and they altered the size of the building." With the stroke of a pencil, the window spacing was shortened, the column spacing was changed, and O&M narrowly escaped having to give some of their employees twenty-four-foot offices.

As well as listening to the tenants, SOM discussed their designs with several other important participants. The developers of course had a say, as did HRH, the company that would manage the construction of the whole project. They would have a valuable contribution to make to designing the building in such a way that it could be built as economically as possible.

By mid-1986 the main elements of the skyscraper were decided. There was to be a classical base rising for three floors from Eighth Avenue. Inside would be an elliptical arcade and lobbies on three sides. The main design feature would be a series of granite-clad columns and precast concrete arches, giving an overall pink-and-deep-red cast to the base. The lobbies would have marble walls and floors, with escalators to a mezzanine floor, from where the elevators rose to the other floors. Above the three floors of the base, the shaft of the building, clad in brick, stretched up to a roof in the shape of a copper pyramid, surmounted by a smaller pyramid of glass in aluminum, with a beacon to light it at night. The building would be forty-seven stories and 770 feet high. It was a massive and ambitious concept for Childs, hailing from a city whose tallest building was no larger than just the roof of Worldwide Plaza. In the summer of 1986, before a piece of asphalt had been turned, Childs gave a picture of how his building would look:

> The materials are essentially of masonry—brick. People were surprised when I proposed this, originally thinking that any impor-

tant building must be out of granite. But I pointed out to them that in fact the true New York tradition is also brick. The Chrysler Building, for example, is a masonry building. It's a wonderful material, in which one can get articulation and details in a much simpler way than one can in granite, which is difficult to carve or to turn corners, being usually a thin veneer placed on a precast backing. But the bottom of the building is stone with glass openings and the metalwork holding it. Then there's the simple rise of masonry up through the shaft of the building, changing color from the slightly pink or warm-white color of the basic building up to the top, where there is a much whiter, brighter cornice of masonry. It then changes to what will eventually be a warm green of the copper roof as it tarnishes over the years, and then finally rises to the whiteness of the crystal lamp at the very top.

With a tall tower we tend first to think about the daytime views, but the night lighting of this building is tremendously important as well. There is a tradition in New York of lighting the tops of buildings. This one will also have stripes of light running up the strong vertical bands of the building, giving it a sort of pinstripe character and increasing its sense of elegance and thinness. Finally, at the top, lights will shine on the copper dome and then radiate out horizontally across the city, and at the very top this glow will give a particular identity to this project, to this small city within a city, but also to the edge of midtown Manhattan between 42nd Street and the Park.

His eloquent description makes it sound like a building that any community would be proud to have in its midst. But that couldn't be taken on trust. A series of meetings with the city planning authorities culminated in discussions during the spring and summer of 1986. The Planning Commission expressed worries about the bulk of the tower and about plans for the subway, and so SOM did more work and submitted more drawings. Finally, in May 1986, the City Planning Commission accepted the SOM design. But there was a further hurdle to be overcome: the approval of the community, as represented by various community organizations set up by the city to monitor and comment on development in their own neighborhood.

The planning of New York became increasingly democratized over the last decade as laws were passed to ensure that communities were brought into the consultation process. Under the Uniform Land Use Review Procedure (ULURP) the developer has first to submit his plans to the scrutiny of a group of citizens called a Community Board, made up of "appointed community activists." Ruth Kahn is one of the volunteers who worked for Community Board 4, which looked after the interests of Clinton. After a lifetime in politics she decided to give some of her time to preserving, or at least controlling, the character of her home district, and was the chairman of its fifty-strong membership at the time the Zeckendorf partnership was trying to gain the Board's approval, an essential part of the planning process. She explained the Board's initial reactions to the project:

> Worldwide Plaza was one issue that no one was indifferent to— they were either passionately against it or passionately for it. I think most people were afraid of the secondary impacts of such a large project. Clinton has been besieged and beleaguered for many years with the developmental pressures that have caused the warehousing of apartments, eviction of commercial tenants, the sort of mom-and-pop stores that you don't find anymore in the city. There has been arson, harassment—all the things that precede the major redevelopment of a community. It is the last urban-renewal area in the borough of Manhattan and so it is a target. And everybody is frightened. Both Chelsea and Clinton are ethnically and economically diverse communities and it's nice. It works. It's nice having poor, middle-income, and rich of all ethnic backgrounds, living side by side, and we feel that it's worth preserving.

The Community Board reviews projects and can discuss its views with the developer, who may then make changes in his submission. As a next step, the plans, accompanied by the views of the Community Board, are sent to the City Planning Office, which listens to their advice but is not bound to follow it. The City Planning Department, who are already discussing FAR and zoning issues with the developer, hold hearings into the proposals and then advise another body, the Board of Estimate,* of their opinion. The Board of Estimate—comprising the Mayor and other senior city officials—has sixty days in which to make the final decision whether to allow the development. Rob Schubert observed some of the dialogue between the Clinton Community Board and the ZCWK partnership: "The Clinton Community was an interesting animal. It's a politically volatile community. Basically, the activists who are involved don't agree among themselves."

For Edith Fisher and the rest of the developer's team, these internal political divisions were of some benefit. Points of division may well have been exploited so that the community missed opportunities to score points in the complex and time-consuming wrangles over the final deal. Schubert saw what went on:

> There were times when I would go to these meetings and I would say to myself, "God, if the community just said this, they would be able to get more." In the end it turned out that they got far more than I ever thought they would, and I think that was basically to do with Zeckendorf. I have never encountered a more honorable man. Where other developers would say to somebody who asks for something, "Go screw yourself," he would listen. He would go to meetings and talk to these people in a manner that other developers I don't think would ever do. He's genuinely

---

* The Board of Estimate consisted of the five borough presidents of New York City, each with one vote, and the Mayor, the Comptroller, and the President of the City Council, each with two votes. It has now been abolished in favor of a more democratic method of consultation.

concerned about what he's doing and the effects that his projects have on people. But do I think the community got what is best for it? No, I think this project is too big, but that has nothing to do with Bill Zeckendorf, it has to do with the economics of the United States.

Much of the discussion between ZCWK and the community centered on a plan by which the developer would donate housing for the poor as compensation for the large amount of housing for rich people that the project would provide. ("To mitigate the project's gentrifying effect on Clinton," as the *Clinton News* described it.) The community wanted the equivalent of 20 percent of the apartments in the residential part of Worldwide Plaza to be handed over to them, but Zeckendorf persuaded them to accept off-site housing, in the streets nearby. When Gulf and Western sold the old Madison Square Garden, they "threw in" six buildings in the vicinity; three were burned-out shells, three occupied by tenants. With Zeckendorf's consent, Edith promised the community that the gutted buildings would be renovated and made habitable, and the three inhabited buildings would be upgraded. This would be done without increasing the rent of the apartments.

The apartment buildings were dismal: shuttered and barred; narrow, brown-painted corridors with front doors leading to walk-through apartments, with rooms like the compartments of an open railway carriage; walls, floors, and windows all suffering from structural neglect. With an average income of $8,000 or $9,000 a year, most of the residents paid less than $200 a month in rent. What could be more welcome than the news that these apartments were to be rehabilitated at no increase in rent, and that new ones would be provided for other Clinton residents? Well, that's not how it turned out. There were sticking points: some of the residents were reluctant to believe that, having moved out during the renovation, they would be let back in; the community was concerned about exactly how many apartments there would be, and who would secure the extra apartments. For Ruth Kahn the battle had to be fought on two fronts: Edith and ZCWK, and her own volatile coalition of community groups:

There was great despair in the community, because they didn't seem to be getting anyplace. Edith would offer something and the next thing take it away. Her manipulation of the community seemed to be in the direction of "Either you take what we give you or you will get nothing and we will build anyway." I think that I always knew that Bill Zeckendorf would be very nice to the community, and I thought we might get much more than Edith was willing to offer. I think sometimes you send your advance person in, who acts very tough, and then Bill comes in and says, "Yes, of course we'll give you 20 percent [the numerical equivalent of 20 percent of the new apartments to be built on the site], not the six buildings, which are only 10 percent. Of course we'll consider that. Of course we'll consider smaller-size stores in keeping with Ninth Avenue, rather than the gentrified stores of a Fifth Avenue. Of course!" And this seemed to be the way that they manipulated the community. There has been talk, of course, that he contributed heavily to the local Democratic party, and that is why that whole group became very strong adherents of Edith Fisher and of Zeckendorf. There was a group who was utterly opposed—the Clinton Coalition of Concern. They felt that the very least they should get would be six buildings that they had already been offered *plus* 20 percent, because it was such a gigantic development. Their demand for much more brought the agreement down to 20 percent: the six buildings plus an acquisition of other sites which would come to the 20 percent. One hundred and thirty-two apartments. But this was up and down and up and down, and I finally said to the chair of the committee, "This will not be decided until the night of the Board of Estimate meeting. Then we will have an agreement."

Thursday, July 17, 1986, was an important day for Bill Zeckendorf for two reasons. The city of New York was to decide between a number of companies who had applied to build on the site of the South Ferry Plaza, the Staten Island ferry terminal on the southern tip of Manhattan. Zeckendorf's group was hoping to build a new ferry terminal topped by a sixty-story skyscraper. On the same day, the Board of Estimate was to meet to make its decision about World-wide Plaza. ZCWK had invested $25 million in the project and, if the decision went against it, that money could be entirely lost. The Community Board and some other Clinton residents would be quite happy to see Zeckendorf lose his $25 million if they didn't get what they wanted. Unfortunately, they weren't entirely in agreement over what they *did* want.

In the afternoon Ruth Kahn received a call from Edith Fisher: "I said to Edith: 'I want a letter from Bill Zeckendorf that he will adhere to the agreements that we have made on the housing and on one or two other issues before I go into that meeting.' She said, 'OK.' The meeting started at seven. We rewrote our resolution to include the negotiated agreement, which was basically 20 percent off-site housing, which was a better deal than 20 percent of a major building, because tax abatement on an apartment in the building would only last for ten years, whereas, if you renovate old buildings, you have *permanent* housing for the poor and middle class, which for me was the most important item."

The Board of Estimate itself contributed a new element to the confusion. Edith was there: "The issue that came up that was totally unanticipated was the following: that it was decreed that there was a policy that the awarding of this very precious housing in the city of New York had to be done on the basis of a city-wide lottery." For the Community Board this was a bombshell. In their negoti-ations for the best deal with the developers, they had always as-sumed that the apartments would go to native Clintonians. Now they were told that homeless people from all over New York could be entitled to one of the apartments. Ruth Kahn was as surprised as everyone else:

> That stopped everybody dead cold in their tracks. There were little pockets all over, negotiating and trying to work this out with the various voting members of the Board of Estimate. But city policy, as it was perceived, prevailed at that given moment. The Mayor made his announcement that he wouldn't vote for it unless all these apartments were given away by a city-wide lottery. We begged him. We said, "At least give a weight to Clinton." He said, "No, city-wide." "At least give weight to Manhattan." "No, city-wide." It was almost as though this great victory had been taken away from us. But it did have one positive result. It was the first time that all the warring parties in Clinton, the developer and the Borough President and the Community Board, were united totally against the irrational demand of the Mayor.

To the *Clinton News*, Kahn described this decision as "the shafting of Clinton."

Edith Fisher analyzed the Mayor's demand: "This was an issue that had merit on all sides. Some areas of the city don't get development and I think that there was a sense that the people in these areas will never have an opportunity to get a different type of apartment. By the same token, I think the people who are affected deserve something in response to the changes in their own neighborhood. I think that what prevailed was actually something that was inherited from federal regulations which was then the policy in this city."

Early in the the morning of July 18 the Board of Estimate indicated its approval of the development, along with the city-wide allocation of new apartments. For the time being, the ZCWK partnership, and Edith, could heave a sigh of relief. However much the approval of Worldwide Plaza was a foregone conclusion, there had always been the small possibility of an unpleasant surprise.

The following day the *New York Post* printed a story mistakenly illustrated by a picture of Bill Zeckendorf's father, with the headline "ZECKENDORF'S $884M DAY." At the same time as Worldwide Plaza received the final go-ahead, the city had chosen Zeckendorf to be the developer of South Ferry Plaza; the two projects totaled $884 million. But the first priority was Worldwide Plaza. Now that their first $25 million was no longer at risk, the partners would have to start spending real money on the detailed design and construction of the building.

Two SOM partners held joint responsibility for the Worldwide skyscraper. David Childs was the *design* partner, who decided on the shape, color and materials, the lobby, and so on, while his colleague Leon Moed was the *management* partner, charged with devising the best system for nursing the project through from the earliest ideas of how to use the site to the day SOM took their last fee and signed off. Once the project was past the preliminary-sketch stage and seemed likely to happen, Childs and Moed assembled the in-house team that would generate the huge amount of drawings and other paperwork containing instructions that would determine every single detail of the entire building.

In any large building project three main teams address the three major tasks of design, structural engineering, and mechanical engineering. The mechanical engineering was organized by a company called Cosentini Associates, whose founder, Marvin Mass, summed up the different tasks in anatomical terms:

> If you take the architect, you can say that he designs what the skin looks like, what the face looks like, what the hair looks like, the cosmetic portion. Then there's the structural engineer. He designs the bones of the body, how to keep all these things together. Then along comes what I consider the most important part, which nobody wants to know about, which is the heart and

the pumps and the valves and the veins which make the body tick. We design the mechanical systems and the electrical systems and the elevator systems and the lighting systems and the plumbing systems: all the things that are very mundane that nobody wants to know about, but without them the building can't function. As a matter of fact, that's one of my biggest problems. I think we're the unsung heroes of the industry.

Frequently a firm of architects creates only the design—the appearance—in-house, relying on outside structural engineers and mechanical engineers as consultants. SOM have in-house structural engineers, a practice that improves day-to-day communication but is not without its drawbacks, as Rob Schubert found: "Structural engineers in the New York office are a pretty new phenomenon—we used to just go out and hire consultants. If I hired a consultant and he screwed up I could call him up and scream at him. Now I've got people who are our own employees who I don't have the same clout with." Clearly someone with Schubert's management style could still scream at in-house consultants, but there was one major difference: if told to get something done, an in-house engineer would do it by hiring more staff and spending more money—out of a budget for which Schubert was responsible.

Schubert had no illusions about human fallibility. In his mid-thirties, he had already acquired a knowledge of management psychology that was to stand him in good stead as he observed and tried to control the actions of the people around him. Tall and moon-faced, Schubert had a jaunty cheerfulness for much of the time, but would indulge himself occasionally in a trenchant, and profane, summary of a colleague's character or of a particular suggestion as "horseshit." Although not the most senior member of the team in the SOM hierarchy, Schubert set the tone of the weekly meetings, by a matter-of-fact appreciation of all the details of the project and a usually correct judgment of what could be done in any developing situation. This project was Schubert's biggest so far, and he was to make the most of his opportunities. For the quieter members of his team, he could be a great source of comfort and inspiration. Every team needs someone to express what the group is thinking in an articulate and forceful way. Occasions arise when there is no time for niceties, and Schubert was usually to the fore at such times. But unlike the motivation of some of the other characters on this project who imposed their will by force of personality, his motives never seemed suspect. He just wanted to get the building built, and was infuriated by things or people that stood in the way. He was also very organized about meetings and schedules and agendas, a part of the job that bored some other members of the team, including Jim Bodnar, the senior designer.

Bodnar had worked with David Childs in Washington for the previous twelve years and had come to New York with him. He was proud of his close working relationship with Childs, and whenever design issues came up in the day-to-day running of the project, Bodnar would deal with them first, and decide whether they were important enough to involve Childs. There was a coolness about his personality—some saw it as arrogance—but he was well liked by the senior members of the firm, even if his colleagues sometimes found him standoffish. Bodnar was an associate partner in the firm, a step nearer than many of his colleagues to the coveted partnership status of Childs, Moed, and others. In August 1986 Schubert was *not* an associate partner, and he was impatient for the same promotion:

> For what I do, my services are undervalued, in terms of my standing within the firm and my compensation. I have a lot of friends who are no more or less intelligent than I am, who chose a slightly different profession and make a helluva lot more money. I'm being used; we're all used; I'm a user; I use the people on this team to the best advantage to get the best product. There are people in the project, in this organization, who are using me to the best of my advantage, and I've got a certain amount of

resentment for that. When's the next promotion? It damn well better happen next year—if it doesn't I'm going. I said that last year, though. . . .

Whatever Schubert's feelings about Bodnar, and there was some resentment of his status, their working relationship was usually perfectly manageable. But Bodnar sometimes gave the impression of using his closeness to Childs as a shield against the rest of the team: "Often with David conversations don't have to end, or even sentences, and I understand where his interests are and what he wants done, and how he wants it done. And I think that part of the reason I was brought here to work on this job was that the efficiency, reliability, trust, expectations made his job easier."

A third member of the team was Gary Steficek, one of SOM's in-house structural engineers. He was lanky with a dark complexion and brown eyes that stared unblinkingly across the table at meetings, suggesting either quiet puzzlement or a total absence of thought. Usually it was neither—he simply didn't speak unless it was absolutely necessary. Steficek was one of the quietest members of the team, but had one of the most important responsibilities. He and a more senior engineer, Dick Rowe, had the task of devising the steel skeleton for the tower, on which everything else hung, and of following the intricate plans for the steel, nineteen thousand tons of it, through the convoluted process of milling and fabricating and assembling. Although some tall buildings can be constructed of reinforced concrete, the usual method, particularly in New York, is to design a steel framework, as Rowe explained: "A composite building of steel plus concrete is extremely difficult to achieve in New York City. It's done very easily in other parts of the world, but it's extremely difficult to do here. The two trades—steel and concrete—have very different working requirements and so they don't want to work in close proximity to each other. So you either have to do the steel first and then the concrete or the other way around. It may be an extremely efficient structure, but an extremely efficient

structure that is extremely difficult and time-consuming and complicated to build doesn't lend itself to the overall construction of a
project."

It may seem fussy for a concrete worker not to want to work
in close proximity to a steelworker, but "close proximity" usually
means underneath, and however careful a steel erector is, bolts,
wrenches, and even whole pieces of steel have been known to fall
accidentally from the steel floors onto the workers below. It's simply
another constraint on the final design and engineering of a building
that has less to do with architecture and more to do with human
psychology.

A fourth architect made up the inner circle of the team—Ed
Narbutas, the technical coordinator, or "job captain," as he would
be called in some companies. And Narbutas certainly had a lot to
coordinate. While Bodnar and his team design and refine the drawings for the lobby or the main office floors, mechanical engineers
will be planning complex systems of piping and cables, elevator
shafts and ductwork, and the structural engineers will be making
sure that their steel skeleton can hold the lobby walls or provide
openings for the ducts and the pipes. Thin, wiry, with streaks of
premature gray in his hair, Narbutas was the quiet humorist of the
team, whose jokes could be so subtle that they passed unnoticed
in the hubbub of a hectic meeting. One of his tasks in the design
and planning of this building was to coordinate the three main
teams—designers, structural engineers, and mechanical engineers—so that they all built the same building. With the myriad
small changes that take place in the evolution of the drawings for
a building, it is easy for a tiny shift in the position of a beam to
impinge on the layout of the granite or the pathway of a steam pipe.
It was Narbutas's responsibility to see that everybody knew about
such a shift and was aware of its impact. He also had the unenviable
task of dealing with the many city authorities whose approval is
needed before certain tasks can be carried out. He explained: "New
York has probably more codes and regulations to follow than any

other locale in North America. Whether that's good or bad I'm not quite sure, but because there have been places in other municipalities where they have terrible fires with loss of life and so forth, they have tried to avoid that. With the amount of construction going on in this city, and how few very serious fatal accidents on highrise commercial construction there have been, it reflects the strength of the code that we have to follow."

Narbutas also had to translate the design architects' elegant concepts into practical instructions to the men and women who would actually build each detail of the building: "The designers have an ideal image of what they want the building to be. I take it and put a little dose of reality into it."

At its most elementary, the role of Narbutas and his team could be to take a corner as shown on a drawing—two lines meeting at an angle—and decide on the best way of making that corner. And it's not as simple as it might seem: "When the designers design a corner—in pre-cast concrete, say—they think, 'This *looks* nice.' I think of it as a corner that will be chipped when it's pulled out of the form, shipped to the site or after it's erected, during construction. If it's low to the ground I worry about it once the building's finished. A famous example is I. M. Pei's museum down in Washington, where they have a very sharp corner and everybody comes up and touches it and it's wearing it away." While he talks, Narbutas sketches the different ways you can build a corner. To the designer, they will all look like the corner he drew. But for Narbutas, the best corner is the one whose components suffer the least damage during manufacture, transit, erection on the site, or the day-to-day life of the building. A corner made of two pieces having sharp points that can be knocked off is not as functional as one of the other designs shown on page 56.

Backing up the efforts of Schubert, Bodnar, Steficek, and Narbutas was the unsung heroine of the Worldwide Plaza design process, Suzanne Smith. Suzanne looked after the drawings, most of them computer-generated, and knew at exactly what stage everything was—on days when everyone else was running around like headless chickens. Like Steficek, she sat through meeting after meeting, answering questions when they were put to her, but not imposing her quiet personality. Suzanne's job involved a single-minded devotion to the SOM computer and its design system, one of the most sophisticated in the business. In the early months of the project her job was to translate the hand drawings into computer drawings that could be refined and changed, and serve as the database for the whole project.

This group of architects met officially every week; and unofficially, in twos and threes, every day. Their lives were complicated by the fact that each was working on other projects at the same time. Narbutas was looking after a massive project to expand Dulles Airport near Washington. Schubert was supervising a number of large construction projects in and around New York, and the others also had tasks on other buildings that meant that during the design of Worldwide Plaza they were all being pulled in a number of directions.

On Worldwide Plaza the team faced design tasks beyond the construction of the building. Because Zeckendorf had acquired a bonus for rebuilding the subway, they had to integrate the base of the building with a new subway station they had designed. And this meant a tempestuous relationship with the city authorities, in particular the Transit Authority—the TA—who runs the New York

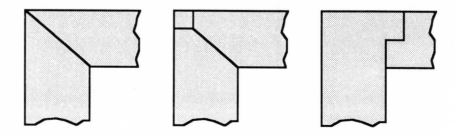

subways. "The Transit Authority is their own worst enemy," Schubert said, trying to convey the full horror of dealing with them. "The Transit Authority meetings are a sight to behold. It's astounding that anything ever gets built. Going to a TA meeting is like going to a Fellini movie. You'll get twelve people in a room, and it's never less than twelve, none of them agree with each other, they're each a separate department. I was talking with the owner's rep, and he said, and I think quite rightly, 'Get rid of 40 percent of these people and the subways would run better.' "

Schubert ran the regular team meetings, usually once a week. From the beginning of the project, when the team members were meeting on their own, or with colleagues of their own age and background, there was an easy camaraderie, with the tone being set by Schubert: "For the four of us, Jim, Gary, Ed, and myself, this is our first project as true adults, our first mature project. We're all approximately thirty-five years old, and we're not as jaded as somebody who's done it six or seven times. Also there's an underlying affection for each other."

Often Leon Moed came into the meetings, sitting back from the table for much of the time but leaning in occasionally to interject some obvious but devasting observation that the others seemed to have missed. Often, in fact, the observation was as obvious as it seemed, and such interventions seemed more like Moed's necessary display of authority than a major contribution to the discussion. But given Moed's mantle of ascribed authority, Schubert found him difficult to ignore:

> I admire Leon a great deal. He just scared the daylights out of me when I was on the technical floor, because he used to come out and basically do terrorist raids. He would scare the living daylights out of everybody, and they'd sort of run for cover, and I didn't know who this guy was. I eventually learned not to fear him so much. Leon has a lot of bravado but he's also got a very

good intuitive sense of what can get screwed up. I've found that on this project he has a very great degree of trust in me, and if I tell him something is wrong that's fine.

The project was announced in September 1985, at a press conference with models and realistic colored renderings—architectural illustrations giving a perspective view of the project against its city background. Such renderings always show pleasant sunny weather, and slim and elegant people walking in corners of tree-lined plazas.

In New York architectural circles there are two or three critics whose reactions are important to any new building. Paul Goldberger, architectural critic for the *New York Times*, is one. He has written the definitive popular work on the history of the skyscraper and takes a great interest in new additions to New York's skyline. Goldberger's favor is quite difficult to earn. He is frequently contemptuous of new buildings, however distinguished the architect. It must have been quite a relief to David Childs, when he opened his *New York Times* on Tuesday, November 26, 1985, to read:

> It looks . . . like a set of . . . buildings that have been designed by an architect who has walked the streets of New York, understands the architectural language with which the city of New York was put together, and endeavored to speak that language himself. . . .
>
> Like the best architecture in Manhattan, it is not directly imitative of the architecture of the past, but it is consistent with it in spirit; it combines a certain zest with a strong sense of classical order. . . .
>
> This stands at least a chance of being one of the few big projects that heals wounds in this cityscape instead of deepening them.

Having Goldberger on his side was a good start for Childs, but there were already other opinions. Even some people in SOM had reservations. Rob Schubert actually said as much: "I try not to comment too much on the design. My job is to get this project built. But I think that the building is going to be forever dated as being a brand-new old building. I think that the design is physically a bit too large, the scale of it, it's a big building and you can't hide it. But there's a texture and there's a use of material that is, I think, sympathetic to what a building romantically is. It's got a base and a middle and a top with a scale and a quality and a texture that I think is very good."

Whatever the range of opinions about the appearance of the building, by 1986 the die had been cast. A workable and distinctive design had been arrived at and agreed upon by the main partici-pants in the project. Now there was the task of turning those neat and elegant renderings into a construction with the floor area of the Empire State Building and with an uncountable number of components, each of which would first have to be specified in its own accurate, dimensioned drawing.

3

STANDING UP

I n 1984 a book written by Robert Byrne told the story of a New York skyscraper blown over by a high wind. It was a seven-hundred-foot building, topped with a yellow metallic pyramid, built on the old Madison Square Garden site by a man whose name began with Z. As a result of some shady dealings, the building included a lot of substandard concrete. One night, in the type of storm that rarely but occasionally hits New York, the lateral pressure on the building overcame the resistance of the foundations and the building toppled over in the midtown direction, taking with it the owner—a Mr. Zalian—who had become a homicidal maniac in the closing stages of the collapse. Byrne's book is fiction, a novel with a weirdly prophetic quality to it, and it embodies everybody's fear, or at least curiosity, about the stability of skyscrapers: a curiosity fed by the occasional sensation many of us have experienced when visiting a high building, as the top floors move a foot or two from side to side.

Stability is of prime importance in a large building but not actually very difficult to achieve—one way might be to anchor the building to the ground, fixed in some way to the underlying foundations. But in fact it doesn't need to be fixed at all; the sheer weight of all the components—steel, masonry, concrete—can be enough to keep it firmly in position, provided the foundations are strong enough to support the weight. New York has little trouble supporting the weight of its skyscrapers, since the island of Manhattan consists of large areas of extremely solid bedrock, called "Manhattan schist."

One of the first tasks for the architects of Worldwide Plaza was to determine the geological makeup of the site. Rob Schubert explained this exploratory work done by SOM:

There were various approaches—one was to try and find the plans for the old Madison Square Garden. Based on those drawings we determined that the rock was somewhere around seventeen feet down on average for approximately five hundred feet, or two-thirds of the way down the site toward Ninth Avenue. Then we had to work out how deep we could actually go at various points, before we started digging rock. Rock excavation is obviously very expensive. The Zeckendorf Company retained a company to do borings and to drill test holes in the site, in a regular pattern to determine exactly where we thought rock was. In addition, some investigation was done by examining old records to see whether there was any archaeological significance in the site. Was there an old Indian camp here, for example? Based on some of the old records, we saw there used to be a stream bed running about midway through the site, and it was determined that since it fell within the footprints of the old Madison Square Garden it was probably obliterated when the Garden was excavated so it didn't pose any archaeological significance.

It was fortunate for ZCWK that there were no archaeological remains. Had there been, the developers would have been required by law to delay excavation work long enough for archaeologists to excavate the site and extract the most useful information before it was obliterated by the building.

So, beneath the site of the office tower, there was rock at seventeen feet. To make basements, truck loading bays, and car parking, they planned to excavate to a depth of thirty feet—nine or ten meters. At the lowest level, they would pour concrete foundations and install steel baseplates to support the bases of the columns that made up the steel framework. Gary Steficek and Dick Rowe had the job of designing that framework so that at every point it would support the weight of everything in the building, as well as the weight of all the steel above it. But they had another requirement: to make sure that this was done safely with the minimum amount of steel. Every unnecessary pound of steel meant several unnecessary dollars added to the cost.

Steel made skyscrapers possible. Before the steel skeleton, tall buildings were made of stone. You can of course pile stones as high as you like, as the Egyptians demonstrated with the pyramids, rising to nearly 150 meters (480 feet). But if you want something other than a large monument—something that is hollow, for example— stone is useful only to a certain point. In Chicago there's a building that still stands as a demonstration of how far you can go with stone in building a habitable structure. The Monadnock Building is a highlight of an architectural tour of Chicago, a city with many more impressive buildings but none as central to the historical development of the skyscraper as the Monadnock, a sixteen-story office building built in 1891. The walls are made of brick, and a key

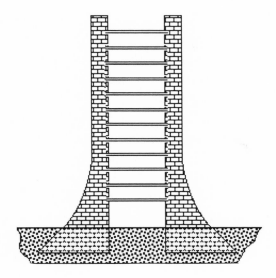

feature of its traditional method of construction is that the lower levels of masonry support the weight of the upper stories.

The walls are load-bearing, just as in any much smaller stone or brick house. However, strong as stone or brick may seem, there are limits to the weight it can support. A foot-square block, say, might support a total weight of three hundred thousand pounds on its upper surface before cracking or being crushed. To support more weight, the block must be wider. A tall building with a great deal of weight higher up must therefore have very wide blocks at the bottom—in other words, very thick walls. The Monadnock Building demonstrates this clearly: its ground-floor walls are six feet thick and the windows are set back in dark recesses. As the building rises, the width of the walls decreases, because they do not have to support so much weight above them, and eventually the rooms on the higher floors receive a decent amount of light from walls of an acceptable thickness. Looking at the Monadnock makes it clear that to build much higher than sixteen floors with masonry would result in ground-level walls of an impossible thickness.

The first attempts at a new method for building tall buildings used cast iron as a framework. Indeed, there were notable cast-iron buildings in Britain and continental Europe two hundred years ago, principally warehouses or factories. But cast iron had severe limitations. It could bear a strong load under compression but was brittle if stretched. So, though suitable for vertical supports—because the load of the building above would push down along the length of the column—it was of little use for horizontal beams, where a load from above could bend or snap the beam.

Cast iron is hard and brittle due to the presence of various impurities, including carbon, resulting from the process of producing metallic iron from the crude ore dug out of the ground. In converting iron into steel, the important discovery was that carefully burning off the impurities, including *some* of the carbon, resulted in a metal that was still largely iron but vastly superior in structural properties. The key factor was the amount of carbon left in the iron: too much and it would be as brittle as cast iron; too little produced a soft, weak material. It transpired that if 0.75 percent of the material was carbon, it would have the correct properties needed to make a versatile skeleton for buildings. As Lewis Mumford has pointed out,* "the gap between stone and steel-and-glass was as great as that in the evolutionary order between the crustaceans and the vertebrates." Lowly creatures like crabs, relying entirely on their surface covering to provide support, evolved far less than creatures with backbones and lightweight, rigid interior members, such as giraffes, just as the pyramid and the four-story house gave way to the skyscraper.

Steel is strong under compression *and* tension, so that it can be used for a linked framework of horizontal and vertical members that encloses a volume the size of a building without any of the problems that stone produces. If steel is stretched with a force of

---

* Lewis Mumford, *The Brown Decades*, Dover Publishers Inc., Mineola, N.Y., 1955.

about 22,000 pounds per square inch it will resume its shape after the tension is released; at about 36,000 pounds it will stretch and not return to its original shape; and at 45,000–60,000 pounds per square inch it will break. Under compression it will usually support a load of 30,000 pounds per square inch quite easily—fifteen times as strong as stone. Even at the bottom of a very tall steel structure the width of column needed to support the weight above is measurable in inches rather than feet.

But the weight of the building isn't the only force the steel must support. Quite strong forces are exerted on the side of a tall building. These lateral pressures come from the wind that swirls around any building, and the higher the building the more significant they become. At the top of Worldwide Plaza they would be about fifty pounds per square foot and such a force, applied to the whole area of wall, will tend to swivel the tower, using the lowest point as a pivot. Like a ruler held at one end, the top floors will move to the side under the pressure of the wind until the rigidity of the building stops it from moving any farther, and then it swings back.

The city of New York has codes of practice that specify the maximum wind force a building should be able to withstand. Expressed in pounds per square foot, the code ensures that a building can stand up to a wind of a strength likely to occur only once in a hundred years in New York without suffering major damage.

There are various ways of designing a steel framework to stand up to the vertical and lateral forces. The first principle is that somehow or other all the forces that impinge on the building at any point must be transmitted from that point down to the ground, where the building is anchored, or where it has enough strength to resist the sum of all the forces. And forces can be transmitted only by the solid elements of the building: the walls, columns, and beams. They can't be transmitted through the air, for example. The engineer must ensure that every force on the building, wherever

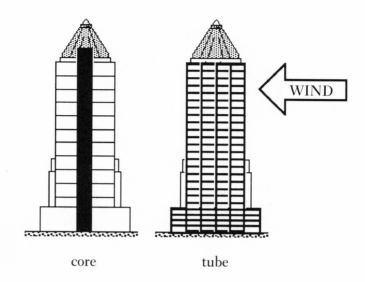

core   tube

it arrives, can find its way down to the ground along the interconnecting network of solid members, each strong enough to resist
and pass on that force.

One possible structure is to build a strong core all the way up
the center of the building, like the mast of a ship, and "hang" all
the floors from the core. The outside walls would then be quite
light, and would receive the wind forces and transfer them to the
central core, built to bear the total forces on the building. Another
way is to make the building into a steel tube that receives the forces
as they arrive at the walls and transmits them along the steel beams
and columns down into the foundations. For an office building this
can be a better solution than the central core, because it leaves a
bigger area of each floor as rentable space.

Worldwide Plaza has a little of both. A tubular structure for
the outside framework keeps the top of the building stiff, and a
braced core gives the necessary stability at the bottom.

Buildings are stiffened for various reasons other than avoiding
their collapse. There is the question of comfort: people working on

the top floors of skyscrapers might suffer bouts of motion sickness on windy days, which could affect the rentability of the space. The current comfort standards for movement of all buildings are derived from a series of tests carried out on people standing in suspended rooms. In addition to human discomfort, there's the problem of potential disintegration of the skin of the building if too much wind movement leads to windows falling out or masonry cracking. Finally, the elevators: in a tall shaft an elevator could well scrape against the side as it descended, or even become stuck as the building leaned over. For all these reasons, engineers prefer to design a reasonably stiff building. In fact, the best design is a compromise between stiffness and materials costs. A building *can* be made not to move at all, but it means spending a lot more than necessary on steel or concrete.

Unfortunately, it's not that easy to predict the effects of particular wind forces on a building. Even if the average wind speeds in an area of the city are known, the actual effect of that wind on a particular part of the building depends on several different factors. First, the wind blowing down the canyon of a New York avenue and bouncing off various buildings on the way may have a very different effect from a wind of the same speed blowing on the side of an isolated building in the middle of a flat field. Second, the building itself may have particular design features, such as grooves, curves, or setbacks, that turn an otherwise steady wind into vortices or gusts of a much higher force. This can happen at every level, from skirt-raising eddies on the pavements around the building to window-cracking jolts on the top floor.

Mathematical calculation will provide general answers about the stability or stiffness of a building, but for a more detailed picture of how a building will behave in a high wind, a model must be tested in a wind tunnel.

Wind-tunnel testing is a technique that reproduces quite accurately the effect of New York winds on the building. There are two wind tunnels within a hundred or so miles of each other in

Ontario, Canada, where many of the largest skyscrapers from around the world are tested. Early in 1986 an accurate 1:500 scale model of the Worldwide Plaza tower was placed in a wind tunnel at the University of Western Ontario. The model was surrounded by a wooden replica of the streets around the old Madison Square Garden site, to generate the turbulence the surroundings would be likely to create in the area of the skyscraper. At one end of the tunnel a huge fan, about eight feet in diameter, created a wind that could be varied to match the wind speed stipulated in the city of New York's code. Just as the model is scaled down, so is the wind speed: someone standing in the tunnel while the model is being tested feels a pleasant breeze rather than the hundred-mile-an-hour gale it represents.

The wind-tunnel engineer, Nick Isumov, actually built two models of the Worldwide Plaza tower. One was a simple wooden structure carved in the shape of the building. This rested on a pivot incorporating a strain gauge, so that as the wind speed increased the engineers could measure the degree to which the building leaned over or twisted, and the forces that would be exerted at the foundations. These early tests revealed some accelerations across the diagonal of the top of the tower that seemed to imply an unexpected snag in the design. Because the building was perfectly square, there was a cumulative effect as the wind arrived at two adjacent sides of the building. Almost like a pendulum or a seesaw, the building's movement would increase progressively in a high wind, because the pressure on one side of the building would reinforce the movement caused by pressure on the other.

Since the problem was due to the symmetry of the building, and in particular the symmetry of the stiffness that was built into each side, the solution was to make one side stiffer than the other. This meant changing the plans for the steel skeleton so that the size, strength, and connections of the steel columns were made different on one side, to break up the self-reinforcing response to wind. For the SOM engineers, there was nothing surprising about

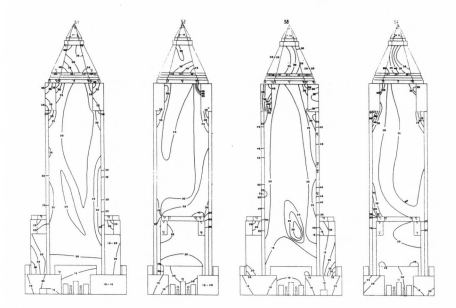

making such major changes in their design on the basis of a simple wooden model two feet high placed in the path of a fan. Wind-tunnel predictions have been remarkably accurate over the years, and any skyscraper engineer would be foolish to ignore a warning about his building.

The second model Isumov tested was far more complex. It still reproduced the shape of the skyscraper but was carved out of per-spex and incorporated in its surface more than a hundred tiny brass nozzles, each attached to a thin plastic tube. These tubes were fed from the bottom of the model to a battery of pressure detectors, each registering the wind pressure at one of the nozzles. During the test, each pressure detector fed its reading into a computer, which then built up a contour picture of pressures over the surface of the building.

Each contour line connects the points on the surface of the building where the wind pressure is equal. Drawings like these are produced for each wind speed, and they show how a steady wind arriving at the building can produce a very variable range of pressures on the surface. The engineers look out carefully for any unusually high pressures around corners or parapets, in case they would be strong enough to shake stones or bricks loose or break windows. Worldwide Plaza turned out to be quite a stiff building as skyscrapers go. Its combined core/tube design meant that it would move about fourteen inches at the top in a high wind, compared with some that can move two or three feet.

While ZCWK were sorting out the financing, and SOM were beginning the process of designing the building and perfecting its structure, HRH, the construction management company, began to play its part. Buildings, even skyscrapers, don't *need* construction managers. Some projects have a general contractor—one company that actually builds the building—receiving a construction budget from the developer and hiring subcontractors as necessary to do the specialized jobs. This can lead to higher costs for the owner, since the company will build whatever the architect designs and have no interest in suggesting possible cheaper ways of doing things. A construction manager, on the other hand, passes on the fees from the owner to the subcontractor but receives no share of them. So the company has no financial interest in keeping the budget high, and if it wants to please the owner it will look for savings. As part of its service, therefore, HRH was expected to contribute its expertise and experience at the design stage and suggest ways of doing things more cheaply if it saw the opportunity. In fact, in the earliest stages of the project, before the building was approved, HRH received nothing; the work it did then would be included in the fee for actual construction.

HRH had no financial involvement in the project other than its fee, and to complete the project at or under budget would enhance only its reputation. The converse was also true: if the project were to lose money and run over budget, HRH would be blamed for poor management and cost control. This could jeopardize future work from the same developer or from the others in New York, since word spreads quickly in the industry. In fact, as the World-wide project progressed, the relationship between Zeckendorf and HRH was severely tested, although at the beginning of the design phase, in 1985 and 1986, all was sweetness and light.

The tone of the relationship in those early months was set by Arthur Nusbaum, known to most of his colleagues as Artie, a vice president of HRH. Artie is one of the most experienced construction managers in New York, and that probably means in America as well. Alternately profane and charming, sometimes both at the same time, Artie has been in construction since 1946—even longer if you define construction more loosely: "I'm probably the only person you've ever met who wanted to do what he's doing since he was seven years old. Several times they brought my mother to kinder-garten because I was stealing all the blocks from the other kids, and they would find all the blocks piled up on my side of the room. So I think I've wanted to do what I'm doing since I was a little kid."

One of the things Artie most enjoyed about construction man-agement was being an important member of the small group that discussed how the building was to be designed: "The excitement comes in the planning of a job from its very birth. And what con-struction management does that is different from general contract-ing is that we get a chance to work with the architects from almost the first moment. I don't want to say that we affect the architecture, which we try our best not to; we just help them build this archi-tecture for a more reasonable amount of money and in a more easily built way."

David Childs usually ended up finding Artie's contributions helpful, where another architect might have seen them as an in-terference in his artistic freedom:

> My relationship with HRH and Artie Nusbaum is that same kind of creative tension that you have with the owner. Their opinion is most valuable on how things can be built. We do a drawing and they say, "That poor man up there in the air cannot build

that within the budget that we have." And we suggest some other alternatives, and they will cost those. So they have a design input as well—they won't just say, "No, that's too expensive." Artie has been part of meetings throughout the design process, saying, "Not only is that not possible in our budget but here are three ways I've done it before and I think this is the best way to do it." And I will gasp with horror and say that that'll be the worst thing for the design of the building, and we will have a dialogue back and forth until finally the right solution, both from his and my point of view, will emerge. And we've never failed yet to come to a conclusion that I feel is aesthetically well chosen and he feels is buildable and the developer feels that he can afford.

If you design something that requires a man to lie on his back seven hundred feet in the air and do an overhead weld, that is more expensive than just taking a prefabricated piece and putting it in place. So those decisions are consciously a whole part of that design process, from the very first sketches. It's easy to make wonderful scribbles on a piece of paper, it's simple to do in a warm room, but when you think about the winds and the cold in the upper regions of a skyscraper during the construction—even in the spring, when where it can snow up on top and it's warm down the bottom—you have to think about how those people are actually going to move around and construct it.

In the summer of 1986 Artie weighed 279 pounds. One year later, when Worldwide Plaza was rising out of its hole, Artie weighed seventy-seven pounds less: "We have about five guys in the office on these liquid diets, and I know very well that when they finish them they'll put all the weight right back on again. So I wouldn't bother with anything like that. But I've been to a hypnotist and I'm very lucky. I'm a good subject, which is not true of everyone—either you are or you aren't. He programs you to eat half a meal, so I have three other people living on the food I leave on the plate." In spite of his diminishing bulk, Artie still weighed enough to make an impression on everyone.

Striding the high floors of one of his buildings, Artie looks
everywhere, searching for signs of shoddy work or delayed schedules, stopping to pat someone on the back or bawl him out. Over
the years these walkabouts have led to a stream of inventions that
now pepper construction sites all over the city. Some can be held
in the hand, like the patent, easy-to-use standpipe seal to speed up
access to water in an emergency. Another is a type of safety net
that in 1986 was made mandatory on all construction sites. Artie
has masterminded the construction of many Manhattan buildings,
most notably Philip Johnson's At&T building and the Citicorp building with its distinctive wedge-shaped top. With any big project
nowadays, a construction management company like HRH is
brought in at a very early stage, even before the final design is
fixed, to make preliminary estimates of cost. With Worldwide Plaza
there were probably only two or three construction management
companies to choose from, and Bill Zeckendorf chose HRH.

As the leading participants assembled for this project, it was
difficult to escape the impression that securing a major contract in
New York was a mixture of inertia and friendship. Inertia operates
to carry someone from a project for one particular developer to his
next project; friendship is the sort that grows up in an industry
where at a senior level only half a dozen people are serious contenders for the big contracts. Marvin Mass, the mechanical-
engineering consultant for Worldwide Plaza, organized a regular
poker game with various friends of his who were senior figures in
the construction industry:

> The game has been going on for about ten years now. It includes
> a lot of friends of mine in the industry, contractors, architects—
> my accountant shows up once in a while, probably to make sure
> I don't lose too much money—and we play a very friendly game
> of poker. It's so friendly that Artie Nusbaum, who's really not a
> great poker player, but he loves to play, he loves to kibbitz, he
> loves the food—if Artie can't show up he sends you a check for

$30, for what he would have lost. It's really a fun type of thing. It's amazing: we see each other socially every two months at this poker game and during the day we're fighting with each other. People say New York is a tough city, but we really have a community of very, very close family members, even though we live different lives. And that's the way we've built in New York over the years.

As 1986 unfolded, a series of meetings refined the design of the building and also made it more buildable; at the same time the other pieces of the jigsaw puzzle began to fall into place. ULURP hearings were successful; most community opposition had been dissipated; the city departments and Transit Authority were being dragged toward consent; a major tenant was on board; the initial financing had been raised successfully; and, at the Board of Estimate hearing, the unthinkable had *not* happened and the project had cleared its last hurdle. While Artie was batting back and forth between HRH and SOM, other HRH staff were starting to put out for bidding the drawings that were being produced by Ed Narbutas and his architectural team, so that an accurate price could be calculated for the whole project.

Artie and his colleagues had already come up with some early estimates of how much the building might cost, although these were based on what seemed fairly flimsy information, as Artie explained: "If you build enough you are able to put together the cost of a building without ever having seen any architect's designs. I never see a full set of plans. I only work with sketches and preliminary drawings. My superintendents and project managers deal with the final set of drawings. I think now I'd get confused if you gave me a big roll of drawings on a building."

But that kind of "seat-of-the-pants" judgment needs firm calculations as soon as possible to confirm that the figures were correct. The HRH bids office would send out detailed drawings of each of the elements of the building to those contractors most likely to want to do the job. Arnold Kriegel, thin and perpetually cheerful, was in charge of the process. He has a healthy lack of respect for drawings he receives from the architects to start the bidding process: "The architect is a designer, basically, and his training is a visual, sculptural concept. However, they do have to draw detailed drawings that depict the pieces and parts so we can determine what they are looking for and try to build it. There's an old joke that the architect will take his drawing and stand up on his stool and see how gray it became by the number of lines he drew. He'll stand up there and say, 'Well, looks like this drawing's complete.' " Kriegel also finds that architects are rather attached to shadows in their drawings, and this produces problems when it comes to pricing:

A piece of sculpture or a piece of architecture is really nothing but an object in space that needs light to depict its facets. What would a diamond be without its facets? What would a piece of architecture be without deep recesses so that when the sun strikes it there'll be dramatic shadows and a visual attractiveness? Unfortunately, Worldwide Plaza has got recesses, and recesses are much more expensive. We've demonstrated to the owner that he could save a lot of dollars if he didn't have these little corners or facets. But he has made a financial decision that he can afford the facets. "I like it," he says. "I can sell my building. I can have more clients come in. I can rent more apartments."

There were six hundred drawings of Worldwide Plaza and, on February 13, 1987, at the height of the bidding-and-pricing process, Kriegel seemed to have all of them in his office at the HRH headquarters on Third Avenue. His job was to identify the tasks to be done and find the right subcontractor to do them. Some fifty different types of work needed to be done to complete the building. SOM circulated the following list:

Structural steel

Excavation and foundations

Superstructure concrete

Masonry

Heating, ventilation and air
conditioning (HVAC)

Lighting fixtures

Material handling
equipment

Fire protection

Copper panel system

Precast concrete

BMS security

Roofing and waterproofing

Miscellaneous metal

Foundation waterproofing

Roll up doors

Louvers

Hollow metal

Reinforced fiberglass

Drywall and carpentry

Spray fireproofing

Painting

Toilet partitions

Sitework and planting

Vertical transportation

Metal deck

Windows and glass

Plumbing

Testing and inspection

Apex curtain wall

Electrical and FMS

Exterior and lobby stone

Stairs

Hoist

Elevator entrances

Scaffolding

Storefront and entrys [sic]

Convector enclosures

Window washing equipment

Lath and plaster

Hardware

Elevator cabs

Ceramic tile

Acoustical ceilings

Toilet accessories

Graphics

Each of these tasks would be carried out by a different company. Most were outside New York, some in other countries. Many of those companies would in turn buy materials and services from yet other companies, placing Worldwide Plaza at the center of an expanding web of interconnecting companies, some very large, others very small. And the information and the paperwork and the salesmen and the accountants would all arrive in Kriegel's office. Here's how he describes his job:

To obtain prices from each of those subcontractors, I solicit proposals from anywhere from five to ten. I review each of the proposals, I go over the drawings with each of the subcontractors, determining if they have a complete scope. To "determine the scope" means: "Do they have all the things that are necessary to build the building the architect wants? Do they understand how they are going to build the building? Do they understand what our problems will be in the building and the coordination of it?" That's basically what I call the scope of the work. As an example, just recently I received two proposals for some piping that's going out on the street. The difference in cost, just from the proposal, was 50 percent. In speaking to them, one of the subcontractors, obviously the lower one, didn't have all the pieces and parts in his estimate. Now he claims he didn't see it. All the drawings flow through this office. Every piece and part that goes into the building is put into the structure by individual trade contractors. We, as construction managers, manage each of those subcontractors to ensure that they get their materials there on time, they put their materials in in a workmanlike manner, and in a sequence that allows ongoing work to continue without interruption.

On the same day that Kriegel was trying to keep his head above a sea of drawings and bidding documents, Rob Schubert over at SOM was a little unhappy with HRH and with him. He suspected that all sorts of decisions were being made without reference to the architects, because Kriegel thought it wasn't necessary or because he couldn't find time to do the necessary paperwork: "Arnie's got a hell of a lot in his head and I'm worried about the flow of information. There's—what—six hundred documents in this project? Plus the contract specifications on top of it. I'm a little concerned about the lack of information about what HRH was doing. Arnie, having more experience than either Ed [Narbutas] or I, makes certain assumptions based on that experience, and I haven't been through that yet."

During the six months following groundbreaking, much had to be done to establish effective working relationships between the team members in each of the three companies, SOM, ZCWK, and HRH. In a high-pay, high-stress environment like the construction business, there are a number of egos battling for their own way. And, as often happens with clever people jostling for supremacy, part of the cleverness was never letting people know what you *really* think or feel. This approach can have two opposing effects: it produces people who fume inwardly but appear outwardly calm, or, as with Jack Schuster, ZCWK's project manager and representative at all the job meetings, the type who bites everyone's head off and then betrays his soft center with a joke directed against himself.

Schuster described himself as a "surrogate" for the owner in all matters relating to construction. It was his job to think "What would Bill Zeckendorf say or do in this situation?" so far as the effect on his budget or schedule was concerned. He was intimately involved with many of the most contentious issues in the three years of design and construction. He is outspoken, witty, occasionally vulgar, and when he smiles his whole face lights up. But you can also tell when he's angry or depressed, which he had reason to be on many occasions.

Schuster had a background in engineering, essential for the detailed understanding of the project that he would need for working his way through the labyrinth of decisions, events, and items of expenditure he would have to approve. He joined the project in the spring of 1986, when much of the design work was under way at SOM and some of the major budget figures had been determined—or, rather, estimated—by HRH. And Jack wasn't entirely in agreement with what he saw:

> When I saw the budget I thought it was a crazy-low budget. And remember, a job of this size, we have 1.6 million square feet of space, roughly, round figures. Construction very often is analyzed

on the basis of so much a square foot. For every dollar more than the budget, you're talking about $1.6 million. If you've made a mistake or if you have given a low budget that is $10 less than cost, you're talking about $16 million above the budget. That's a very sizable piece of change.

This wasn't entirely unexpected. In the early stages of a project there's a lot of game-playing that can lead to underestimating the budget. When a construction manager helps to estimate the cost, he can sense what total figure would be too much for the owner. Since both owner and construction manager want the project to happen, a certain amount of wishful thinking and finger-crossing helps them to arrive at pleasing rather than entirely realistic estimates. The owner needs good figures to show the financial institutions he is approaching for construction money, and the construction managers are tempted to provide him with those figures and with a schedule that looks good. Schuster has seen these pressures operate often in the past:

> The combination of a low budget and a short period of construction as submitted by all construction managers is very good news to the developer. He takes that joyously down to the bank and they very happily loan on it and then the project starts. Now, because the budget is usually prepared on a preliminary set of drawings, when the project is approved and the budget has been fixed and it's gone up to the bank, the architect and the engineer start really putting the hard pencil to it. That's when the cheese gets a little binding. That's when the extras start coming in and the developer finds out what the cost of that project really is. Most developers are sophisticated enough to know that they were being kidded up front, but "To what extent?" is the question.

The forum in which Schuster found out what some of these costs really were was the job meeting, where representatives of SOM, HRH, and the owner met every couple of weeks to consider current progress on the whole project, including the areas on the rest of the site, away from the skyscraper. Three main headings covered the skyscraper construction—Subway, Mechanical/Electrical, and Architectural—and a meeting rarely passed without some unpleasant surprise: a cost overrun, a subcontractor behind schedule, an overlooked design feature. It was in the face of such unpleasant surprises that Schuster earned the money Zeckendorf was paying him by his forceful flair in handling the situation.

Artie Nusbaum is an experienced Schuster-watcher:

> He watches what we do. He comments. He's a counterpuncher. He doesn't have to originate. He doesn't have to develop the plans. He does have input—I'm not trying to diminish what he does—but the basic responsibility is that we helped develop the plans, we go out and get the subcontractors. He approves what subcontractors we go to. We sit down together and review which subcontractors we would prefer on the job. Because Jack has worked around New York a lot, he has his own opinions. I worked with Jack fifteen, seventeen years ago. I'm older than he is. I say that because he sometimes says to me, "You have to do it, Artie, I'm the older," and I say, "No, Jack, I'm older, by about a week."
>
> Of course he's tough. What kind of business are we in? We're all tough and we're all pussycats. You can't be tough all the time. You couldn't live with each other. So you're tough sometimes, but most of the time you don't walk around with a gun in your holster ready to pull it and shoot people. You've got to do a day's work.

As with most people, there is always an element of doubt about whether a particular Schuster tirade is a sign of real anger. His true bursts of toughness are reserved for those explosive occasions when numbers come up with several more zeros than expected. Everyone knows then that to all intents and purposes it's just Jack treating Mr. Zeckendorf's money as if it were his own:

I don't think I would be successful if I said, "Well, it's his money and he's got a lot more than me and therefore he's going to spend it." We're talking about hundreds of millions of dollars. We're talking about every project. We're talking about subcontracts that run into—the small ones—six-figure numbers, and the larger ones that run into seven-figure numbers, and the really bigger ones, eight-figure numbers. You make a mistake, or you're overly generous, and it would not take very long for your budget to be a piece of paper with no value. So to do your job, and earn your pay, you really have to be pressing all the time. And the only way to do that is to do a job as though it really is your own money.

For most of 1985 and 1986 it might have appeared that building a skyscraper consisted of a lot of people taking turns to meet in one another's offices to plan what pieces of paper to draw or write next. Down Third Avenue tramped Artie and Kriegel for meetings at SOM; up Third Avenue tramped Schubert, Narbutas, and the others for meetings at HRH; down Madison Avenue strolled or drove Zeckendorf and colleagues in search of financing and tenants; across to Park Avenue tramped everyone for meetings at the Zeckendorf Company. The key players were settling into the pattern of relationships that was to determine the success or failure of Worldwide Plaza as a piece of architecture, a well-engineered structure, an effective office building, and a money-making enterprise.

Meanwhile, at the parking lot between Eighth and Ninth Avenues, office workers parked their cars during the daytime, and theatergoers and diners-out in the evening. Only when the backhoes started scraping away at the asphalt did the team turn their attention away from the meetings and toward the site, where Dominic Fonti, having organized a reasonably successful groundbreaking party, now had to bring the same organizational skills to bear on building the Worldwide Plaza.

4

GOING DOWN

In the summer of 1986 Dominic Fonti was working for HRH on a site on the East Side of Manhattan, when he was told by Artie Nusbaum that he would be HRH's project manager on Worldwide Plaza. He was excited at the news:

> It's one of the biggest projects in the city of New York, so there's all kinds of experiences that you are faced with. I'm going to be with it for the next two and a half years and I'm quite happy to see it through to the finish, whatever the problems. After it's all gone, you forget all the aggravation, you forget all the problems.

You just look up in the sky and say, "Wow, that's a beautiful building." That's the reward. You feel that great sense of satisfaction, and that makes everything else go away.

Fonti is a voluble man, with a fetching smile which disappears for days on end when the pressure is on. Usually rather dapper, with permanently polished Italian shoes. Fonti was always to be seen either at the telephone or with a line of people waiting to see him in or outside his office. Only at the end of the day, as construction workers signed off and subcontractors and developers and architects were no longer in their offices, did he have some time to himself, poring over the table-sized schedule or murmuring memos into his tape recorder. With a salary rumored to be hovering around six figures, Fonti was embarking on the biggest project of his career.

As the man on the spot, he was responsible for the smooth running of everything that happened on the site. He was in charge of the long-term planning of the intricately balanced schedule of construction activities, each of which seemed to depend on all the others; he looked after all the HRH management expenses in running the project—the salaries of all the people he had to help him monitor and supervise the construction, known as "General Conditions"; he organized and attended the job meetings that had started at SOM and moved close to the site once construction was under way; he had to decide when—and how much—to pay the subcontractors on the basis of work they had completed.

In mid-1986 Artie had no doubt that he was picking the right man for this apparently superhuman job:

I've known Dominic about seven years. I don't know many weaknesses. In my opinion, Dominic will be a major executive some day. In my opinion, this will be the last job he builds in the field. He'll be going in the office, and I hope this book doesn't come out in a hurry, so that I don't have problems with him. His problems? He's maybe too quick to kill, but I think that goes away with age, meaning more patience and more reasonableness. When you're younger, there's an automatic desire, when somebody gets in your way, to kill. I mean, those are the attributes we look for, and the people who get ahead have them. But at some point it has to be tempered a little bit, and we'll see if, as the years go by, they get tempered down to more reasonableness instead of just kill, kill, kill.

Just across the street from the site, near the corner of 50th Street and Eighth Avenue, is the Seeda II Thai restaurant. As excavation began, Fonti moved himself and half a dozen colleagues into the two floors above the restaurant and set up his site office. With a view of the site from his window and Tiger beer and Thai food downstairs, he was ready to give his all to ensure that the building was built in accordance with the plans and elevations that festooned every spare surface in the shabby offices. Fonti liked the look of the building, although he didn't see "liking it" as a requirement of the job:

Our major responsibilities are not really to design the building or to critique the building. We are hired to build the building. Obviously we all form opinions of the building, and if we don't like it, well, we'll tell the architect, "It's an ugly building." And he'll say, "Well, you have your opinion, I have mine." In any case, there really isn't much that we could do once the building is set. The building, at least from what I've been able to see in the drawings, in models, and in photographs of models, is very nice. The masonry gives it a nice warm feeling; it's not glass and aluminum, which gives a cold, sterile feeling. It blends in very well with the surrounding architecture, and yet it gives it a nice lively look. The ground floor, the entrance lobby, the rotunda that will be created, is, in my mind, going to be spectacular.

This building is going to attract a lot of people to the West

Side, where people wouldn't come. You have the theater district and Times Square only three or four blocks away, and yet it seems a world away when you're here. It's a fifty-story office tower, where you will have thousands of people working. It will improve this neighborhood a thousandfold.

As Fonti settled into his closet-sized office, the first major subcontractor, Delma, was at work just outside his window, gouging deep into the rubble left behind by the demolition of Madison Square Garden. They would soon lay the bedrock bare, ready for the dynamiters to come in and blast it away to a depth of thirty feet.

Mary Dunn was the superintendent of one of the unappetizing brownstones overlooking the site. She had taken part in some of the numerous community discussions with Edith Fisher, but was entirely unconvinced of any real benefit to her or Clinton. What's more, she was to be one of the closest witnesses to the daily activities on the site, whose southern border was about ten yards from her living-room window—a room entirely dominated by greenery of every description, perhaps to compensate for the drab surroundings. In late 1986 Mary Dunn peered out of her window through the leaves and watched the backhoes scraping away the topsoil revealing the tops of the cellar walls of the old Madison Square Garden, like some submerged city coming to light as the waters recede. What she saw would be the marble lobby of Ogilvy and Mather in two years. At least, that was the intention.

It was a trying time for Mary Dunn. Of the many irritations she had to suffer, none was more disruptive than the blasting of the rock, carried out under Delma's supervision. One of Delma's blasting engineers, Vito, expressed feelings for the rock that were decidedly more favorable than Mary Dunn's: "It's good rock. We used that term, 'good rock,' because, you know, it's nice to blast, it breaks up nice. It's seamy, but not that seamy that you're going to get big rocks when you blast. At the same time it mustn't be too soft, so that the site will hold up. You've got a sidewalk that you've gotta worry about."

Vito and his colleagues had the task of removing enough of the earth and rock to provide a flat horizontal surface that would support at least forty tons per square foot, and sixty if possible. This surface would be the bottom of a rectangular hole 800 feet long by 200 feet wide by 30 feet deep—4.8 million cubic feet in volume— and they would produce it with a mixture of scraping (the dirt), exploding (the rock), and prizing (the various bits of the old Madision Square Garden). To support the steel columns forming the framework of the tower, the construction team would build a series of reinforced platforms, the footings, one for the base of each column. Each footing is made up of a foot-thick steel plate, called a "billet," resting on a solid concrete block poured into a pocket in the rock.

By digging or blasting to the edge of the hole, the excavators would create four vertical sides needing to be shored up. They would also have to take care not to damage or displace the network of sewer, steam, water, and gas pipes, electrical conduits, and other miscellaneous city services that lurked somewhere beneath the surface—where, it wasn't always easy to find. Day after day, Fonti telephoned around New York from his trailer or the site office, trying to decipher the palimpsest that is Manhattan, with the help of people in various city authorities who appeared to know—and to care—less than he did: "In the city of New York, if you open up the street, it's like a bowl of spaghetti. There's a lot of cable, a lot of conduit, a lot of pipe. There's so many that, if you called the specific agency that put the pipe down there forty or fifty years ago, first of all they say, 'That's not mine.' They don't even know if it's theirs. Second of all, if it *is* theirs, by the time they check and find out it'll be at least another two or three weeks." He burst out laughing in a way that suggested the whole business was more amusing than important. But the laugh was deceptive:

I'm laughing now because I have to laugh to keep my sanity—
but it's frustrating. The Water Department has so many other
projects it has to deal with, why is ours more important than
everybody else's? That's OK. Their attitude's OK if that's the way
they want to do it, but they don't realize that this is one of the
biggest projects in the city of New York. All it takes is an hour
to look at the drawings and say, "Yes, this location of the water
pipe is correct. Proceed with it."

Fonti's task was complicated by the fact that, when the city
agencies did get around to looking at the situation, they would
sometimes see the opportunity to get something for the city at the
owner's expense: a new sewer pipe, for example. When HRH
planned to work around the existing pipe, the sewage authorities
asked them to replace the pipe. Fonti asked plaintively: "Why do
they want it replaced? I'm not going to disturb the sewer. I'm going
to be working around it. But the authorities say, 'It's our policy
that, if you work around the sewer and damage it, five years from
now we may have a leak because of the vibrations, and how are
we going to fix it?' The threat is there—it's a good concern—but
what we have said is, if we damage it, we're going to repair it, but
don't force us to replace it now, at an astronomical cost, when
there's no reason for it." But such promises didn't wash. As Fonti
said: "Either we do it, or we do it. It's as simple as that. So we're
doing it."

That tiny episode led to a bill for an extra $25,000 or so, to be
paid by the owner. Even Fonti, himself not responsible for the
expenditure, saw such incidents as unfair: "What's ironic about it
is that we are improving the city system. We are improving the
subway. We are replacing an eighty-year-old water pipe with a new
water pipe. We will be protecting and reinforcing the existing sewer
with an additional concrete seal around it. And yet, when you talk
to them, it's as if they're doing us a favor by letting us spend our
money to build the city's system."

Another factor adding to Fonti's problems was the subway. It wasn't just the complexities of building the new station, but that trains had to keep running while the station and the foundations were being constructed within a few feet of the line. It took a year and a half of meetings with the Transit Authority, starting in 1985, before the plans for the new entrances to the subway were approved. Since these entrances were actually part of the lower floors of the skyscraper, the approval of their design was important to confirm the final layout of the ground floor and basements. But while HRH were waiting for the approval, they had had to blast away and act as if it were a certainty.

Although the site itself was in private hands, the excavations inevitably impinged on the surrounding streets. And, like the subway and the sewers, the streets are full of jealously guarded accoutrements that acquire great importance only when somebody wants to move them. On February 11, 1987, Fonti was tearing his hair out over a lamppost and a fire hydrant that needed to be moved a few feet:

> I've been trying to move a light pole for well over a month and finally started moving it yesterday. Now, the physical act of moving the light pole would take three or four days, but the procedure to get approval has been six weeks. It is absolutely crazy. At the same time I started approvals to move a fire hydrant, which is even more critical. I don't even have approval on that yet, and six weeks have come and gone. That has strictly been red tape, paperwork, with the city agencies: the Fire Department, the Street Light Division, if nothing else. It's just one small item.

While Fonti made endless telephone calls, wrestling with a thousand problems like these, the hole in the ground was nearing its final depth at the east end of the site, where the tower would stand. It had taken three months to excavate down to the bare rock. Now the rock itself had to be blasted away to produce a thirty-

foot-deep rectangular pit for the foundations of the tower. Tony
Raffiniello was out and about on site as HRH's general site superintendent. He and Fonti work hand in hand—while Fonti is hidden
away in his office worrying about money and schedules, Raffiniello
is the visible face of HRH, available to any one of the thirty-odd
trades and with enough knowledge of all of them to nip any bull-
shitting in the bud. If a city agency were suddenly to point out that
a permit had the wrong wording and work on a particular task
couldn't start, Raffiniello had to deal with the little problem of thirty
men with nothing to do but all having to be paid.

It was a springlike day, warm for February, and the site was
already active at 7:00 A.M. as the day's delivery of dynamite appeared on site in a small red van with the word "EXPLOSIVES" in
huge white letters on the side. There was no secrecy about its
contents, although it is delivered in limited and carefully controlled
amounts. The excavation gang was working systematically at several points around the main site of the tower. The center of the
hole had reached its maximum depth, but the edges were still at
the level reached by the excavation of the rubble and foundations
of the old Madison Square Garden. Now, with dynamite, the excavators were nibbling back each outcrop farther and farther away
from the center.

The edges of the hole were like a series of ten-foot-high cliffs
being eroded away by each explosion. Over near 50th Street, just
down the road from the Krakatoa Indonesian restaurant, Vito and
his team were preparing the ground. Huge drills would first bore
a cylindrical hole about eight feet into the rock. Several of these
drills were running at the same time, so that it took only an hour
or so to produce two or three rows of holes back from the edge of
the "cliff" and parallel to it. Then the box of dynamite arrived and
Vito and a colleague lowered several sticks into each hole, carefully
calculating how much explosive was needed at each point. The
sticks of dynamite were covered with a pink plastic skin. Inside
was a gray mush that cut easily with a knife, so that, when nec-

essary, a final half-stick could be added to the hole. After cutting a stick in half, Vito's colleague would throw the knife into the dynamite box, where it stuck, quivering like Excalibur.

By deciding on the placing of the holes and the number of sticks of dynamite used in each, Vito could determine how much rock would be blasted and where it would fly after the explosion. If the same quantity of dynamite were put in each hole and all were detonated at the same time, the rock would fly in all directions and the blast and vibration would be deafening and possibly damaging. By varying the amounts of explosive and delaying the detonation of some of it, Vito could shape the explosion in time and space. Delays could be set of up to four-thousandths of a second after the first detonation. This would mean that the vibration and noise would be spread over only a fraction of a second, but even this would be enough to dilute the shock waves. Also, the order in which the individual loads of dynamite were detonated determined the principal direction for the flying debris. If the dynamite nearest the interior of the site were detonated first and the rest delayed slightly, the rock would follow the path of least resistance and explode away from the streets and houses around the site.

To someone whose only familiarity with dynamite is derived from Tom and Jerry cartoons, the robust way in which it is treated can come as a surprise. Only when each stick has a detonator cap embedded in it and is attached by wire to the next stick does dynamite become really dangerous. Nevertheless, the instruction leaflet in each box has a few pieces of helpful advice: "In cold weather NEVER thaw dynamite by open flame or other direct heat," "NEVER put explosive material in the pockets of your clothing," and "Keep from children."

Each hole is ready when it is filled to the top with the right number of sticks each with a detonator, linked to the next by wire. The top stick of dynamite is covered with earth, leaving the wire poking through. After the holes are filled, one of the excavation team joins the individual protruding wires together and feeds the whole bundle of wires toward the trigger device.

While the explosives are being prepared, Henry Morrison, an engineer employed by the city, is down in the 50th Street subway station. He bypasses the turnstile and goes behind a partition that separates the platform from a space behind it. Here, on the floor, is a small flat cylinder with a spirit-level bubble in the center of its top surface. It is linked by wire to a briefcase-sized electronic device fifty yards away. This is a portable seismometer. The subway station is separated from the site by a wall a few feet thick and, each time there is an explosion, the bubble in the cylinder moves slightly with the vibration in the ground. The seismometer registers the number of the explosion and the time and date, and it sounds an alarm if the explosion has exceeded a certain threshold. One of the thousands of city ordinances controlling Manhattan building specifies the limits of vibration from explosions, and Morrison monitors the readings at the end of the day to make sure those limits haven't been exceeded.

Above ground, Vito's latest explosion is imminent. When the

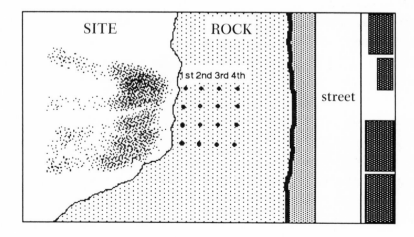

dynamite is in the holes, one of the backhoes picks up a series of woven steel mats, each weighing a ton or so. These mats cover the area of the explosion to prevent small stones from flying in all directions. A minute or so before the explosion, an alarm sounds. After the alarm, a burst of voltage is sent down the wires. (This is where years of exposure to Tom and Jerry cartoons pays off: the detonation *is* triggered by a box with a T-shaped plunger.) A quick push on the plunger turns a dynamo that sends a surge of current down the wire, creating a small electrical explosion in each detonator, which in turn causes a chemical explosion in the dynamite. Such a current could conceivably be triggered by a side effect of radio waves, and notices on the streets around the site warn taxi drivers to turn off their radios as they drive by.

When the plunger is pushed down, there is a dull thud and the mats rise gracefully a few feet before subsiding onto the pile of rubble that a moment before was solid Manhattan schist. As Sonny, the rock super, explained: "The mat is only to protect you from the small pieces that will fly up, not to hold the blast back. If I overload the shot, the mat will take off with the shot. It's been known for a mat to go off four or five hundred feet in the air—into the street, sidewalk, everything like that. But that's things that you gotta judge, you know? It takes a lot of practice."

Sonny and the other excavators are typical of the men, and a few women, who will put their muscle and brain power into this building as it goes up. However hard-bitten the site workers seem, for many the task of blasting rock to smithereens is a source of pride, and they see the job as forging a personal link with a permanent part of the city of New York. And all the way up the building, each of the hundreds of craftsmen guards jealously his own preserve in the form of the skill that only he and his colleagues in the same union can supply.

Every construction trade has a union—unlike, say, the automobile trade, where one union covers all. A hundred different trade unions may be represented on one site. A contractor or construction manager like HRH hires specific workers from the union. The union has rules applying to that trade; for example, no flexible pipe longer than five feet shall be brought on site by anyone other than a member of that union. The contractor must ensure that the regulations are met. HRH may hire a subcontractor who might in turn buy the materials from someone else and have them assembled on site by a third company. The subcontractor would be responsible for the success of the work and would have to cope with the specific union regulations. In a sense, the unions can act like the employers of the worker, so they also deal with many of the welfare and pension issues, as well as setting pay levels. Sonny seemed happy enough with his lot:

It's a tough way to make a living, but the pay isn't bad. It averages from $600 to $900 a week. We have seven different pay scales in the union, and mostly, including myself, we're not formally educated. I mean, I went to high school; that was it. So where's a guy, in this day and age, going to go out and earn $600 to $900? Plus you've got fringe benefits. We've got a very, very good pension-and-welfare plan in the union, and that adds to the incentive of coming to work. The only thing we have to put up with is the elements, where people who work in high rises and inside, they don't have to contend with the cold weather, wind, snow, and ice.

Nor must they contend with the noise. A construction site is noisy all the time, and when you add the regular "crump" of blasting during the excavation, the noise level destroys the fine hairs in the inner ear in people without some form of protection. That often includes the workers on the site: "Well, in the past," Sonny said, "being an egotist, I guess, I didn't like to put cotton in my ears. We didn't have earplugs—they just come out relatively recently, six or seven years ago. By that time my ears were shot. I'd say 90 percent of the union is half deaf. It's one of our main hardships in the union."

Mary Dunn, in her brownstone on 49th Street, had no union to protect her ears from the commotion. Day after day she peered through the lush greenery of her front-room plant collection that all but obscured the view through the window, and observed the inexorable progress of the hole and the devastating effect on her personal environment:

When they first started digging, the rat problem was unbeliev-able. In our tenant association, instead of having the exterminator once a month, we had him come twice a week and bait for rats. When they blast, the rats jump out of the sewers and then dive back in again. In fact, we've been known, when the rats start to come across the street, to stamp our feet and say, "Get back! Go back to Mr. Zeckendorf! We don't want you here, rats!" And one of the pleasures of life is lifting up the liner from a garbage can and having a rat jump out and land on your head. I screamed, the rat screamed. I don't know which one screamed louder. We went in different directions. Of course, after the exterminator leaves, the next day or the day after, it's no fun shoveling up the dead rats.

The effects of the project inevitably spread far beyond the boundaries of the site. The constant stream of trucks to and from the site, some bringing concrete, others carrying away rubble to dumps in New Jersey, disrupted the already busy traffic on 49th and 50th Streets, main arteries across the city. Fonti had to play a cat-and-mouse game with the traffic authorities, who had forbidden the trucks to unload from either of the streets, even though con-struction would come to a halt were that enforced. Of course, they *did* unload, traffic was slowed down, and buses sometimes had to mount the pavement to skirt around the trucks, making life yet more unpleasant for the inhabitants of the brownstones.

While the explosions were sounding off regularly on site, the atmosphere in the SOM offices was equally explosive. It stemmed from the shock of finding that some of the drawings that had been completed and sent to HRH for bidding had now to be redrawn, and fast. The expression "back to the drawing board" originated in precisely this situation, and the fact that it's common in the industry made it no easier to accept the sudden spurt of activity demanded of the team in late 1986 and early 1987. Everybody thought the first, main stage of the drawings had been completed. Indeed, in October they'd had a party to celebrate, after word went around that the drawings were out for bids.

Rob Schubert saw it as "the sprint to the finish" but, unfortunately, the team had already started celebrating the fact that the race was over. But this was a stage in the design where some of the complex interactions of one part of the process with another were only now becoming clear. The pressure to issue the steel package, with its detailed drawings of the steel framework, put pressure, in turn, on the technical team, to produce a definitive specification for attaching the skin of the building to the steel. With the complex in-and-out variations in the wall, this was no easy task, and the architects often worked late nights and through the weekends to complete it. Finally, there was the architects' "artistic license" to reconsider aspects of the building before it was finally set in concrete, as Schubert explained:

> David [Childs] and Jim [Bodnar] and their people were going through and restudying all of the last, nitsy details. Part of the roof was being looked at in terms of how everything lines up and butts together and fits and looks from six different ways. That affected how the steel was placed. A lot of pressure was put on people, especially Gary [Steficek], to get the structure out but get

it right, when there wasn't the information to do that at the time. And meanwhile the owner was coming at us, and the construction manager was coming at us to answer questions which we weren't yet ready to answer.

There are two main problems with fast-track projects: design changes and cost overruns. A complete schematic set of architects' drawings had, of course, been available from late 1985 to start the task of estimating costs and seeking bids from subcontractors. These consisted of plans of each floor and elevations of each of the four sides of the tower.* But the sheaf of drawings produced by the architect—to the layman a complex, highly detailed, and apparently complete description of the building—is only the starting point for successive generations of drawings providing further layers of information that couldn't possibly be incorporated in that first level of description.

The schematic drawings are used as the basis for bidding. HRH first identified companies to carry out each of the tasks necessary to build some part of the building. Those companies able to do the job and wanting to bid were supplied with a set of drawings relevant to their specialty, on which they bid. The successful bidder, usually the lowest, then prepared what are called "shop drawings," showing in more detail how he would do the job; these might include his interpretation of how to do things—using different types of fastenings, different materials, even suggestions for changes in the design of some component of the building. The architects had to approve such revisions, to ensure that they conformed to the overall plan, and HRH was then supposed to check them to make sure that some seemingly insignificant change wouldn't produce a problem with the work of another subcontractor. Any single cubic foot of

---

* "Plan" refers to drawings showing a horizontal cross-section of the building; "elevation" refers to drawings that present a vertical view, of the side of the building, say.

the building might require the attention of several subcontractors, none of whom necessarily knew what the others were doing.

This is the way it works in principle, and with a "slow-track" building many such problems can be spotted and ironed out before construction starts. But Worldwide Plaza was fast-track and the team was under considerable pressure to confirm and circulate final drawings as soon as possible, since backhoes were already digging and steel was already being fabricated. In addition, the continuing discussions between architect, contractor, and tenant might reveal the need for other changes. If SOM saw such a need, they issued what's known as a "bulletin," describing the change. This had to be approved by the owner before being sent to the subcontractor, who might then have to prepare his own, more detailed revisions and send them back to SOM and HRH for approval of the way the changes would be incorporated into the original work.

One of the problems with the Worldwide Plaza tower was that Ogilvy and Mather's early participation in the project led them to feel that there was plenty of time for customizing the building to make it more suitable for their needs. They had signed the lease in December 1985, and during 1986 their own team of architects started to look at their floors to decide how best to use the space. Because the site was still nothing more than a hole in the ground, it was perhaps easy to think that changes in the design and structure would cause no problems. In fact, with many of the steel drawings already being worked on at the fabricators, the O&M changes involved about $3 million of unnecessary expenditure, which would not have been incurred had the design process been allowed to reach a more finished state before construction started. But that would in turn have created another problem: had steel design and fabrication been delayed until O&M's changes were incorporated in the later drawings, O&M's date for moving in—and paying rent—might have been delayed by about six months. The extra $3 million to keep the project on schedule would be more than offset by the loss of six months' rent, perhaps $5–6 million.

(Not to mention the interest on the money borrowed to construct the building, running at over $3 million a month in January 1989.) So changes were clearly a fact of life, and everyone on the project had to live with them, however reluctantly.

Whenever a new version of an architectural drawing is issued following a change in design, a balloon is drawn around the altered section of the drawing, so that nobody overlooks the change. In October and November 1986, balloons proliferated, each one leading in turn to new changes. Every change highlighted on the drawing of the whole building had to be carried through by the drafting team to all the other drawings, to give the contractor the detail needed for carrying out the revised work. According to one of them, "every drawing had to be changed." In a series of meetings at which the technical group were told about these changes, feelings ran high. Much of the tension focused on Jim Bodnar, who, as David Childs's lieutenant, was the purveyor of the bad news. Some of the team couldn't escape the feeling that not all the changes were really necessary. As one of them put it: "David Childs got nervous when he traveled around the country with a client and saw the buildings of one of his design partners. He began to wonder, 'Is mine as good?' "

Certainly, at this time Childs made some important aesthetic changes to the appearance of the building, changes that might be seen as an attempt to make the building more interesting. The parapets at each setback level suddenly acquired a new feature: a layer of lighter-colored brick, like snow running a little way down the walls, emphasizing the three-dimensional changes in the tower as it rose and narrowed. But for Childs, speaking in early 1987, changes like this were an expected consequence of the design process:

> I wouldn't say there's been radical changes, compared to any
> other project. It's been an ongoing process of evolution, not rev-

olution, in terms of refinement of design, rather than in major programmatic changes.

The parapets at the top of the building were one of those elements that you get a closer and closer focus to, and I felt that they needed some further transition between the top of the occupied portions and the penthouse. Those have changed considerably. To the extent that we recognized in the design that they're going to be viewed from seven hundred feet away, they are still crudely proportioned compared to the details that we have been working on down at the base of the building. They are nevertheless an important element, like the epaulettes or the shoulders on the base portion of the building as well as up at the crown. As they step down through the building, they reappear in finer and finer detail until they appear into the main oval form at the lowest element of the building.

Although Rob Schubert was a daily focus for much of the team's discontent, he had enough experience to take a more practical view of the situation: "These kinds of changes desperately had to occur. It was demoralizing to a lot of production and technical people that they had drawn something and then it went out to bid, was priced, everything seemed hunky-dory—'We love it'—and then people changed it. As a manager, looking back at it, I wish I could have made that occur four months earlier than it did. But it just didn't occur, and everyone was stressed."

And in any case, what could be done about it? Architects are paid to design, they have learned to design, and they will seize every opportunity to design. Jim Bodnar said that he would love to go on designing forever, and Childs was unrepentant about the flood of changes that made life so difficult in the autumn of 1986:

You *never* stop designing, and we haven't stopped now. As much as the technical people would like to think that we've stopped, it will continue to be refined. Now, I do recognize that architecture is that which is built. To get it built, you must decide major decisions in proper sequencing and order. I won't have new ideas about the top of the building all of a sudden—"Let's do a dome rather than a peak." But particularly in the lower portions of the building, where people can walk up and touch it and they see it from a three-foot distance rather than from a seven-hundred-foot distance, we need to keep refining those exact dimensions of the joints in the stonework or what the ashtrays look like in the elevator lobbies. All those elements are tremendously important, and as we have time, including during the review of the shop drawings, we will continue to make refinements in the design.

I think that we're falling into an expected period of hard, "slug-it-out-in-the-trenches" type of work, but there are those moments of design activity that make it all worthwhile. It's terribly important to make these drawings, these images, that we have on paper and in our minds, become real. If we don't tell the contractor exactly how to put that screw in or to lay that piece of stone, which aren't on the drawings as they come back in the shop drawings, then it will turn away from a really classically designed building, classical in the sense of thoughtfully designed, into something which is not fully coordinated in a design sense either.

Ed Narbutas used the same battle metaphor when talking about the stress on the team: "When the morale flags too much and people start getting crazy, we go out and have a three-hour lunch with lots of margaritas. You just have to have good communication between the team. You tell them why it's happening. There's a lot of camaraderie. You're fighting it out in the trenches, and everyone supports one another. They know the ultimate goal is a good-looking building. That's really what keeps people going."

The person who might have been more affected by the design changes than the SOM team was Arnie Kriegel, who had already based a number of price estimates and some preliminary contract discussions on the earlier drawings. But Kriegel was more sanguine:

> As an architect refines the drawings, from small details to large blowups depicting exactly what he wants and what visual effect he's looking for, some details have crept in that have caused some cost increases. For example, the top of the building had, at one time, only one color. Now the architect has requested to price out two colors that would give some different visual effect on the top of the building. He's also included some corbeling. Corbeling is where brick sticks out of the wall at the top of the building. It is almost duplicating the 1930s look at the top of some buildings, such as the Daily News Building. That's what the architecture is trying to look like. That has crept into the design. Not very costly, but there is some cost involved. Once again, it's an owner's choice.
>
> As an architect or an engineer or anyone starts developing any sort of a project, the initial detailing is vague. But this detailing becomes very, very important to the pricing. There is a cost difference from an ordinary door buck, or doorjamb, which just laps the Sheetrock, versus a door buck, which needs to have a little bend, a little space between the Sheetrock and the door jamb, to break the line of the Sheetrock on the door, because the architect may want it. It's a little more expensive, and one doesn't really see that in the early stages. That's the kind of thing that occurs.

For the construction managers, this architect's habit of tinkering with the drawings when everybody thought he'd made up his mind is called "drawing creep," or, according to Artie Nusbaum, "drawing in the closet": "Sometimes the architect will draw without showing anyone what he's drawing and then say, 'Here's the drawings,' and then, if you don't like them, he says, 'Well, OK. I'll redraw them, but we'll lose four or five months.'"

By mid-April 1987 the hole for the office tower had reached its correct dimensions: two hundred feet by three hundred feet by about thirty feet deep. Across the flat bottom a series of deeper pockets had been blasted into the rock. Some were elevator pits, to accommodate the lowest components of the elevator machinery and the underside of the cabs when they reached the subbasement level. Many of the other pockets in the rock were waiting to be filled with concrete to form the "footings," as they're called, for the bases of the steel columns.

Each steel column in Worldwide Plaza had to support about two thousand tons at its base. Although the column acted as one seven-hundred-foot-high piece of steel, it was, of course, a series of sections joined together, each section two stories in height. To make sure that the footings for each column would support the load, the rock was cut away and filled with concrete of a known strength, reinforced with steel bars, and surmounted by the thick steel billet plates. At least, that was the idea. But to produce a concrete footing of a known strength and consistency needs a great deal of care and attention, and depends on the skills and actions of a number of people, including members of the Mafia who are known to control the industry and are often more interested in cost than quality. At several points in the concrete process a mistake could weaken the strength of the final product.

First, there is the mixing of the material itself. The history of concrete is almost but not entirely without interest. The ancient Romans discovered a mineral on the slopes of Mount Vesuvius that produced the first true Portland cement, the key component of modern concrete. They used it in many buildings, but these declined and fell with the Roman Empire, leaving a few traces of the substance but no real guide as to how to produce it. The next high points in the history of concrete came in the nineteenth century: the rediscovery of Portland cement, the invention of reinforced concrete boats, a French patent for concrete flowerpots, and the beginnings of pre-stressed concrete as a load-bearing substitute for steel.

In the construction industry, concrete is big business. Every major site needs a constant supply of this slurry of cement, stones, gravel, and water. But the supply must be carefully organized to fit the pattern of use. It must be mixed in the correct proportions, to be neither too stiff to pour nor too loose to set with the right strength. The crucial factor is the amount of water in the mix. Water performs two functions when added to a concrete mix: a small amount of water causes the cement to bind the other elements tightly together; a much larger amount of water is then necessary to make it possible to move the concrete from plant to truck and from truck to site. The strength of the final product is closely related to the ratio of water to cement: the more water, the less weight the concrete can support, even when the excess water has evaporated to produce the solid final product.* And since concrete has to perform different jobs in different parts of the building, the specifications laid down for the proportions of the ingredients and the hardened strength vary depending on whether the concrete is to be used for footings or for pumping to the top of the building to pour on the floors.

There are all kinds of ways by which the concrete in the footing can end up the incorrect strength: it might be mixed wrongly at the plant; it might have water added to it on site to make it flow more smoothly; it might be poured from too great a height, so that the aggregate separates and produces an uneven mixture. There are safeguards against each of these possibilities. When the Worldwide Plaza footings were being poured, on April 15, 1987, Carlton, a concrete inspector employed by an independent inspection company, US Testing, was on hand to monitor each stage of the process.

---

* A change of 10 percent, from 40 to 50 percent, can reduce the strength of the concrete by half a ton per square inch.

Each truckload of concrete arrived from the plant with a certificate listing its ingredients and proportions. Then, while the truck was pouring its load down a chute into the footing pit, Carlton took a wheelbarrowful of concrete from the slowly flowing stream and wheeled it to a nearby patch of ground. He first put a thermometer into the concrete to check that it was warmer than fifty degrees. If it was too cold, the "curing reaction" that turns the mixture rigid would simply stop, until it warmed up again. Carlton then took a small scoopful of concrete and shook it up with alcohol to see how much air was dissolved. He was checking that there was just enough air to form sufficient bubbles in the concrete to make it workable without destroying its strength. He then performed what's known as a "slump test"—as though making a sandcastle on the beach, he put several trowel-loads of concrete into a kind of bottomless rubber flowerpot, filling it to the top. Then he tipped the pot of concrete upside down onto a board, lifted the pot, and left behind a moist mound of concrete in the shape of the pot. Because it was wet, this concrete slowly subsided until the top was several inches lower. The distance it subsided was the "slump." The regulations allow only a four-to-six-inch slump in seven to ten seconds after removing the pot. A slump of more than six inches means that the concrete is too wet, and cannot therefore set at the right strength. If this happened, Carlton would reject the whole load and send the truck away. This is not a popular move with anyone, since it holds up the work—certainly not with truck drivers, who have been known to threaten to throw an inspector off the site if he declares a particular load to be faulty. What has sometimes happened is that the inspector has waited a week before drawing anyone's attention to the problem, by which time the mistake is set in concrete. It's then no longer a problem for the driver, and it's up to the structural engineer and the contractors to decide what to do about it.

There were two options if these tests showed that the concrete was substandard. The engineer could recalculate the stresses in the light of the new value for the weaker concrete and, with luck, would find the overall strength still adequate to support the load, particularly if only one truckload was faulty. But without this margin of safety, he would have to find a way of adding strength through some form of structural bracing or, as a last resort, have the concrete dug out with jackhammers and replaced.

As each load of concrete arrived, it was poured straight into one of the footings, with half a dozen men helping it on its way down the chute and spreading it in layers. Concrete is extremely strong when compressed but has no strength at all when pulled apart. To give it strength in compression *and* tension, steel rods were embedded in the concrete. It is a fortuitous accident that steel and concrete behave in a remarkably similar way: they expand and contract at a similar rate; they are *chemically* compatible, so that, in close contact, neither corrodes or degrades the other; and they bond very tightly together when steel is surrounded by wet concrete. If steel and concrete were incompatible in any of these areas, reinforced concrete would sooner or later degrade. For example, if they responded differently to temperature, after a few years of hot summers and cold winters the mixture would eventually tear itself apart.

When the pit was full, two large bolts were embedded in the right position to receive the baseplate and the steel column to be eventually lowered onto the footing. These bolts must be located exactly, since the plates and columns have holes pre-drilled to slot snugly over the bolts.

One spring morning two anchor bolts were inserted in the footings that were to receive the first steel column. Unfortunately, the tops of the bolts were one inch lower than they should have been. To the naked eye, the bolts looked just like the others that protruded from other footings around the site. This tiny hitch would be discovered only five weeks later, when the first steel columns arrived on site.

As the individual pits were filled, Carlton followed them around the site, testing temperature, slump, and air. These tests generally reassured him that the concrete was as near as it should be to the ideal mixture for the job. But there was a further safeguard, a more direct test of strength, that he had to perform on each footing. For every fifty cubic yards of concrete, Carlton took four samples and pressed them into plastic cylinders. These were left out in the open for a day, and then taken to a testing laboratory in Long Island City. Concrete can take about six months to reach full strength, but it is designed to be used at the strength it has after twenty-eight days. After seven days, by which time it should have reached about 70 percent of its target strength, a sample from each footing is put in a hydraulic press and crushed. Three weeks later more samples from the same batch are crushed, to make sure they will support the required load. If a sample fails this test, the safety regulations insist that a section of hardened concrete from the actual site be cut out and tested. If the section is not up to scratch, the final sanction is for *all* the substandard concrete to be cut out and replaced.

The long list of safety measures operating in this one area of a major building might suggest that, left to their own devices, every subcontractor and construction worker would cheerfully go about his business in a perpetual spirit of knavery or incompetence or both. But the history of technology is littered with disasters that were in the end nobody's *fault*, but an accumulation of tiny human failings, any one of which was insignificant.

When Robert Byrne, author of the novel *Skyscraper*, looked for a potential weak point that would cause *his* skyscraper on the old Madison Square Garden site to collapse, he was advised by his engineering consultant, Charlie Thornton, to choose the concrete, and Thornton suggested the use of a lighter concrete than was required. Once there's a single weak link in the system that transmits forces throughout the building, an intolerable strain can be placed on the rest of the system, straining some of the other components beyond their limits. A skyscraper has a vast quantity of components, each needing its safety-inspector equivalent of Carlton, either in the field or at the factory or plant.

Two weeks after the footings were poured on the Worldwide Plaza site, a building under construction in Bridgeport, Connecticut, forty miles northeast of New York City, collapsed, killing twenty-three workers. The investigators, a company run by Charlie Thornton, looked closely at the concrete and the footings, in case they had failed in some way and contributed to the disaster. The design specifications had called for the columns to rest on bedrock that supported a weight of seven tons per square foot. In fact, some of the footings had rested on soil, not bedrock. In the end, a combination of factors turned out to be responsible for the collapse, and no one factor could be blamed. But it was a chilling reminder for the people working at Worldwide Plaza that safety measures weren't just a series of bureaucratic obstacles.

5

STEEL

Once the decision had been made that Worldwide Plaza was to be a steel-framed building, HRH had to find the steel contractors to do the job on schedule and at the right price. Since HRH were looking for the lowest price, they didn't really care where the steel contractors were located, provided they came up with the right package. Mosher Steel, a company with several large steel plants in the South, including Houston and Dallas, were eager to secure the contract, because times were hard in the steel business.

The steel contractor's task has four elements: buying the raw steel in the form of beams and columns of various cross-sections;

carrying out a preparatory process, called "fabrication," on the beams and columns; transporting the fabricated steel to the site; and erecting the steel framework in accordance with the plans. Although one company would be responsible for all this, it would be expected to subcontract such tasks as transporting and erecting the steel, while itself doing the fabrication. The basic units for any steel-framed building are columns and beams. Columns are usually vertical, and their cross-section is designed to support forces that compress them along the long axis or bend them from the side; beams are usually horizontal and have to take loads from other directions, often at right angles to their length. A girder is a beam that supports other beams or is made up of separate beams joined together. Steel fabrication can be simply a matter of cutting beams and columns to exactly the right length and drilling holes in the right places so that they will fit neatly together. Alternatively, it can involve a large degree of pre-assembly—several pieces of steel are cut and drilled and fixed together into more complex shapes away from the site, to make the task of erection easier.

The headquarters of Mosher Steel's Houston fabrication plant is a windowless two-story building not far from the city center. Standing outside the building, you get a good view of downtown Houston, a monument to the role of steel in modern high-rise buildings. Mosher have supplied the steel for many of these skyscrapers as well as other major buildings in cities throughout the United States. But late 1985 was not a good time for American steel companies. Construction was declining and foreign steel fabricators were taking much of the available work. Over the previous two or three years the amount of work had dropped by 30 or 40 percent. As one steel contractor put it, "Domestic U.S. steel got fat and sassy. Now it's on the outside looking in."

Gene Miller is a senior vice-president at Mosher Steel's Houston plant, and an engineer. He radiated quiet enthusiasm about the task facing him on any large steel-framed building. As someone who could be the *cause* of a major construction disaster or the means of preventing one, he gave the impression that the weight of the building sat on his shoulders until he was entirely satisfied that every connection in the framework would resist the load it would receive once the building was up. Whenever Dick Rowe or Gary Steficek drew on the framing plan two steel members meeting, Miller and his colleagues had to design the right connection for those pieces of steel, with the right number of bolts or strength of weld to do the job. To ensure that the connection would support the load anticipated when the building was complete, involved calculations of all the forces meeting the connections, and a knowledge of the strength of each of the components—steel, bolt, or weld.

Miller's principal colleague in Houston was Haskell Ray, whom Gary Steficek had gotten to know very well by telephone over the early months of the contract: "Haskell's a very pleasant fellow to deal with. He's always cheerful. I haven't talked to him yet when he was in a depressed mood, so I look forward to meeting him some day." But both Ray and Miller took their jobs very seriously.

The history of construction is littered with disasters caused by a failure to appreciate the impact of loads and forces on steel connections and supports. In July 1981 two walkways in the lobby of the Hyatt Regency Hotel in Kansas City collapsed, killing 113 people, and injuring more than 180. One probable cause was a departure from the engineer's original instruction about how to support the walkways: one component rather than two supported the loaded weight of the two walkways. As Steven Ross, author of *Construction Disasters*, pointed out: "The steel fabricator . . . said the structural engineer made the change, the engineer said it was the fabricator's idea, the contractor has blamed the engineer . . . the construction manager has blamed the contractor or steel fabricator, and the architects have blamed the engineer or steel fabricator or both."

That disaster was a reminder of the importance of a single connection in a complex structure and of the engineer's responsibility to design it correctly and see that the work in the field was carried out as the drawings specified. As Miller remembers that disaster, his eyes moisten, as if he were himself responsible for all the actions of his colleagues and fellow engineers:

> I always worry about collapse, very much so. I know the engineers for the Hyatt Regency in Kansas City. In fact, I had a collapse once. I designed a beam and didn't put the proper stiffeners in and the beam collapsed under a huge pile of gypsum. Luckily, no lives were lost. It's a fear. When a structural engineer recognizes that he's got a good team behind him that's aware of public safety, aware of competency of designs using basic laws, using the laws of God, if you will, free-body diagrams, and the principles of engineering, there's a great deal of comfort in that for all of us.

The engineer's job concerns forces and how to withstand them. Some forces travel *through* structural elements and compress them, like the vertical forces in columns; some push on the sides of columns or beams and bend them, or pull on their ends and stretch them; others twist material in various ways. Forces are transmitted through connections, and the combination of materials and connections has to withstand any anticipated force. Even the strongest substance has its breaking point; even the most firmly bolted, welded, or glued connection will give way eventually under some force.

The structural stability of a building is a *requirement* rather than a design aim. It has to be achieved once the architects have decided how they would like the building to look, and so engineers respond to the design process rather than initiate it. In the early stages of design the developers and architects are more concerned about the job the building should do and how to make the most aesthetic, most efficient enclosed spaces for that job. The engineers must shadow the designers as they carry out this early process, to see that the choices of materials and the way those materials are

joined together lead to a building that can withstand the expected—
and not always easy to predict—forces. The Hyatt Regency walkways collapsed while several hundred people were dancing on
them. There's a tall building in mid-Manhattan that sways a little
more than it should when there's a dance on the top floor. It may
seem unreasonable to expect engineers to anticipate the stresses
of any conceivable mass human activity, but in the light of the
unpredictability of human behavior, it's safer to do so.

Miller and his colleagues worked really hard to secure the
Worldwide Plaza contract:

> It was very important to Mosher. The market for structural steel
> has been quite limited, and it's no secret that construction in
> Texas has declined over the past few years, so it was necessary
> for us to look elsewhere. We had established a very good repu-
> tation in New York City in the last two to three years with three
> high-rise buildings down in Lower Manhattan, so we were al-
> ready rolling, and this just continued to assist us to maintain our
> momentum here in New York City.

Mosher had to think hard about their bid for the Worldwide
Plaza job when it came up. Too high a price would result in another
contractor's securing the contract, too low and Mosher would make
no profit or even take a loss. On the other hand, even a no-profit
price would serve to keep the plant running and keep people at
work who had fabricated steel for decades and to whom Mosher
felt a duty. They made a series of trips to New York to talk to HRH
about the "scope" of the job—the overall figures for tonnage of
steel, type of structure, and complexity of design. For Miller, there
was a different quality about working with New Yorkers:

> I think we're more genteel down here in Texas. I should talk—
> I'm originally from New England—but there is more gentility
> and more of a handshake type of situation here in Texas than in

New York. But I think New Yorkers put up a front. I think they put up an outer hard crust that you can crack. I've been stranded in New York a couple of times over the past few years over weekends with snowstorms, and people's tensions are relieved and they know they don't have to be busy and they can relax. But they have a hard outer shell. They try to be tough.

At a meeting in New York, Dick Rowe and Gary Steficek put on the table the drawings that would be used to carry out the pricing of the job. These showed a simplified version of the steel skeleton in plan and elevation, with each of the steel members drawn as a straight line.

Every floor had a drawing like the one at the top of page 114, because it would be required to support a different distribution of loads, both downward through the floor itself and sideways from the effects of the wind.

There were about forty-five of these basic drawings, containing enough detail to estimate the amount of steel needed, provided Rowe and Steficek had made their calculations correctly. Since each beam or column had a specified weight of steel per foot length—103 pounds in the lower example—it was simply a matter of multiplying all the lengths by their appropriate pound-per-foot figure to arrive at the total weight of steel. Mosher also had to suggest to HRH how they would fabricate the steel, and that depended in turn on the way in which all the separate elements shown on the preliminary drawings would be connected together. At one extreme, every single connection could be made on site—"in the field," as it's called. At the other, unlikely extreme, the whole nineteen-thousand-ton framework could be connected up in Texas and dropped on site in the most dramatic display of prefabrication New York would ever see. In fact, much fancy fabrication would be done away from the site, and Miller and the others showed how they would do it with a set of DCs, or "design-concept" drawings. These showed, for example, how they would design some of the

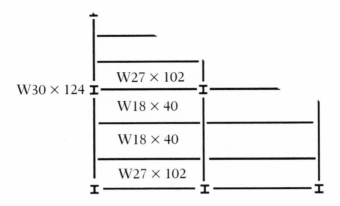

angled connections around the arcade area that would be needed to carry vertical forces *around* the arcade rather than through it.

Together with the drawings Mosher had to submit a total price for the job. Several steps were needed to arrive at this figure. First,

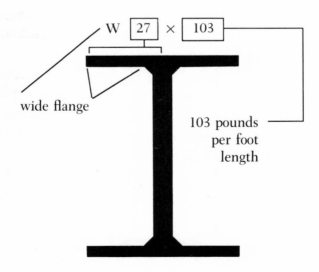

The symbols on the framing plan indicate the shape, thickness, and weight of steel in each member. So W27 × 103 means a wide-flanged column with a depth of 27 inches and a thickness of steel that weighs 103 pounds per foot.

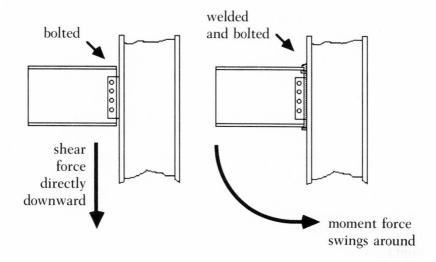

of course, there was the material cost of the steel—where could they buy it from, and at what price per ton? (Korea? Belgium? Luxembourg?) Then they had to fabricate it, at their plants in Houston or Dallas, and then transport the steel to the site. (By road? Rail? Barge?) Finally, they had to find a subcontractor to erect it. Mosher would work for HRH and in turn retain other subcontractors, to work for *them* on some of these tasks.

One important element in the costing was to calculate how much work was involved in designing the connections, which was Mosher's job rather than SOM's. SOM supplied simplified plans showing a beam butted against a column or against another beam. Mosher examined each of the points where the steel members met and designed a connection. They had to take into account what load each connection had to bear, and whether it had to support only a vertical load—known as *shear* force—or whether it would also have to resist the tendency of the connection to bend away from a right angle—a *moment* force. Dealing with these forces might involve extra pieces of steel—angles or plates—and Mosher had to decide whether the connection should be welded or bolted or both.

At the stage of deciding the price to quote, Mosher had only a general feel for the type of connections they would have to design and fabricate, but they could estimate well enough to know that they wouldn't be far out on the final cost. They chose to buy most of the steel from Trade Arbed, a Luxembourg company, and to ship the unfabricated steel from Antwerp to a port on the Houston ship canal. This would take four weeks, and they would not have the option of quickly calling up extra pieces if there were mistakes in supply or fabrication. A U.S. supplier who was days rather than weeks away would have been better from that point of view, but the price of steel, $400 or so per ton, was so much better, even taking into account the shipping costs, that they had no other option.

They also had to estimate how much it would cost to transport the steel to the site and erect it. Since good navigable waterways run from Houston to Pittsburgh, they decided to ship the fabricated steel in barges. It would then be sent by road to the site, where a company called Atlas-Gem would hire teams of ironworkers to erect the steel.

After months of work and many meetings, the Mosher team put in their bid. Their total figure for the job was about $25 million, broken down as follows:

- $11 million for the erection of the steel.
- $7 million for the raw steel, milled into columns and beams.
- $800,000 for detailing and fabricating.
- $600,000 for transport.
- $5.5 million for labor, overhead, and profit.

Mosher's bid was the lowest of four, though by quite a small amount, and because their paperwork was thorough and detailed, they were awarded the contract, in mid-1986. They estimated that the whole job of design, fabrication, and transport would take about seventeen months.

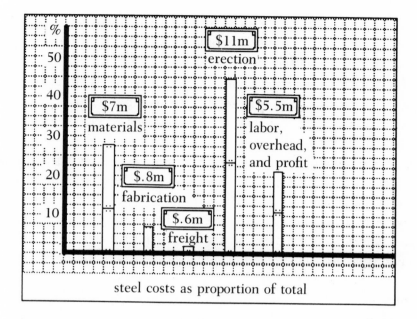

steel costs as proportion of total

Gene Miller and Haskell Ray started by translating the basic plans and the design concepts they had drawn up into a number of detailed shop drawings of pieces of steel. Each of these drawings had instructions for fabricating an individual piece of steel, with a unique number and a unique position in the framework. Unlike a toy-construction kit, even identical pieces were labeled with a unique reference mark. This began with "37000," the identification number of the project, followed by a reference number identifying the floor level at which it would be placed and the position in the steel grid. Part of the estimating process had involved calculating how many detailed drawings were needed. Miller and his colleagues used a simple rule of thumb: for every five tons of steel in the building, they guessed one detailed drawing would be required. Knowing the costs of their draftsmen's time, they could work out how much to cost into their estimate for drawings, merely on the tonnage of steel in the building.

These drawings specified all boltholes and welding sites to a fraction of an inch, based on complex calculations and allowing for a margin of safety. Here there's an obvious question of compromise. After the engineers have combined all the estimates of the weight a building will have to support and the required resistance of the thrust of the wind, the result is still an educated guess. After all, who knows what the tenants will do in fifty years—perhaps they'll take up communal dancing—and how strong the New York winds will be in the winter of 2020? To ensure safety, all the connections are designed with a specific safety factor built in, laid down by various industry safety codes that usually require the connections to support about 50 percent more than the expected maximum load. This load depends on factors such as where the connection is in the building. Although many of the column sections look identical, they can't be made identically. At each level of the building, the steel members can experience different forces from higher up or lower down. The gravity load on the columns decreases as you go up, for example, because they have less of the building to support. And the wind loads can vary widely from one part of the building to another.

Some figures, however, were unknown at the beginning of the project, because they depended on design decisions that were still being made. Because Worldwide Plaza was a fast-track building, many aspects of the building were still not fixed at the time the steel was put out for bids. Some decisions about the brick or stone had still to be made, and there were already the ominous beginnings of changes in the overall design that would swell to expensive proportions later in the schedule.

While Mosher were working on the original steel plans in late 1986, Bob McGarry at Ogilvy and Mather started formulating definite plans for customizing their space, involving changes that O&M were required to—and, fortunately, were happy to—pay for. Less fortunate was the effect of these changes on Mosher. McGarry rather liked the idea of building an interior staircase to connect the

O&M floors, to avoid having to use the elevators. He discussed his ideas with José Lambert, the architect for the O&M interiors, who pointed out that the fire regulations prevented an entirely open staircase all the way up through the O&M space. But Lambert thought about the problem and came up with an idea he was rather proud of, that created the illusion of openness while meeting the regulations. McGarry was delighted: "The stairs José has designed are most unique and a number of the contractors working with us have told him he really should try and patent it. As long as we incorporate the fire-code requirements for smoke alarms and safety detectors in there, the stairways look like they're open at all times. It's wide and it's inviting. People don't even realize they're going up and down the stairs."

McGarry and O&M's architects also took a look at an area of the building they were to use to a television studio and decided to embed a floating slab into the floor at that level, to reduce vibrations transmitted from the steel framework. Neither the stairs nor the floating floor were part of the original plans, and so O&M would have to pay for the extra cost. McGarry saw these changes as taking place early enough to be of real benefit to O&M:

> One of the advantages of being involved with the Zeckendorfs and with Skidmore since early on was that we were able to make these changes while the building was still being designed, so the alterations to the steel beams were able to be done while they were manufacturing the steel at a saving to us. If this building had been up already and we just came along and decided to become a tenant, the costs would have been three times as much as they were.

For the steel fabricators at Mosher, who had detailed drawings of the floors *without* a large staircase cut through them or a floating floor for a television studio, these imaginative and unique design concepts meant a flurry of change orders and revised drawings carried by Federal Express couriers between SOM and Houston.

Another factor led to frustration, annoyance, and an unnecessary expenditure of about $800,000. In early December 1986 Mosher were notified that they could go ahead on the basis of a complete set of drawings from SOM. Miller, Ray, and the Mosher team set to work breaking down the "broad-brush" designs into the individual pieces to be fabricated. On the day the set of steel drawings was handed over, SOM issued another set of drawings, an updated version of those Mosher were working on, that incorporated a whole lot of changes in the connections and sizes of the pieces of steel.

But Mosher had already started work on the basis of a now out-of-date set, planning in detail how to make pieces of steel that in minor but essential ways were shaped wrongly. Why it happened is anybody's guess, and everybody can find reasons why each of the parties should have behaved differently. Schubert should have made it clear that another set of drawings was in the pipeline—he thought he had. Schuster shouldn't have passed on and approved out-of-date drawings—he thought they were the latest. Steficek should have made clearer to Schubert how far behind he was in "catching up with the architecture"—he probably thought there was nothing he could do to speed up. The result was that a great deal of expensive design work had to be redone, at unnecessary additional cost.

Looking back at the first few months' design and fabrication, Ray, his cheerfulness muted, said: "My personal opinion is that the project was started too soon, as in any fast-track project like this. The designs are not completed and already we're starting to buy materials and make details and there are still changes being made. You've got to stop and fix it. There's no way around it. It either has to be fixed in-house or in the field. Those revisions that we're getting late are going to have to be fixed in the field, which is just money. Time and money."

In the face of these changes the Mosher team still have to see that the steel framework did its job: "Schedules are our nemesis," said Miller, "there's no doubt about that. They keep us awake at night, along with public-safety concerns. When you're trying to maintain connections that have integrity and also race the clock, it causes butterflies in your stomach at three-thirty in the morning."

For Rob Schubert, steelmen's worries about schedules and pressure were an occupational hazard—he had seen them all before: "Only if you've been through this event before of getting the project out and getting it bid and into construction do you know that the minute you go out the steel guy's going to say, 'My God, the damn shop drawings are late.' He's going to say it no matter. He could have every shop drawing in the world returned, every drawing, we could have spent a year on the drawing, and he's still going to say, 'I don't have enough shop drawings.' Every project is like that."

Though it's useful to picture a steel framework as a giant child's construction set, the image can oversimplify the task of design and construction. Children's construction sets have extremely simple components which are bolted together "in the field," so to speak, where the field is the bedroom carpet. But the components for Worldwide Plaza were already highly complex when they arrived on site. The fabrication work done in Texas was precision assembly work that would have been almost impossible in the open air high up on the framework of the building. What is involved, for example, in making one particular type of steel member, called a "tree column," makes the point clearly.

There were about seven hundred tree columns in Worldwide Plaza, about half to be fabricated in Houston, the rest in Dallas. The central vertical element is just one of the columns shown on the basic plan. The branches of the "tree" are other pieces of steel, attached to the trunk in the fabrication plant. There are *two* side arms on each side, because each tree column occupies the height of two floors of the building. Each tree column consists of about *forty* separate pieces of steel, including the main column and all

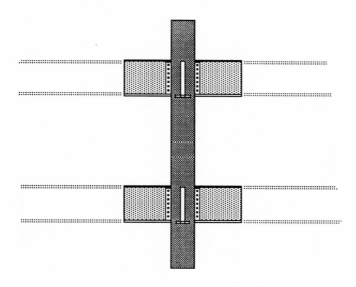

its arms and associated ironware, to be welded and bolted as specified on the DCs. When the tree column is lowered into place, ideally
it should nestle snugly to the top of the column below and be in
exactly the right position to fit against the four beams on either
side and the bottom of the column above. Each tree column must
fit those six points in space. To prevent the return of pieces to the
plant for minor changes, the design incorporates a method of adjusting some of the components so that, with a little squeezing and
twisting, the piece can be made to fit.

On April 7, 1987, the main member to be fabricated at the
plant was tree column 724 Y1 R, destined for a position near one
corner of the eleventh and twelfth floors. To fabricate one tree
column took about three hours and a team of about ten men. Column 724 Y1 R began as a piece of W36 × 280—wide-flanged, 36
inches deep, and weighing 280 pounds per foot—an inch or two
longer than the final cut length should be. It was now to be cut
down to approximate size. A circular saw was lowered onto the
column and the quarter-inch-thick blade slowly, almost sedately,

tree
columns

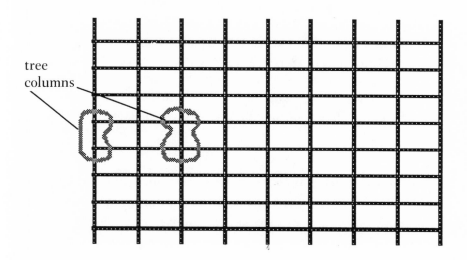

ate into the cold steel, and sliced an inch or so from the end. What it lacked in speed—you could see the individual teeth, instead of the expected blur—the saw made up in strength as it scraped through the steel.

Then a hoist carried the drilled column to be reduced exactly to length, either by milling—eroding away the last fraction of an inch—or "burning"—cutting off a slightly larger slice with an oxy-acetylene torch. One of the burners was Johnny Hunter, originally from Sweetwater, Texas: "Rattlesnake country—they have a rattlesnake roundup every year in March." Hunter, a tall polite black man, has worked at Mosher in Houston since 1946 and likes his work:

> I enjoys it all. I think it's become a part of me. I like it. You know what I mean. It's a job where I can get up at twelve o'clock at night and come to it. It's very enjoyable. I like burning, welding, you know. The foremans,* they're excellent. I think that I've got to be a part of this city and part of this nation. I can look right

---

* "Foremans" seems to be the recognized plural of "foreman" in the construction industry.

over many highways and say, "Look, I had a hand in all of it," you know? It makes me pretty proud. I knows nothing about Worldwide Plaza. I's just heard about it. I would like to take a trip up that way to see it. I was in New York during the time when I went to England in '43, in the Army. Then I caught a ship out of there going into Belfast—Belfast in Scotland, Scotland in England.

In an industry fraught with hazards from falls, burns, and electric shock, Hunter has seen people do some pretty stupid things: "The dumbest thing I ever saw anyone do was sit on one side of a beam thinking he was at the right place, cutting it half in two. So when he cut it half in two he found out he went one way and the beam went the other way, but no one was hurt, though." Only when pressed does he admit that he was the subject of this story.

After being "burned," the trunk of the tree column went to a jig, a set of clamps arranged on the ground to hold the various elements of the column while they are fastened together. Other pieces were slid under a computerized drilling rig, to have boltholes drilled according to the shop drawing. Then a team assembled the column. The "shop-floor man" read the drawing and checked that the right number of components was there, down to eight bolts and eight washers. The layout man used ruler and chalk to mark on the beam the positions for the welds and some of the components, like stiffener plates. The fitter brought the separate components into the correct position by the trunk. If any cutting was necessary, to change the shape of the steel from the basic I-beam, a "burner" would do that, according to plan.

Though accurate design and skillful fabrication are important for a well-constructed building, it was interesting to observe how often mistakes occurred, and were corrected or incorporated into the building with no significant detriment to the building. The intimate knowledge many of the craftsmen possessed of the ways of steel, stone, brick, or concrete meant that a lot of ingenuity and

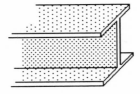

skill went into improvising in the face of minor problems, rather than bringing the whole system to a halt. One small example out of many illustrating this flexibility occurred as a result of a piece of steel's having been slightly misfabricated by Mosher.

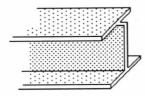

There were often small variations in the assembly and fabrication of otherwise similar pieces. The team on the shop floor did whatever the plan told them to do, but occasionally one of these minor variations was missed, and discovered only months later, when it turned up on the site.

When steel beams are rolled at the mill, they all have the familiar "I" cross-section. Often, at the fabricating plant, this I-shape is maintained so that the flanges run all the way along the beam. But sometimes the flange needs to be cut back to allow it to fit a particular feature of the column it will be attached to. Somehow, one particular beam left Houston without that half-inch cutback. Only when it reached the forty-second floor a year later was the mistake noticed, and it had to be dealt with in the field.

In the fabrication of a complex piece of steel like a tree column, after the pieces are assembled and final changes made to the individual shapes, the welders tack-weld the pieces, fixing them lightly in place, ready for the final welding that attaches the side arms, or spandrels, firmly to the column.

Welding two pieces together creates one continuous piece of metal, unlike *glueing*, where the adhesive is a different substance from those being glued. An electric arc, or continuous spark, flows between a metal electrode and the steel. This is so hot that it melts both the steel and the electrode, which is continually eaten away. Moving the electrode with its arc at a temperature of more than a thousand degrees centigrade along the meeting place of two pieces of steel creates a pool of metal that is a mixture of the electrode and the steel. This hardens as it cools, and the joint is stronger than either of the pieces of steel. Often, two pieces of steel that are welded could also be joined by bolting, but the business of drilling the right number of holes and fixing them with high-strength bolts can be more cumbersome than welding. On the other hand, in the field it's easier to bolt than to weld, particularly because bolting is less vulnerable to bad weather.

Because a welded joint is so strong, it's important that the steel underneath is fault-free. Sometimes steel leaves the rolling mill with invisible laminations beneath the surface, where the rolling process creates voids within the steel, rather like the air between the layers of a *mille-feuilles* pastry. Normally this wouldn't interfere with the steel's ability to support the forces transmitted along it, but if a beam were welded to a column at the point where there were laminations underneath, the force on the welded joint could cause a layer of steel to peel away at the point where the lamination had occurred. The way to reveal laminations is to use an ultrasound device, similar to that used to explore the womb of a pregnant woman, which sends high-frequency sound waves into the steel. Like radar or sonar, these waves are reflected back into a detector to show areas that are more or less dense than the surrounding steel. Laminations—essentially fissures in the steel—appear as layers or boundaries on a visual display, just as the outlines of the soft tissue and skeleton of a fetus show up in the womb because they are different in density from the amniotic fluid. Each steel member is checked for laminations in the area marked out for the weld, and rejected if any are revealed.

Gary Schmedt is plant manager. Young and slow-speaking, he knows each stage of the fabrication job, including the tricks steel can play on you:

> It takes several years' experience working with steel to be competent enough to know what you're doing. Steel has a lot of properties that through experience a man can know as second nature and work with it and make it look easy. A lot of these operations out here look easy, but they are not really. Steel is sometimes very unforgiving. You can't always second-guess it, especially when you weld on it or you burn it. It'll move to you, especially a tree column, or anything else. If a spandrel moves it's not going to fit in the field, so we check all the spandrels after welding them, and if they have moved on us we've had to apply heat to them to pull them back around to make sure they will fit.

For about a year, the Mosher workers received the flow of milled steel pieces from Luxembourg at one end of the plant and turned them into intricately crafted components at the other. It may seem odd to use the word "intricate" about pieces of steel weighing twenty tons and measuring six or seven meters but, as Schmedt said, steel is unforgiving. The accuracy of measurement required to ensure that two pieces of steel fit together, with the right number of holes in the right position for further pieces of steel to be attached, is high. Even an error of a tenth of an inch in the position of a bolthole drilled in Houston will make the steel erectors disgruntled when they discover it three months later, several hundred feet up in the air in Manhattan.

As the steel pieces are finished, they are given a reference number, tied around with a piece of colored tape, and collected together in truckloads to be driven twelve miles or so to another Mosher plant, off the northwest tip of Galveston Bay. Here the barges from Luxembourg arrive with raw steel and await a load of fabricated steel to take on the next stage of the journey. Each barge weighs about 850 tons and carries about eleven hundred tons of steel. All day the trucks arrive and the hoists lift the steel piece by piece and place it carefully in the hold of the barge. Although the journey will not be at breakneck speed, each piece of steel needs to be supported firmly in the barge, and secured against toppling over; its own weight is enough to bend an arm or the corner of a flange, and this could mean a long journey back from the site for repairs.

Once on the barge, the steel is towed out into Galveston Bay and toward the Gulf of Mexico. It doesn't actually go into the Gulf but travels along the Intracoastal Waterway, the ship canal linking Houston with New Orleans. At Baton Rouge, Louisiana, the barge is maneuvered among fifteen or twenty other barges carrying other goods assembled from elsewhere in the South, and a tug begins to haul the load northward up the wide Mississippi River.

6
TENANTS

Terry Soderberg was the Zeckendorf employee with the job of supervising the leasing of Worldwide Plaza, and during the first two years of the project he rode an emotional switchback from elation to despair. On his best days, he claimed that the building sold itself by the sheer appropriateness of its location, rental rates, and design: "There are so many holes on the Broadway corridor, which is Broadway, Seventh and Eighth Avenues, that no one knows if they're real projects. The minute steel got above the street grade it was real and everybody knew it was real. Also, since we signed Ogilvy and Mather, everybody knows that we're building a

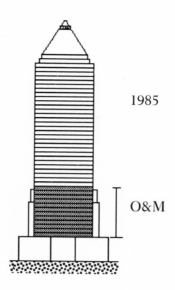

1985

O&M

project. Ogilvy and Mather, by being a partner and the first major tenant, helped to sell the building. The entire brokerage community knew we were building the building."

Soderberg was of course being modest when describing the building as "selling itself." From the early days of the project he and his colleagues at the Zeckendorf Company spend a considerable amount of time and effort trying to find tenants who would commit themselves as soon as possible to renting the thirty-thousand-square-foot floors.

Tenants matter to skyscrapers because of their close interaction with the design and construction of the building. At its most basic, a building sometimes acquires the name of a tenant as part of the bargaining process. While Worldwide Plaza rose on the old Madison Square Garden site, a smaller skyscraper was rising three blocks to the north, on Broadway. One of the advertising companies that had been interested in Worldwide Plaza in the days when it was short and fat, D'Arcy Masius Benton and Bowles, decided instead to lease three hundred thousand square feet of the Broadway building, 40 percent of the whole. That chunk of floor space gave them the leverage to persuade the landlord to give the building the name of the company, and it is now the D'Arcy Masius Benton and Bowles Building, a somewhat less euphonious name than Worldwide Plaza.

In the tortuous procedures that accompanied the search for and capture of tenants, the exterior and interior design played an important part, as did the appearance of the rest of the site and even the wider community. For example, the days of the nearby Adonis Theater were numbered, once it became clear how distasteful the potential tenants found the prospect of being near a theater showing films like *Well Hung, Brothers Do It* and *The Hot Rods*.

So far as financing the building was concerned, the most important factor was the early participation of Ogilvy and Mather, who were interested in taking nearly six hundred thousand square feet. To imagine what that means, if the average office is ten feet by fourteen feet, this space would have accommodated three thousand rooms, spread over fourteen floors and the associated lobbies and corridors. At the time it was a perfect marriage—a large company finding the space it needed to move all its offices into one building at a reasonable cost, and a developer with more than a third of his building leased before construction had even started.

A tenant leasing a large amount of space in a new office building is presented with a shell: floors, ceilings, and partly finished interior walls and windows. A power supply is provided, and a central supply of heating, air conditioning, and ventilation. The tenant will want to impose his own style on the premises and to design the interior office space to suit his employees and directors.

The money that changes hands can take a bewildering variety of forms and flow in various directions. It's not simply a matter of the tenant's paying the landlord, for example; the tenant could ask the landlord to pay for the unexpired leases on his existing premises. One prospective Worldwide Plaza tenant asked for $6.5 million to compensate its existing landlord for leaving the premises early. This could also have been expressed as a six-month rent-free period. In this case, ZCWK didn't feel the potential deal was worth the outlay.

Part of the negotiations with a tenant addresses the fact that the tenant must pay for a great deal of interior design and construction to make the offices suit his needs. The contract includes something called a "work letter." In the unhurried days when developers leased buildings only when completely finished, the landlord would write a letter describing what the tenant would get for his rent in addition to four walls and a floor. This would specify ceilings, carpets, a certain amount of lighting per square foot, and so on. But when the tenant has signed up while the building is under construction, it is pointless for the landlord to supply all the interior fittings when the tenant can do it himself and end up with something closer to his needs. What now happens is that the *landlord* pays the *tenant* an agreed amount per square foot to use to equip the bare shell of his office space with the interior he needs. The figure varies and can be a closely guarded secret, like the rest of the figures in a complex leasing deal, but can easily amount to $30–60 a square foot. When multiplied by half a million or so for a big rental, this is a lot of cash to have to hand back to the tenant.

In addition, tenants in a good bargaining position, as O&M were, can get the owner to pay for some of the more substantial structural work that they want done. O&M managed to prize more than $600,000 worth of structural work and electrical improvements out of Jack Schuster, or, rather, out of the owner—with Schuster grudgingly overseeing the work.

Factors like this made the leasing process a protracted and convoluted business in which potential tenants came and went. On a good day, the building would be almost entirely rented—apart from the small matter of signing the contract. On a bad day, six hundred thousand square feet of space would be available because someone had dropped out, or threatened to. Each of the prospective tenants took part in a dance with Zeckendorf that was part serious, part tactical. "It's a gut-wrenching business," said Soderberg later, looking back when the building was fully leased. "One minute you think you've got a deal. The next moment you haven't. The worst thing you fear is opening the building without some floors leased."

Yet, as he also pointed out from time to time, he *had* had it easy on this project. The combination of word of mouth, Bill Zeckendorf's contacts, alert and hungry real-estate brokers looking for million-dollar commissions, and, perhaps, leaflet mailings and advertisements produced a long list of interested tenants. Indeed, although ZCWK had hired an advertising agency to spread the word, they sometimes had doubts about the agency's approach. It took only a five-minute walk around the block to realize that there was a mismatch between the Clinton area in 1986 and the image the agency wanted to promote. Soderberg was concerned about this:

> The image that the PR people first came up with was this Parisian garden and London town houses. I said, "Guys, it's Eighth Avenue, Ninth Avenue, Manhattan, it's not London, it's not Paris. We can't move the building from Eighth Avenue to Park Avenue, and we've got to show an area map, so why not be firm about it: Here it is, Eighth Avenue." I mean, we can't move the site. I said, "You know, we're spending a lot of money building a class-A building, one that's going to have a major presence and major amenities, that could be anywhere in Manhattan." They wanted to stay away from addressing the "Eighth, Ninth Avenue area" and I felt we had to be up front about it. Some of these things were almost caricature brochures, and I'm adamant that if you're dealing with corporate America you've got to present yourself in a way that corporate America is used to seeing—very formal, polished, and straightforward. I guess they finally saw the light—they're creative people and they wanted to have their two cents, and I'm a creative person and I wanted my two cents' worth, and we sort of struck a balance.

Although it's easy to see why people pay a lot of attention to the surroundings when contemplating a move, companies are prepared to pay only so much above a basic rental figure as a premium for that particular aspect of their new premises. Indeed, if they were really keen on good value they might decide to leave Manhattan entirely—many companies do. For many office activities it seems a sheer indulgence to choose premises on an expensive piece of land in Manhattan rather than a cheap piece in, say, Poughkeepsie.

The major companies who were to move into Worldwide Plaza had obviously decided on a potentially uneasy compromise by opting for a site that was still far more expensive than out-of-town but which showed a considerable savings over the most fashionable area of Manhattan, with the hope that their area would eventually become fashionable if they only held on for a few years. Companies choosing to rent space in Worldwide Plaza might save about $5 a square foot, $150,000 per floor per year, compared with a few blocks farther east. But they still needed to be reassured that they weren't moving *too* far down-market, and that reassurance was enthusiastically supplied by Bob Salomon, an energetic sixty-two-year-old who had forgone retirement to sell the mid-West Side to potential clients of the Zeckendorf Company.

Salomon was perpetually smiling. Thin and tanned, he tackled with gusto the job of persuading people to believe two things: that they were heroes to consider settling as pioneers in a frontier land, and that there would be no murderous Indians when they arrived:

> One day people will look back at Zeckendorf and say, "Look what he did, he created an entire new area." I explain to people that we're not creating just one building, we're creating a city, a dynamic city. We're the forerunners on Eighth Avenue; ultimately we will change the whole area, and if they're smart enough, and a lot of them are, they'll get on the bandwagon. Eighth Avenue has been a sort of a seedy area, between the Port Authority on

40th and 41st Streets and 49th and 50th, which is our building, there are a lot of pockets of difficult areas. That's going to change. I believe there will be some people that ultimately will have to move. There's a lot of poverty in that area, and that's an unfortunate thing. We hope that there will be some way of finding homes for these people. But change is going to happen. There's no question about it.

One reason that the neighborhood matters to a tenant is the need for a high standard and variety of "food outlets," as they are called, in the vicinity. And if people want to eat at their desks, as many do, they require an astonishing range of fast-food varieties, preferably food that can be ordered by telephone or, in a recent late-1980s development in office life, by fax.

On May 20, 1988, in Bill Zeckendorf's office, an earnest discussion took place about the types of restaurants and shops that would be most appropriate in the retail space on the first three floors of Worldwide Plaza. Soderberg, Salomon, and Zeckendorf, all in shirtsleeves, were looking at one of the floor plans, and Soderberg overlaid a sheet of yellow architects' drafting paper with various penciled suggestions as to how the retail space might be allocated. They displayed an impressive knowledge of the nuances of clients' tastes. Soderberg spoke in terms of brasserie versus bar, "tablecloth" versus fast food, and from time to time Zeckendorf would interject with some query about the eating needs of the different professions. "What are you going to do about takeout? You have a lot of takeout lunches. . . ." Salomon pointed out that Ninth Avenue would have takeouts, but Soderberg dismissed that idea. Clearly he thought that busy office workers would not wish their messengers and secretaries to travel six hundred feet in search of sustenance, or to wait the time orders would take to be delivered from so far away. "If you're dealing with a law firm," said Zeckendorf, "they're going to be sending stuff up all day long." Plans were made for a fast-food restaurant across the Plaza at the foot of the office tower. Soderberg then pointed out another professional characteristic that had to be satisfied within the building: "This building's got to have a bar because of the ad agencies and the attorneys."

As the discussion continued, the group considered whether some of the spaces allocated to restaurants should have shops instead—a women's-wear shop, for example—but the inner man prevailed over the outer woman and they penciled in a deli here, an ethnic restaurant there. Soderberg, from Kentucky, suggested a Cajun restaurant—"good Southern cooking"—and they all laughed.

The size of the whole Worldwide Plaza development effectively meant that it could promise to rectify on site some of the deficiencies of Clinton, at least until the area itself went up-market. And having gone slightly down-market by choosing Worldwide Plaza, the tenants could allow a little more money for actually equipping and running a thriving corporation with a staff of thousands. Even in this aspect of budgeting, it might seem an indulgence to spend the equivalent of $80 per square foot on furnishings, carpets, lights, decor, and ancillary space—waiting areas, washrooms, and so on—when far less could buy a few desks, bookshelves, typewriters, and electric coffee makers, with some attractive posters on the wall—all you need to carry on your business as an advertising agent or a lawyer. But this is to ignore the key fact about office life, particularly in a city like New York. Providing conditions in which the work will be done is only a small part of the function of office premises. No one would deny that equivalent work could be done in less opulent premises, but your clients would think much less of you if you tried to do it, as would your competitors, your investors, and your staff. The psychological value of the money spent on city-center office space is rarely made explicit.

When O&M appointed an internal management team to supervise the move, much of their time was taken up with the design and furnishing of the individual offices themselves. To help visualize the implications of some of their decisions, and to sell the decisions to the staff and partners, José Lambert designed and built an imposing visual aid, a life-sized mock-up of a corner of one of the floors of Worldwide Plaza as it would look when decorated and furnished. It was just like a large movie set, with walls and doors and windows, and cost over $100,000 to build. But the team felt it was worth every penny, because it enabled them to be confident about decisions whose implications would not otherwise have become apparent until they moved into the building. Bob McGarry feels he saved several times the cost of the mock-up with one decision: "We had an estimate for a back-lighting of our ads and we were talking about something like $30,000 per light track built into the ceiling. We installed it in the mock-up and discovered that it really didn't add anything to the look of the thing, so we replaced that $30,000 light track with four wall washes. Multiply that by fifteen floors and I've paid for this mock-up many times over."

At regular intervals in late 1987 and 1988, groups of Ogilvy and Mather employees trod carefully across the cobbled paving of West 22nd Street, a mile south of Worldwide Plaza, toward a corrugated shutter in the wall of some old brick buildings. The shutter was lifted with a rattle, revealing a small graffiti-covered door. In single file, a couple of directors, a photographer, perhaps, a secretary or two, a copywriter, and some account executives stepped gingerly around piles of rubbish across echoing bare floorboards and walked toward a small door in a plasterboard wall erected on the floor of the warehouse. As the door was unlocked, a collection of "Oohs!" went up from the group as they peered through the door and glimpsed their future.

Inside was a lobby, furnished and decorated exactly as if it were the reception area for one of the O&M departments. Through a door on the right of the lobby, unlocked with a card-key, was a corridor that wound around the mock-up and off which opened several sizes of office to allow the visitors to judge what their offices would be like, and to compare them with their current premises. Overall, the reaction of the group was positive. People asked questions about the lighting and the elevators. An O&M staff photographer looked at the type of space that would be allotted to her and said that it was "night and day" compared with what she had.

Lambert showed off the design of the offices and discussed the amenities that would be available to the company. Someone asked if there would be a bar; indeed there would: "There's an old bar at Albany that has closed and we want to go and buy the bar and install it as a sort of antique bar." The most striking feature marking out these offices as typically Ogilvy and Mather was the bright-red carpeting everywhere, a design constraint imposed on Lambert from the start as a key element in the appearance of the new offices. McGarry, for O&M, described the importance of the color: "Red is an Ogilvy and Mather color. In every office in the forty-nine countries we operate in, when you walk off an elevator or in an entrance lobby you will see red carpet, white walls, and in most cases black doors. I believe at one point when Ogilvy was doing some renovation work in their headquarters building, the designers asked Mr. Ogilvy what he wanted and the story is he said, 'I like red carpet, white walls, black doors,' and it's been that way ever since."

Lambert did not seem entirely comfortable having such a strong design decision imposed on him from the start of his relationship with the project, and McGarry was certainly willing to consider breaking with tradition, but not for long: "Early on we said, 'Let's see if we can get away from the red carpet. Maybe we'll have it in our reception room but let's do our corridors in a different color. Let's just put a stripe of red in.' But we sat in a meeting one day with about eight people from our management sitting around, and one by one they said, 'Gee, shouldn't we have more red carpet?' So now, if you look at the mock-up, you'll see that all the gray we had in the corridors is gone, the red is in, and we're all much happier."

There were three sizes of office: A (twelve feet by twenty feet), B (twelve by fourteen), and C (ten by twelve). Although these were smaller than many of their existing offices, the general feeling among the group was that it was worth exchanging a little territory for an improved quality of life. As one of the visiting senior vice-presidents looked around an office similar to the one he would have, he commented, "It's pleasant, a little sterile, requires a personal touch. I'll cover the walls, *and* I'll cover that dreadful carpet with something else."

Though it's efficient for a large company to have a lot of offices on the same floor, there are drawbacks. The huge, thirty-thousand-square-foot floor in Worldwide Plaza meant that, apart from those offices in a twelve-foot-wide strip around the perimeter, most of the working space was away from natural light. Lambert had hoped to compensate for that in some way: "I happen to like a lot of glass and I love light and I love sharing that light with the people adjacent to the core. I like the transparency you can get with a lot of glass as you're walking through it, and I like seeing people doing their jobs. O&M decided 'No,' but I haven't completely lost it, because although they don't know it they'll never close those doors, and as you walk through the space you'll look into the peripheral offices and you'll get the light."

From time to time the architects of O&M and SOM had to meet and coordinate their activities, particularly when O&M decided that they didn't like something SOM had planned and decided to change it. They had every right to do so and had the extra clout of being an equity partner in the building, but Lambert felt he ought still to handle things carefully, particularly when it came to the lower floors of the building, the escalators and the lobby, which O&M wanted to change: "There's ways of dealing with a corporation like Skidmore, I have great respect for Jim Bodnar, and I would go in and say, 'Jim, here are my problems,' and then offer him a solution. I guess I led him down the path until he came up with a solution that was acceptable to Ogilvy." There was endless scope for arguments about who would have to pay for changes, and a whole range of people in SOM, HRH, and the Zeckendorf Company would need to be consulted. This made communication between

O&M and the rest a tricky business, to be handled very carefully.

Bob McGarry's first meeting with Schuster nearly ended in disaster:

> It was at one of our regular Skidmore meetings and this man, who turned out to be Jack Schuster, was sitting across the table. When we were about four minutes into the meeting, he started banging on the table and saying, "I don't care who you are, this is what you will do." I left, picked up the phone, called Terry Soderberg at Zeckendorf's and said, "Who is this guy? I never want to go to a meeting with him again." And Terry said, "I'm sorry, we'll take care of that," and I guess we had two or three encounters after that on a similar adversary basis. Then, all of a sudden, I sat down one day and had lunch with Jack and he said, "OK, I realize now that, in addition to being the major tenant, you are a partner in the building, and the partners have told me that there's a different relationship there and we're supposed to be working together," and since then I think Jack has been a real godsend to the project. He can cut through things very quickly. We can pick up the phone and say, "Look, there's a discrepancy here, Jack; how do we resolve it?" and it gets done.

Another group of tenants was finding Schuster difficult to take during 1986 and 1987. Per square foot of space, three elderly ladies in apartments on 49th Street probably generated more nervous excitement for Schuster than all the O&M changes. When Zeckendorf offered the community 132 fully modernized, renovated buildings, he may not have realized the complications involved in making such a gift. First, to the surprise of the Zeckendorf Company, some of the residents were not all keen on the idea of moving, even if it was only a temporary move while their own apartments were renovated. Schuster was particularly surprised:

> Those apartments are something you read about but you can't imagine one unless you see it. They're horrendous. The floors,

the walls are in a horrible condition. The plumbing system and electrical system are, in my judgment, substandard. I'm not even 100 percent sure that they're legal. There's no such thing as painting, I mean, the plaster is coming off the wall, the roofs leak, the windows leak, and the rooms are very tiny. You see children living in rooms that are in really bad shape. I have children; I have grandchildren; the thought is just scary. I mean, the rooms are like rabbit warrens, with two and three people living in a room that you wouldn't use as a walk-in closet.

Certainly some of the apartments had barely changed from when they were put up in the last century. From one room overlooking the street they stretched back into the gloomy depths of the building, with no daylight apart from a glimmer through a window onto a well in the center of the building. Such an environment doesn't necessarily encourage good housekeeping. But there's another factor in the equation which is easy to ignore: whatever the external appearances of a home, there's a deep human need for attachment to familiar surroundings. And that attachment, when it has grown over the years, can make someone blind to things that are all too apparent to people from outside, who see with fresh eyes.

The three ladies on 49th Street were called Mary, Dolores, and Bella. Mary was tall and dignified with curly gray hair, and showed some willingness to consider what was on offer, although she was a long way from accepting it. Bella, short and plump, was making no concessions to the possibility that she might end up better off if she did what Zeckendorf and the community wanted. Dolores was thin and small with gray hair in a bun and a wicked smile. She probably understood the realities of the situation better than the others but was still determined to put up a fight against the disruption that they would be caused.

Among them they harbored a selection of fears and anxieties that were sometimes contradictory but nevertheless bolstered them against the assembled might of the evil developers—"the power of the billionaire," as Mary put it. They didn't trust anyone. They were being asked to move out of apartments they had lived in for up to fifty years so that the apartments could be renovated. Then they would be able to move back in—or so Zeckendorf *said*. Mary, Dolores, and Bella chewed over the subject for hours, rehearsing their objections to the scheme and telling anyone who would listen how bad they felt about the situation:

"I may consider moving," Mary said, "if I get something in writing that seems like it's a fair and just settlement. The option is that we relocate to the other building and they will completely refurbish this building and then we would have the option to move back . . ."

"That's what they *said*," Bella butted in.

". . . but it's only words on paper; nobody's really sure what's going on."

"But I will *never* move," said Bella.

"Like Mary said," Dolores added, "it's not really a promise just because they wrote something on paper. They would have to show us more proof, I think."

The three ladies dismissed the entire world of contracts as "just writing on paper," although it's difficult to see exactly what other sort of proof would have allayed their fears. In any case, there was a fundamental mismatch between the developer's view of what he was doing *for* them and their view of what was being done *to* them.

Schuster was puzzled: "I really don't know how we are going to be able to accomplish a complete first-class renovation while people are still in the building. We may end up doing a cosmetic job on some of the apartments, which is really not fair to those people who are in there, since everyone else is going to be getting new kitchens and new bathrooms and new walls and new ceilings and new appliances, new everything."

Bella didn't quite see it that way: "We *have* new bathrooms.

What is he going to put in new bathrooms for? When I was living in this house in 1938, the bathrooms were out in the hall. We had a tub in the kitchen. We didn't have no showers, no nothing. In 1938 they put the new bathrooms in—sink, tub, shower, every-thing—and they took the tub out of the kitchen and gave us com-bination sinks and everything. *Now* what are they going to do? We already *have* a private bathroom."

There was one important reason that Schuster *had* to worry about whether Bella and a few like her might refuse to move out of their apartments. Satisfying the old ladies and the other residents, every single one of them, was a condition of the permit the devel-opers had received from the city. One resident holding out, however perversely, could place unpleasant obstacles in the way of com-pleting the project. And it had been known, in slightly different circumstances. While Worldwide Plaza was going up on Eighth Avenue, another, smaller skyscraper was rising on the other side of town, on Lexington Avenue. This particular building was being constructed around and on top of a three-story house whose owner had refused to sell out to the developers at a market price. Her suspected motive was to squeeze more money out of the developers, but they refused to give in and pay her off. Although Schuster's problem was different, he didn't want to become involved in any-thing resembling *that* situation:

> We are pushing to get some apartments completed so that the people who are worried can see what they would be moving into. Also, we'll let them know that we have no intention of making them rich by asking them to move, because I think that in some cases that's what they expected. They expected someone to drop a purse of gold in order for them to move, which is not going to happen.
>
> I think, if we go to the wire and can't move these people, we intend going to the Borough President or city agencies and

telling them that it's absolutely impossible for us to fulfill our commitment. We would hope at that time that perhaps the city would intervene as a friend of the court and try to get these people to relocate. And if they don't, then the city has no option but to let us off the hook.

7

FRAMING THE STEEL

A t about eleven o'clock on the morning of April 10, 1987, the tugboat *Bessie Walker* eased her way slowly up the Ohio River from Cairo (pronounced "Care-o"), Illinois, toward Newburg Locks, a few miles from where the states of Indiana, Illinois, and Kentucky meet. The river was high because of heavy rain in the previous few weeks, and the sky was overcast. The scenery on either side of the river was fairly flat, and in the area of the lock the banks were lined with expensive houses owned by some of the better-off people who worked in nearby Evansville, Indiana.

The *Bessie Walker* was pushing eighteen barges, lashed together in six rows of three abreast, with a total weight of some thirty-three thousand tons. This made for tricky maneuvering as Greg Hart, the captain, moved toward the locks. In his words, these conditions made things "a little touchy." It was rather like pushing a pencil from the eraser end toward a quarter-inch gap in front of the point. Two-thirds of the way down the rows was the barge that had left Mosher Steel's plant in Houston about two weeks before with its thousand-ton load of fabricated steel for Worldwide Plaza. There was little to distinguish this barge from the other seventeen. If you opened one of the hatches and clambered down into it, you'd see bundles and bundles of rusty steel, each with the appropriate colored ribbon around it. Here, some hundred yards from the tug, all was silent and there was little sensation of movement. But from the hatchway you could just make out the relative movement of the trees on the southern bank of the Ohio, a quarter of a mile wide at this point.

It's a lazy existence, drifting along at five miles an hour and covering 100 to 120 miles per day, and, to put it mildly, it might seem to lack excitement. For Hart, though, it can be addictive:

You're on a boat for twenty-eight days. We don't touch bank. We're in the middle of the river and we run twenty-four hours a day. Of course, it's just normal, people get homesick. You think about your family, especially if you're married and have kids and all. It's a lot easier to be working at home every day than it is being out here on the boat. I've seen people get on at twelve o'clock, and at one o'clock they're on their way back home, their twenty-eight days cut short real fast. But then there's people out here who don't want to do nothing but ride the boats. I know people that ride 100, 106 days at a time. I don't know if they feel more dependable on this than they do off on the bank or what, but I guess they just enjoy it. It's a good job, once you get it in your veins. I've tried to quit two or three times, but I've always found myself back out here.

There's a crew of nine: a mate and four deck hands, one engineer, a pilot, the captain, and a cook. The cook is Brenda McKinty,
a jolly, plumply pretty woman who joined the company after her
husband died and encouraged everyone to believe that she could
cook. In fact, her presence as cook may well have provided the
main point of interest on those early voyages, by the sheer novelty
of what she put on the table at mealtimes. "When I'd make gravy
in the morning—I'd never made it before—they'd keep telling me,
'You're not putting in enough flour. Take it away.' Then the next
morning it'd be so thick you could do it on the wall and it would
just stay there. Then they'd say, 'Don't put in as much.' I had a
horrible time with gravy."

If you spend much of your day behind a desk, it's tempting to
romanticize the working lives of people like Hart. And with plenty
of thinking time, he romanticizes for himself about the variety of
loads the barge train carries and the way they link one part of
America to another:

> We've got a load of fertilizer, got a load of lime [his accent makes
> it sound like "lamb"], and, let's see, there's a load of zinc in these
> two. Zinc I haven't seen a whole lot of, but you see a few barges
> of it every once in a while. Basically it's large commodities that
> we can travel with at the cheapest expense. I often wonder where
> some of this stuff does go. I know the fertilizer. I can place the
> farmer, working in the fields. The chemicals we haul to the dif-
> ferent chemical companies that make different things, you know.
> A lot of stuff that you read on your cleaning supplies and stuff,
> we haul it, we haul it by barge. It's amazing, you know; it keeps
> you thinking sometimes.

Water transport emphasizes its economy of scale when the
barges reach Pittsburgh and are offloaded onto trucks for the next
stage of the journey. The steel in each barge needs about fifty trucks

to carry it to the marshaling yards in New Jersey; all the steel for Worldwide Plaza would have filled 750 trucks.

On May 18, the first steel columns arrived at the site, marking the next stage in the growth of the office tower. The foundations had been dug down to leave enough space for two huge basement floors with parking and unloading bays for trucks that would be lowered in truck elevators. At the moment this was all open to the elements, and dotted around were the concrete and steel footings—the platforms, each of which had been designed and constructed to receive about a hundredth of the weight of the fully loaded building. The concrete poured four weeks previously was now awaiting the load of the first column, a fraction of what it would eventually have to bear. Two weeks before, the weekly job meeting, held at SOM's offices, had heard that "low concrete strengths in some footings have been received," after the test cylinders had been sent back to the laboratory and tested by crushing.

The columns that were arriving weighed about twenty tons each. Made of the thickest-gauge steel in the building, each had an I-cross-section about four inches thick. Waiting on the floor of the excavation was a team of ironworkers hired by A. J. Ross to erect the steel. They would stay with the building until topping out, the traditional ceremony that marks the completion of the steel skeleton. That was estimated to be just under a year away, making an average erection rate of just under a floor a week. One "fact" that has become widely known about ironworkers on skyscrapers is that many of them are Native Americans. Getting to the root of this belief is not as easy as it seems. Even the people involved in the design and construction of Worldwide Plaza gave differing stories.

It's certainly true that the steel erection gangs working on Worldwide Plaza were dominated by Mohawk Indians, all from the same reservation, Kahnawake, meaning "at the rapids," near Montreal. It was really a family concern: many of the ironworkers were cousins; one was the grandson of an ironworker on the Empire

State Building, and at one stage he and three cousins had been working with their uncle on the Worldwide Plaza job. It didn't take long for the "sidewalk superintendents," the construction industry's name for passers-by who watch the activity, to pick out the Mohawks, as the building rose during the spring of 1987. In his essay "The Mohawks in High Steel," printed as the first chapter of Edmund Wilson's *Apologies to the Iroquois*, Joseph Mitchell describes the Indians from the Kahnawake reservation, also known as Caughanwaga: "They have high cheekbones and jut noses, their eyes are sad, shrewd and dark brown, their hair is straight and coal black, their skin is smooth and coppery, and they have the same beautiful, erect, chin-lifted, haughty walk that gypsies have."

Pete Marquis was one of the Mohawks working on the site, and Mitchell's description could have been of him. Both he and his father worked on the tower, and when work finished on Friday, four or five of the Mohawks would share a car for the five-hour drive back to Kahnawake. The reservation now has the appearance of many small Canadian towns, apart from its self-referential iconography; a main street parallel with the Saint Lawrence along which the police car—with a Mohawk Indian head on the doors— cruises past a supermarket with a Mohawk Indian head on the sign outside. There are a Catholic church and schools, reflecting the fact that most Kahnawake Indians are Catholic. Weekends are spent playing lacrosse or hockey, or drinking and socializing, discussing the events of the week in New York.

After a weekend at home, the ironworkers would leave the reservation at midnight on Sunday and arrive at about 5:00 A.M. in Brooklyn, where many of them lived during the week, ready to start on the steel at about eight. One or two of them suggested that the work they did on Mondays might lack some of the efficiency of the other days because of the Sunday-night drive.

Mitchell dates the Indians' involvement with high steel from the time when, in 1886, Mohawks were hired as day laborers on a railroad bridge being built across the Saint Lawrence near their reservation, and he quotes a letter from an official of the Dominion Bridge Company:

> It was impossible to keep them off [the bridge]. As the work progressed it became apparent to all that these Indians were very odd in that they did not have any fear of heights. If not watched they would climb up into the spans and walk around up there as cool and collected as the toughest of our riveters, most of whom were old sailing ship men especially picked for their experience in working aloft. We decided it would be mutually advantageous to see what these Indians could do, so we picked out some and gave them a little training, and it turned out that putting riveting tools in their hands was like putting ham with eggs.

From then on there was no looking back, or down. Every new bridge in the area was built with the participation of the Mohawks, until on August 29, 1907, a span of the Quebec Bridge under construction collapsed, killing ninety-six men, thirty-five of them Kahnawakes. During the weekend, Marquis and his children sometimes visit the cemetery in Kahnawake, where the bridge-workers whose bodies were recovered are buried. An arch over the gate is made of miniature steel columns and beams, and each man's grave has a cross made of steel members instead of stone. This tradition continues for any Mohawk killed while working as an ironworker.

Marquis's father, Frank, has always been used to running around at height: "We started off like kids, we got on a bridge, and we play on a lintel, play tag on there and run around and don't, well, you know there's water at the bottom, you're not gonna get hurt if you go down. Then you get used to climbing up anywhere you want. I never get scared. The higher I go, the better work I do, I think." Pete Marquis also took to the job readily; he didn't see what the fuss was about:

Well, it's just natural. People say you're an acrobat, but if you see a squirrel jumping in the tree there, you don't say he's an acrobat or anything. That's just what he's used to living in. That's what we're used to living in.

My son? Oh, I don't know, he still have a couple more years to go. You have to be around twenty-one-years old to be able to get a union book to go to work, but first you have to go to training school to start off.

We were always meant to be ironworkers and just one disaster like the Quebec Bridge couldn't change our whole way of life. But when we're working on Worldwide Plaza, we have roughly maybe forty guys, forty-five guys working there. If something ever happened it would probably turn out to be as disastrous as the Quebec Bridge, you know, so . . .

It's a compelling idea that the Mohawks have an inherited ability to adapt so readily to walking on six-inch-wide beams eight hundred feet up in the air. But what possible circumstances in their ancestral past could have provided that quality? Perhaps necessity and habit simply led to the suppression and eventual elimination of fears that everyone has. Like seasickness, fear of heights can diminish with experience. But Edmund Wilson's essay contains an intriguing reference to much earlier evidence of special abilities in the American Indians. In 1709 John Lawson wrote: "They will walk over deep brooks and creeks on the smallest poles, and that without any fear or concern. Nay, an Indian will walk on the ridge of a barn or house and look down the gable-end, and spit upon the ground, as unconcerned as if he was walking on terra firma."*

On the day the first columns arrived, those special skills weren't needed, rooted as the ironworkers were to the ground. Their job was to see the first thirty-foot-long column lifted by crane safely from the back of the truck on 50th Street to a position lying flat on the ground in the excavation, propped up on pieces of wood to

---

* John Lawson, *History of Carolina*, 1709.

prevent damage from its own weight. There it was inspected to see that it was intact and undamaged by its journey from the steel fabricators. In fact, one of the "tags" with boltholes for connecting a beam to the column had been bent, and one of the ironworkers hammered it back into position with six or seven blows of a sledgehammer.

Next, the cable loops that had lifted the column horizontally from the truck were slipped off and a metal peg with another cable loop put through two boltholes in the top of the column. Then the giant hook on the end of the crane was hooked into the loop, and the signal given to raise the end of the column.

When the end of the column was over the steel baseplate, the crane operator lowered it slowly into position. Two tags protruded horizontally from either side of the base of the column. These had to slip over two threaded bolt shafts sticking up through the billet plate—the anchor bolts that had been positioned wrongly the previous month. They had been embedded in the concrete an inch or two lower than they should have been. Had they been left that way, when the baseplate was put over them there would have been a shorter length of bolt for the column to be bolted to. The bolts were not crucial to the stability of the building—once the network of columns and beams was in place they would be superfluous—but they were necessary to anchor the column to the ground for the next week or two, until the rest of the basement steel was erected. John Kleinschnitz, in charge of the steel erectors, had two options. He could erect the column on the shortened anchor bolts, and hope that there was enough thread to hold the twenty-ton column upright, or he could arrange for concrete to be hacked away from the footing until the surface was low enough to expose the correct length of bolt. This would mean setting the whole column lower in order to make it stable, and then lifting it a couple of inches in a few weeks once the rest of the framework had grown around it. Kleinschnitz decided on the latter course.

The final stage of slipping the boltholes over the bolts is not always as smooth as it was with the first column. Sometimes the bolts are displaced or bent sideways and have to be hammered underneath the holes; sometimes the end of the column simply won't lower neatly over the holes—after all, it's being manipulated by a crane driver thirty yards away who can't see the inch-wide bolts and is relying on hand signals from one of the team.

One final task remained before the first column could stand alone on the site. The peg that had been put through the top of the column had to be removed. With a flick of the wrist one of the ironworkers sent a wave along the cable up to the peg and whipped it out. The first of the building's two thousand lengths of steel column was in position, and the ironworkers gave a small, ragged cheer before retiring to a corner of the site to cluster around a cooler of beer and celebrate.

While the lower floors of steel were under construction, much of the rest of the steel framework was being laid out on a patch of ground thirty miles away from the site. Keasbey, New Jersey, is not a place one would willingly visit without a very good reason. Like much of the area along the New Jersey Turnpike, it seems

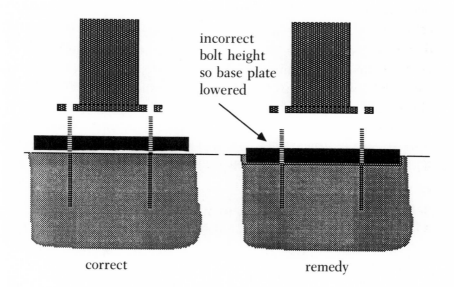

correct   remedy

a flat and industrialized wasteland. From exit 11, a mile or so along Route 9 you reach the traffic lights by Fee's Delicatessen. Turn left and you arrive at the A. J. Ross Logistics Plant, the penultimate stop of the steel's journey. Sixty-five acres of cinders surround some single-story office buildings and several large warehouses. Laid out on the cinders were the steel beams and girders for some of Manhattan's current skyscrapers, in an order that might seem random to the unpracticed eye but made perfect sense to Virginia Edelstein, A. J. Ross's dispatcher.

Edelstein challenges any preconceptions one might have of what a New Jersey steel dispatcher should look like. Young and tall with long blond hair and a thin pretty face, she deals all day with the yard men who lay out the steel pieces and the truck drivers who take the steel into Manhattan, and she calls them all "my men":

> I've been doing this for about thirteen years. I went to college, became a physical-education teacher, started to work in physical education in schools, and realized it's what I wanted to do, but it didn't pay very well that long ago. And I answered an ad in the newspaper that was for a trucking company and that's where I started out. It was different. Everything changed, every day. You didn't have a nine-to-five job. And it was exciting, I progressed from there to working right now with the erectors in New York City. They taught us the ropes. Every building is different, so when you start a new building the erector actually helps you along. He works with the blueprints and we work with the steel. We can't envision what a building looks like. We just get pictures at the end of a job. We never really know.

The steel arrived by truck from Pittsburgh in bundles. The man in charge of the Worldwide Plaza steel had to see that it was laid out division by division, pile by pile, gathering together all the pieces that would be erected in one particular part of the steel framework. The tree columns, because they were more complex, with branches that might be bent out of shape, were separated from the more straightforward beams and columns.

When the steel erection began, Kleinschnitz made daily calls to Edelstein, giving details of the steel that would be needed the following day. With luck, Edelstein and her colleagues would be able to find it: "It's a challenge. Sixty-five acres of steel to find a three-foot-four-inch piece." Her relationship with Kleinschnitz was one born of years of working together without meeting: "Johnny and I have gone through several buildings together. So we've known each other for several years over the phone. Worldwide Plaza is such a fast-growing building, occasionally he has to make changes that require a certain piece of steel; he'd like it today; I always tell him, 'No problem.' Occasionally I'll call him up for help too. We work very well together, Johnny Kleinschnitz and A. J. Ross, very well."

When Kleinschnitz called, Edelstein passed the instruction to the yard to pick out the steel, selected a driver to take the load into Manhattan, and decided on the best type of trailer for the load:

> There are several different types of trailers: stretch trailers, forty-five-footers, forty-footers, low boys, step decks, drop decks, dollies. A low boy is a trailer that has a higher level and then it drops down to a low level for pieces that are particularly high. We have a height limit to go into the city, because we have to pass the tunnels and bridges. Stretch trailers are kinda exactly what they sound like; those can open up to a certain length to accommodate pieces that are seventy-five-feet long. Most of the loads fit on forty-five-footers.
>
> The drivers are phenomenal. Half these loads you can never imagine that someone could bring into the city, into streets that are as wide as my office, to make the corners. Eighty-five-foot-long pieces, a hundred and fifty thousand pounds. These guys chain these things down and they run 'em just like we drive our cars through a country road.

The city restricts us from making any type of a wide movement during daylight hours in the city because of the traffic
problem. So we have to run them over in the middle of the night,
over the bridges, when hopefully there is no traffic. They're trying
to lessen the traffic and the congestion in the city and it's to their
advantage but sometimes to our disadvantage.

Seven days a week, twenty-four hours a day, this company
doesn't stop. Right now I have eight different buildings going
on—Worldwide is one of my largest and it is really running quick.
It had several different cranes to feed in the beginning and we
had to really push the steel in there as fast as we could. The
building is going to be phenomenal, it's one of the best and biggest
ones that I have right now in the city, and we're doing very well
on it.

During the spring and summer of 1987, the steel skeleton
slowly rose from the ground, but the construction activity was not
without its problems. The lower floors of the building were complex,
representing the architects' attempts to impart subtle elliptical
curves using long straight pieces of steel. The lobbies of the building
were considered by many to be the jewels at its heart. As originally
planned by SOM, they would be clad outside with pre-cast concrete
and granite from Brazil, and would have Fiore di Pesco marble
inside. There would be escalators from the first floor to a mezzanine
floor, where the elevators would rise in three banks of four around
three sides of the building. The escalators would ensure that people
coming into the building would be exposed to plenty of shops and
the restaurants, one at ground-floor level and one on the mezzanine.
But the grand plan was gradually diluted by the desires of the
tenants. Even as the steel for the lower floors was being erected
and the orders finalized for granite, pre-cast, and marble, change
orders were flying around that would produce a somewhat more
cramped, less sweeping vista at ground level. Ogilvy and Mather
had always been eager to have their own lobby, and they also wanted

to impose their own design concepts, so far as was still possible, as José Lambert, their architect, described:

> The Ogilvy and Mather lobby was changed expressly for Ogilvy and Mather. When we came aboard, the lobby as projected had a pair of escalators that took you to a mezzanine, and on the mezzanine you would enter the elevator banks that would take you to the top of the towers. Because of the size of the lobby and escalators, we felt that we could not accommodate a security desk and a milling spot for the number of employees that Ogilvy and Mather has in New York. Besides that, there was rather a grandiose lobby with an awful lot of limestone, pink limestone, and a lot of corbeling, and when you got up to the mezzanine level there were columns and it was all very Palladian and very grand, and that's just not the way Ogilvy and Mather likes to perceive itself.
>
> We had the esclators removed and arranged for the elevators to go down to the first floor, which then created a much larger space for Ogilvy. We lowered the ceiling to make a much more natural, much more comfortable space for Ogilvy, less imposing, but we did maintain the limestone up to a level.
>
> Ogilvy and Mather's philosophy has been that they would rather spend their money for the benefits of their employees. What we tried to do was to make this less imposing. It went from a two-story space into a generous but one-story environment.

If O&M had been a late arrival, they would have had to take or leave the lobbies that Childs and Bodnar had designed, grandiose and Palladian as they were. As it was, the lobby change was one of several niggling problems during the spring and summer of 1987, as the steel rose unstoppably and carried behind it the myriad other trades that had to slot into the crowded schedule.

The construction of the steel framework for each floor was the first of several processes necessary to produce solid, smooth, safe floors. Once the steel columns and beams were in place, strips of metal decking were laid side by side across the gap between two beams. Concrete was then poured into the corrugated surface formed by the decking. Next, all the steel that was still visible was sprayed with a slushy gray fireproofing mixture. After that the mechanical engineering work could start, as horizontal pipes and ducts were hung under the floor above. Obviously these things had to be done in order on each floor. The floors themselves had to be built in sequence from bottom to top, to provide bricklayers, plumbers, electricians, plasterers, elevator mechanics, and so on with solid floors to work on as *they* went up the building.

With a building like Worldwide Plaza, made up of many similar floors, the best way to organize the work was to have all the necessary tasks carried out at roughly the same speed, and avoid having one trade waiting around for another. But as Worldwide Plaza rose, things started to fall badly out of synchronization. This was partly because the building was not at all a uniform straight-up-and-down skyscraper. The bottom floors, with their shops and lobbies and mezzanines, were complex to build and fiendish to synchronize. The task wasn't helped by a series of problems that, in the end, were to land in Dominic Fonti's lap, the usual place bucks stopped.

Fonti traced the problems back to some of the changes O&M had made when they decided how they wanted their part of the building to be built. These changes worried Fonti for two reasons. First, they came so late that they upset that carefully timed schedule of steel erection and floor completion. But, second, the costs of these delays seemed to him to be assigned to the owner instead of O&M, who should have paid for them: "The engineer [at SOM] was making changes to the structural drawings which were *tenant* changes without flagging them and saying, 'This is a tenant change.' It was pricing them as building changes which were paid by the owner, until I finally said, 'Hey, fellas, you can't do that, you cannot issue tenant changes as part of the regular job changes,' because the owner's not responsible for the tenant requests."

Another worry for Fonti was that the wrong size of "trench

header duct" had been ordered for the third floor, a floor whose concrete should have been poured well before. Trench header duct is a type of hollow passageway embedded in the concrete to contain electrical cable in such a way that it is accessible later, when the final cabling is decided. HRH thought the mechanical engineer had told them to order thirty-inch-wide duct. When it arrived, the engineer pointed out that they needed thirty-six-inch. Whoever goofed, there was no doubt that the engineer was right. The correct size was ordered, but this led to a delay of three to four weeks. Since the duct had to be embedded in the concrete, the concrete couldn't be poured and, as Fonti explained, in an even more ex-asperated mood than normal: "By not being able to pour the third floor without the trench duct, we can't spray the underside of the deck of the third floor [with fireproofing]. By not being able to spray the deck, we cannot hang mechanicals underside the deck. So you can see one thing leads to another to another." And there was more to upset the concrete-pouring schedule: a long-running disagree-ment between Fonti and the architects over another component in the engineering for the building, the "risers."

Risers are another type of duct to create passageways through the building for different types of piping. There are risers for various supplies of water, for the condenser water to cool the building, drinking water, fire sprinklers, and so on; to provide routes up and down the building for different air pipes, some of them exhausting the used air from the building and bringing in fresh air. These risers must run all the way up and down the building, the exhaust ducts for the seventeen lower floors expelling the air through the basement, and those for the eighteenth upward through the roof. Risers also carry the sewage from the lavatories on every floor down and out of the building. The pipes for all these facilities are installed later, but the holes and passageways must be created in the floors at the time of the concrete pouring.

Some months before the steel started going up, Fonti had been worried about the positioning and the number of these holes. He'd wanted to cluster several risers together and pass them through a few larger slots rather than many smaller ones. This would have made them easier to construct and interfered less with pouring the concrete on the floors through which the risers had to pass. But to do that would have reduced the load the floor would support.

There were two ways out of the situation. One was to strengthen the holes with extra steel around and underneath the floor. This would be expensive and had not been allowed for in the original plans and bids. Alternatively, the holes could be cut after the concrete had been poured and solidified. The solidified concrete bonded with the steel would then be strong enough to hold up the necessary load even with quite a large hole in it. In either case, a large amount of unnecessary work would have to be carried out.

Fonti's frustration grew when the other members of the team, confronted at a job meeting, didn't seem to appreciate the problem:

> At that meeting certain individuals on the design team refused to acknowledge that it was a screw-up and at that point to correct it and frame the openings. It would have cost money, and obviously the owner's gonna turn around and say, "Well, why should it cost me money, what did I do wrong?" So the engineers and consultants are apprehensive about the fact that the owners are going to turn around and give him the bill, and that's why everyone tried to sweep it under the carpet and hope maybe it'll go away by itself or it will be resolved by the subcontractors. Subcontractors are not engineers. What they're hired for is to install what's shown in the drawings. They do not design systems, and sometimes the engineers think that the subcontractors will resolve the problem, just show it graphically and they'll resolve it. Well, it'll work sometimes; it doesn't work all the time. In this case they don't work.
>
> My main concern is to get the job built. It doesn't matter to me who made the mistake, what, when, and where, just get the job built. That's our goal here, not to cover your ass.

One mild morning in November 1987 the second floor, at least, was ready for concrete to be poured. At the beginning of the week Felix Germano, the superintendent in charge of that floor and the lobby area, had laid out the week's schedule for pouring. Already things were slightly out of hand; concrete had been poured on higher floors, but the second had had to wait until every element of the steel decking and structural steel had been prepared with the right holes and supports. On the lower floors of Worldwide Plaza, the concrete would weigh about 70 pounds per square foot. Multiplied by thirty thousand or so, that's a great deal of weight for the steel beams to support. Since the steel is flexible, the beams will bend under the weight of the concrete, perhaps half an inch in a beam forty feet long. To prevent everybody's furniture from rolling to the middle of the floor, the beams are given an *upward* camber before they leave the fabrication plant so that the weight of the concrete will straighten the beam.

Between the main beams, lengths of steel decking are laid side by side, each hooking into its neighbor. Although they don't support much weight themselves, when locked together by a layer of concrete they form a floor with enough strength in tension and compression to take the total weight of people and equipment that will be on the floor.

Watching concrete pouring sounds only marginally more inviting than watching paint dry. In fact, it's an extraordinary scene of controlled panic determined by the fast setting time of modern concrete. On Friday morning, November 20, the team assembled. Pouring would start with a corner on the south side of the third floor and, barring accidents, continue nonstop until every square foot of the floor was smooth, level concrete.

Outside, on 50th Street, a line of concrete trucks waited, engines running, drums turning. Each truck would drive into the bay beside the tower, replacing a truck that had just been emptied of its load. A high-pressure pump would be fitted to the outlet and the mix pumped along solid piping to the second floor. The other end of the pipe was continually spurting concrete onto an area of floor where a team of men would work to spread, level, and smooth it.

One important thing about concrete pouring: the concrete must never be allowed to come to a halt in the pipes long enough to harden. And since this was quick-hardening concrete, that meant a few minutes. If the concrete were to stop pouring—because of a blockage in the pipe, for example—the already hyperactive mêlée would become frenetic. Men strike the pipe with sledgehammers, trying to loosen the blockage and prevent the concrete from sticking to the walls of the pipe. If it does solidify, the whole process grinds to a halt while segments of pipe are removed and the tube is cleared so that pouring can be restarted.

This relentless need to keep pouring choreographs the whole process. Although the scene seems confused, if you look closer you can see that each of the forty or fifty men has a specific task. First, some of them hold the end of the tube and pour where it's needed, under the direction of the foreman, while others carry out a coarse smoothing process, to get the depth to about five and a half inches. Another member of the team draws a circular patch and sticks a metal gauge, a calibrated spike, into the concrete until it touches

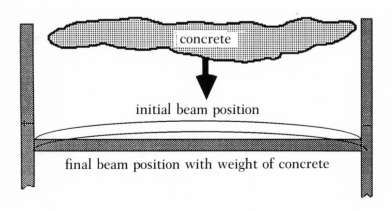

initial beam position

final beam position with weight of concrete

concrete   steel decking

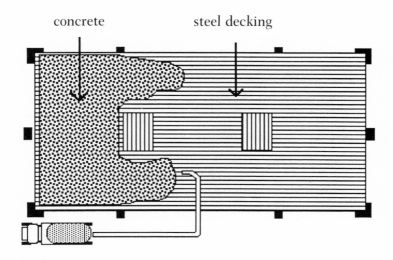

the steel deck. He smooths the circle to the exact depth required and marks it with a big cross. He will make a series of circles like this, and two men will come along with a three-meter strip of wood with a smooth edge. They use this to bring the level of the rest of the concrete, still wet, down to the required five and a half inches, with a comical but coordinated backward shuffle, bottoms in the air. They are followed by yet another "smoother," with a paddle on a long handle, and the final burnish is given by a rotary polisher, as the concrete begins to set. Each stage proceeds simultaneously, accompanied by a continuous torrent of shouting above the noise of the pumps and other machinery. A bystander can easily find himself concreted into a corner if he doesn't take careful note of escape routes up or down.

At about ten-thirty this Friday morning, there's a louder-than-usual burst of shouting. In the middle of the floor, which is really a mezzanine floor, a wooden structure marks the position of the escalator from the lobby. A man using the gasoline-powered polisher to give the final smoothing process to the concrete doesn't notice that some gas has spilled onto the wood. A spark from the engine ignites the gas, and smoke and flames start to rise as the wood catches fire. Although the flames are quite dramatic, and there's quite a lot of wood that could go up, people keep their heads. While the concrete pouring continues on the rest of the floor, some men run over to the fire and use tarpaulins and water to try to put it out. Germano is not unduly excited—such incidents happen from time to time—and his main concern is that the escalator motor already in position not be damaged by the fire.

Once the northeast corner of the floor has been burnished to the required smoothness, the concreting team rush to another section of the floor, dragging the heavy pipe with them. Suddenly all is much quieter, leaving only the rumble of traffic on Eighth Avenue and the muffled crashes, bangs, and whines from other floors. In a day or two, the same area will be the focus of another high-speed activity as the fireproofers move in, followed by a whole succession of trades, each with its own character, traditions, and working relationships. Fonti has seen them all over the years, and observed their characteristics:

Tin knockers, who are the people who put up the duct work for the air conditioning, I classify them as prima donnas. They want everything perfect. If there's anything in the way, they don't want to touch it, or they won't put up a duct because it's in the way. The electricians are also a very particular trade. They're also prima donnas. The stick fitters, who are the people who do the piping work for both the sprinklers and for the heating, are not as much prima donnas. They dirty their hands, whereas the electricians and the tin knockers don't want to dirty their hands. The elevator constructors, who build the elevators in the building, they have their own clique and they usually are very, very safety-conscious, justifiably so. In a shaft six hundred feet high, if you fall you're gone. There's no room for error. And they're very sticky about safety, for good reasons, but they have their own little clique, and they pull for their own basket. Every single trade pulls for their own basket.

As the building acquired a firm steel framework and smooth concrete floors, attention turned to the next important phase of the skyscraper's construction—the walls. Coming up fast behind the steel erectors would be the bricklayers, responsible for the most visible component of the walls of the building and the most controversial. The sad saga of the bricks for Worldwide Plaza began on the day in 1985 when David Childs decided what color he wanted them to be.

8

SHADES OF
DISAGREEMENT

For David Childs, the decisions about the walls of the skyscraper—
what should they be made of? what color should they be?—would
determine what people thought of his building, after they had taken
in its fat pencil shape. He chose brick because he saw it as a way
of shaping and decorating the exterior of the building that would
be impossible with any other material: "I opted for brick because
I felt that the scale of the material would lend itself to the kind of
detailing that I had in mind for the shaft of the building. I want
the sense of play and depth and color and detail and shadow—all
of those things that are going to make this tower read and work in

this particular design. That's what the architect should bring to this."

By choosing masonry, Childs was opting for a labor-intensive method of enclosing the building. He could have chosen to cover the skyscraper with prefabricated panels of metal and glass that would be lifted by crane and hooked into place. A single panel can then cover an area that would have to be filled by a thousand or more bricks, each laid by hand, cemented, and checked for level. In fact, in tall modern buildings a wall made of bricks is in some ways a cheat—a technique designed for load bearing that doesn't. Bricks are a familiar material for building because traditionally they have been a very good way of building low buildings with load-supporting walls. They are small enough to be useful for making quite complex surfaces with angles, curves, and grooves, and strong enough for the bottom layer to support the weight of the layers of bricks above it. It was the first of these properties in which Childs was interested. He had an image of a building with a complex outer surface. The main walls were to have such a large surface area that he wanted to break it up with textured patterns of light and shade, and bricks would be ideal for this. Bill Zeckendorf, who usually believes that when you hire someone to do a job you let him do it, accepted the suggestion in the earlier days of SOM's involvement that the building should be of brick, so SOM prepared a series of color illustrations, renderings, to show how the tower would look. At the same time, SOM, O&M, Zeckendorf, and HRH got together to talk about how much it might cost to build in brick and whether there might be any technical problems. This was the first tiny skirmish in what was to be a major battle.

Anyone who is artistically inclined, or who has some skill whose end product is there for all the world to see, knows what it feels like when something goes wrong and you have to live with the end result. Not only do you feel that everybody else can see your mistakes or misjudgments; you are continually reminded of them yourself, until you decide to put the offending object away in a closet and try to make a better job next time. Imagine, then, what it must be like when a building that you have designed and that will be forever associated with your name turns out to have some major characteristic you dislike intensely, particularly if it was not at all what you intended. It is impossible to hide your disappointments if they are embodied in a 770-foot-high building like Worldwide Plaza.

Once Childs had decided that the walls of his skyscraper should be made of brick, he had to decide on the mix of colors for the three components of the building—the base, the brick walls, and the roof. The roof was to be of copper, and that decision automatically fixed one of the colors. Copper metal acquires a green patina after a few years' exposure to the air, so Childs had to consider how the colors would harmonize with the *eventual* color of the roof rather than with the brown tint of new copper. He decided on a white feel for the shaft of the building with a cool gray in the central panels of each face. This would fit in with the warmer colors of the pre-cast and granite around the base of the building and mark a neutral transition to the pale green at the top.

The issue of color should have been a cozy, in-house decision at SOM, arrived at by David Childs and Jim Bodnar after they had pored over brick samples and color charts for a few days. But it turned into an issue that rumbled on throughout 1986 and 1987, until most of the people who were concerned with the brick turned puce on hearing of the latest developments in the saga.

The word that dominated the discussions about the color of the walls of Worldwide Plaza during the design stage was "pink," delivered in a tone of contempt or approval, depending on who was speaking. When Childs and Bodnar first presented their ideas to the group of developers, there was a subtlety and lightness about them. Beiges and whites predominated in the samples they put on the table from SOM's "library" of materials. The verticalness of the tower would be emphasized in stripes of angled brick that ran down at intervals around the four sides, as those bricks cast shadows.

Then the idea came up of making those bricks darker as well, so that the stripes were even more apparent, and a pinkish-almond color was suggested by one of the owners, Victor Elmaleh. Color is such a matter of personal taste that it is surprising that Elmaleh pushed as hard as he did for his ideas to prevail over those of the architect, the man who, after all, had been hired to embody his own aesthetic view in the building. Although, through his partnership with Frank Stanton, Elmaleh had a substantial investment in the project, he was not usually accorded more status in the project than the other partners, and yet, when it came to the color discussions, the other partners, including Zeckendorf, seemed to hold back and let Elmaleh get on with it.

Elmaleh is a tall, soft-spoken man whose training as an architect led him to develop very specific views about what color the project should be: "I'm a painter, among other things, and I'm very color-conscious, and I wanted this whole complex to look different from any other one in the city."

Unfortunately, what to Elmaleh was a "pleasant pinkish color" was to some of the architects rather unpleasant. There were strong feelings against Elmaleh—as one of the SOM people put it: "Victor wants to put up a great pink penis on the West Side." But the architects' worries seemed to have little effect. All Childs's diplomatic skills were tested to the limit as a series of meetings took place to discuss color, inspect swatches and samples, make a decision, change it, change the changed decision, and, at the eleventh hour, give final instructions to the brick manufacturer.

Over the period of a year or more, the architects used every permissible tactic to try and change the decision and gave up only at the point where it was clear that if the color wasn't confirmed there would be a serious delay in the completion of the building. Until that point, there seems to have been a pretense that this was a subject that could be settled by reasonable men presenting arguments to their colleagues for considered assessment. While the discussions were still going on, at a point where one of the several "final" decisions had been made, Rob Schubert, a constant observer of the process, put a brave face on it:

> The brick color of the building has been a delicate issue. Victor Elmaleh likes pink and he wanted a pink building. I think it would be a terrible mistake to make this a pink building—it is too damn big. If you look at the traditional large buildings— Metropolitan Life, the Woolworth Building, Rockefeller Center— it needs to be a light building. Victor has just got pink in his mind and we'd just been going back and forth, and part of David's approach was to do an avoidance kind of technique in terms of dealing with it. Victor wanted a pink building, David wanted a white building, we had sort of polarized. In the process of going through the budget confirmation, we were getting actual samples of brick. One thing to our benefit financially is that this pink brick that Victor liked costs a lot of money, because it comes from Utah or someplace out west, a lot of trucking costs, and if we can get stuff locally, nearby, the price comes down. We used that as the vehicle and it went back and forth.
>
> Victor trained as an architect but never practices, and I like him a lot, but he wanted to be the architect on the project and was starting to get in the way, and basically what I endeavored to do was get David to make a definite stand. This is one thing that David does not like to do; he likes to win people over. What I had to say was, "David, you have to basically make up your damn mind, tell him what you want and where you want it, and we're going to get it—let's get it done with."

At a key meeting "behind closed doors" in mid-1987, the issue was finally thrashed out, with Schubert clearly itching to get the gloves off and fight with more gusto and fewer scruples than Childs:

> We'd finally gotten this brick which was a sort of a tan with a very light pink cast to it—I think Almond was the trade name.

Then it was a question of whether or not the spandrel panels, the areas beneath the windows, would be a darker pinker color. We had proposed it all be the same color and we set it up in a conference room and reviewed it with Victor. This meeting was a sort of free-for-all. David and Jim made the presentation. Victor said, "I don't like it." I was ready to throw everybody out; my frustration on this one was pretty intense, because I knew that all we needed to do was to say, *"This is what we want,"* and I think we would have got it. In the end, David got as close as he possibly could to saying that, and Jack Schuster and I completed the sentences by saying, "We feel very strongly that this is what it should be." And Victor grudgingly agreed with us. The issue was blown far out of proportion. It really was just the personalities of the people involved, just as this whole project is really a reflection of the personalities of the people involved in it.

Child's reasonable approach, which so infuriated Schubert, seemed consistent with his overall approach to life. Certainly, as he summarized the color decision, he made every effort to play down his own feelings about the issue: "Everybody can look at the color of a piece of material and say, 'I like this one more than that one.' And that's not an unreasonable thing for an owner to want to have a look at. I think that there are other members of the team who have clearly felt much more strongly that this ought to be a highly colorful building. From my side, I think it ought to be a quieter building in terms of its coloring, and that has been an ongoing discussion, if not debate, to a point where I think there is generalized agreement as to what I think would be a handsome solution."

During all this period Elmaleh tried to display the traditional calmness that goes with being at the eye of the storm: "The color that I wanted was a good bit darker, and I think that David had a point in that he thought that a building as massive as this might have been a little bit overwhelming. I didn't happen to agree, but

I think that what we settled on is a very good compromise and I think we'll both be very happy with it."

Among the team, the only puzzling reaction came from Jim Bodnar. As someone very close to Childs, he must have known how strongly Childs really felt about the issue. And yet his was the lone architectural voice that seemed pleased with the final outcome: "I think it's great. It's got a sort of light off-white or pink tone to it. I think it will be a very strong color."

Inevitably, news of the disagreements over color spread throughout SOM, HRH, and the Zeckendorf Company, and aroused the interest, and sometimes the concern, of the rest of the team trying to build the building. After the first "final" approval in September 1986, HRH wanted to get on with finalizing the choice of contractor for the brick. But that depended on whether the particular contractor under consideration could produce that color brick, and even if a contractor was chosen, any changes in color would delay the manufacturing process, a factor that worried Fonti greatly in May 1987, when more "final" decisions had been made and no one was sure where it would end. On May 13 representatives of the architects and the owners assembled on the site to look at a panel HRH had put together to allow everyone to see what the various colors of brick looked like in daylight and in a large area, and to enable them to make a real final decision about color.

The following day, as he waited for that decision, Fonti looked out of his office above the Thai restaurant at the rising steel and gloomily fingered the brick samples colored in the range from which the final colors would be chosen: "The color of the bricks has been an exciting tale. Now, to me, and to my eyes, these look the same, or close, and I find it a little ludicrous that they're worrying about this shade here versus this shade here. Once you expose these to the New York atmosphere for three or four months, you cannot tell them apart. What makes the thing even more ludicrous is that the brick starts on the sixth floor, roughly 150 feet up in the air; no pedestrian is going to tell the difference."

Of course, Fonti would be the first to admit that whatever color was chosen was no business of his. But what did matter was the effect of a delayed decision on his schedule. *That* was why he was annoyed and frustrated:

> I care tremendously what they do, because what's happening is that there's a sixteen-week lead time in getting brick. If the decision's not made this week—today—we as construction managers cannot tell the owner that we are going to finish the building on time. I need brick here on October 1. And sixteen weeks from today is October 1, so I need a decision like today or tomorrow. I'm giving them till tomorrow to finalize it, or else I'm going on record telling them, "No, I will not be held responsible if the masonry doesn't start on October 1." Until they choose the color, we cannot release brick for manufacturing, they cannot decide on the color of the windows that they want, they cannot decide the color of the caulking that they want for the windows. That affects the window manufacturer. That affects the mock-up, or test, of the windows, and it has a snowball effect on other trades.

Fonti's problem was a typical example of the way in which the various aspects of the building were interwoven inextricably together. The story of the masonry* walls of the skyscraper illustrates well how one decision by the *design* architects led to months of work by the *technical* members of the team to finalize plans for the walls of the building.

The main strategic decisions about the brick took place in 1985, but the early estimates for numbers and types of bricks that would be needed were of necessity very rough. To use the potential of brick to the full, Childs had drawn in a number of different-shaped bricks, bricks with points and odd corners that would create the interesting ridges and patterns of light and shade. Originally SOM planned eight or ten different basic shapes for the bricks; by the

---

* The words "masonry" and "brick" are used interchangeably.

time a whole lot of crinkles had been added to the building, the project ended up with fifty-two different shapes.

Most brick buildings have walls that are flat over large areas. In the Worldwide Plaza tower, Childs had designed much more ambitious walls with windows that moved in and out in relation to the plane of the wall, brickwork with projections at various points, such as forty-five-degree corners which project out about four inches. As the building went up, the cross-section changed: the floors became smaller, with more odd angles and corners. Some were 135-degree corners, other ninety-degree corners, and all were to be reflected in the skin of the building, shaped by the various bricks.

In early 1987, when HRH came to look for a company to make these complicated bricks and a subcontractor to lay them, they faced a problem. Although brick had been out of fashion for large modern buildings, it was becoming more popular, and the few masons qualified to tackle a job of such scale were very busy. They could pick and choose their jobs and charge high prices. Arnie Kriegel at HRH solicited proposals from four or five masons, and each quoted a price higher than HRH had originally estimated. Kriegel was determined not to let the cost exceed the estimate without a fight. He asked each of the masons to suggest how the cost could be reduced. He could then present these options to the owner, who would decide whether to accept the cheaper version or agree to spend more to secure what the architect wanted.

It's at times like this that the triangular relationship of architect/construction manager/owner reveals the strains in the system. Each is fighting for something different; each of the parties has views that might lead him to behave differently if he had total freedom to act. As with the color issue, there was a certain amount of misunderstanding about why the architects wanted things "just so" as far as the complexity of the masonry was concerned. Why so many intricate shapes for areas of the building that were several hundred feet up? Wouldn't that add unnecessarily to the costs of the brick? Jack Schuster was very concerned:

> There were between two and three million brick involved overall.*
> If you go ahead and spend 10 cents more a brick, that made
> $200,000–$300,000 in materials alone. The nature of the design
> is rather elaborate. As a result of that, we are spending, in my
> judgment, about $7 or $8 more a square foot of brick than we
> would have in a standard brick job. If you were also to go over
> budget in the type of brick you were buying, it could very easily
> cost $2–$3 million more than a standard job. That's a great deal
> of money.

Awarding the masonry contract was complicated by the fact that there were two parties involved in addition to HRH. Rather like the steel deal, one company would supply the materials and another the labor for putting them in place. Contractually, HRH would deal with only one of those companies—in this case, the masons—but they could specify a particular type of brick from a particular brick company. The mason would then calculate his costs for laying the brick, add them to the price he would pay the brick manufacturer, and charge the total to Zeckendorf. In the case of Worldwide Plaza, one of the main contenders to supply the brick, the company that offered the color-coated brick, was Glen-Gery. If they were awarded the contract they would then work with another company, La Sala, who were contracted to lay the brick.

The Glen-Gery New York offices are in a nineteenth-century brick house, overlooking a tree-shaded courtyard. This is Amster Yard, a rare Victorian oasis in mid-Manhattan, approached by a covered passageway behind wrought-iron gates. There is a small-town charm about the house, part of a complex owned by the Amster family, who still live in one corner of the property. Glen-

---

* In the whole project, residential and commercial.

Gery have brickmaking plants in various parts of the United States; the Amster Yard house is their New York sales office.

The company's customer-service manager is Steve George, a man who was to become a thorn in the side of some of the World-wide Plaza team. George is young, clean-cut, brown-eyed, and with a wary and amused smile on his face much of the time. His manner suggests that he is entirely in control of any situation he finds himself in. He has an answer for everything. In the relationship with HRH and the other Worldwide Plaza participants, George knew right from the beginning that Glen-Gery were, in a sense, the only game in town:

> I think one of the reasons Skidmore came to us is we're probably the only brick manufacturer in the United States that can do this. We can say that now, and we used it quite heavily during the negotiation process. If they wanted us to do it, it would be on our terms. Even during the bidding process, when there were heavy time constraints on the masons as far as having the prices, we had no conception of what certain shapes were going to be, so the prices we gave the masons were very high, exorbitantly high. They had to be—we had to cover ourselves. One particular unit had roughly two hundred thousand special shapes on it that we priced at $5 a piece. That's a lot of money. I believe the actual final quotation to the mason was only about $2 a piece. The owners mistook it for an overpricing structure, which it wasn't, and we finally got that through to Jack Schuster. We did not overprice; we got what the product was worth.

Like everyone else, George remembers the events connected with the color of the brick most vividly. In fact, long before they were awarded the contract to supply brick to the masons, Glen-Gery had been one of the companies consulted about which colors they could produce, and had been asked for various samples for the SOM team to consider:

There was a requirement for colors to happen almost overnight, without the architects' or the owners' realizing the process involved in developing colors. Most architects don't understand brickwork. They understand the thinking behind it and what the finished product looks like, but not what's involved in making a brick. When you have a plant that takes at least six weeks to develop new colors just to run a laboratory sample, the designers find it hard to comprehend. Every time we develop a new color it's about $30,000 for us. So you've got a cost element involved here too. You only go so far before it's not worthwhile from the commercial standpoint. After a lot of hard work they ended up going back to one of the original colors and one of the new colors, which was a buff, almond, pink shade—it depends on who you're talking to what color it is. And a third color was sprung on us out of nowhere—white—which we didn't know anything about. So the project went from two colors to three colors to four different colors and then finally back to three colors.

We ended up in a number of arguments with the architects, trying to convince them why it took so long to develop these colors. It's not paint, it's a ceramic product. We were under a lot of pressure at the plant itself. We're not only working on this project. Glen-Gery is a very, very large company. We manufacture roughly 450 million brick a year. Worldwide Plaza is the equivalent of 4.5 million brick,* which doesn't mean it's not an important order to us, but it is not our total capacity by any means.

It's difficult to escape the impression that at times George and Glen-Gery were playing games with the Worldwide Plaza team. Like other bystanders, they felt the fuss over color was exaggerated, particularly since they had seen it happen before. To the hard-bitten technologists, the aesthetic sensibilities of architects were sometimes carried to extremes, and brickmen like Steve George

---

* The Worldwide Plaza skyscraper would contain 1.2 million larger-than-standard bricks. These were equivalent in volume to 4.5 million standard-sized bricks, the units brickmen use.

were not averse to bringing them down a peg or two: "There've been times where we've shown a specific color of a brick, whether it be a clay-coated product like this project or something else, to an architect and they've said, 'Yeah, I like that but a little bit lighter,' or 'a little bit darker,' and we'll go away for about a week or so and bring back the same color and all of a sudden they like the color and yet it's the same product that we've shown them about a week ago."

Although Glen-Gery were fairly confident that their bricks would grace Worldwide Plaza, a number of companies might have secured the contract to lay them. During the early part of 1987, Kriegel called them in one by one: "I've asked one bidder to come in to go over the scope of the job only, no dollars to be spoken of, just to determine what he has been looking at and what we expect from him; is it the same? We want to make sure he understands where all the brick and interior masonry occurs, what walls are to be left out during the construction, that he'll be responsible for certain means and methods, and to ensure, of course, that the brick and the exterior and the interior are exactly what the architect wants and that there are no deviations in his mind."

As the contractors went away, looked at the plans, did their sums, and came back, it was clear that the masonry would cost more than HRH's original estimates, perhaps because they had assumed the brickwork would be simpler than it turned out. Rob Schubert had seen the evolving complexity of the brick design and knew that it wouldn't be cheap:

> The reason for the high bids is, the brick is extremely complex in the way it's laid up. All that is forcing the cost to a certain level. From what HRH has been telling us, a lot of the brick contractors who install the bricks are very busy in this city. It seems to be a very popular material. If they're busy, they can pick and choose their jobs, so therefore they come in with high prices. Now the fight is developing between HRH and our office

about where it is that we may be able to cut costs. We are trying to maintain the appearance of the building, which we feel is quite important. It's a very large building, and we feel that we've articulated the façade in such a way that it reduces the appearance of a large, bulky mass. If you delete some of the interesting brickwork that we've got, it's going to become very dull very quickly, so that's something that we're negotiating right now.

Over at the Zeckendorf Company, at one of the partners' meetings, the topic of the masonry bids came up, and Bill Zeckendorf revealed a cunning plan to try to make the subcontractors reduce their prices. They would *pretend* to be considering an alternative, cheaper way of cladding the building, in the hope that, faced with the possibility of the building's using no bricks at all, the masons would bring down their prices. Zeckendorf described the tactic: "We'll look at stone, pre-cast stone, everything necessary to see if we can't break this jam. There's no reason why the brick should be coming in at the price. Now, we have some details that are very expensive, and we're gonna have to look at alternatives to get this in line, because I think we're over by $2 million. We just say, 'There's nothing in the budget that can take that. If it's going to take some major design change, we're going to have to do it.'" Terry Soderberg added that they had "put the word out, just to watch them drop their prices a little bit."

They even elaborated on this little piece of theater. To convince the intransigent masons that they were serious, Kriegel commissioned the Canadian company that was making the pre-cast concrete for the lobby to mock up a pre-cast concrete panel with the appearance and color of the brick they wanted for the building. This was then driven to the site and put on display for all to see.

In fact, nobody seriously considered covering forty-five thousand square yards of the building with pink concrete molded to look like bricks, but in the construction world you sometimes have to go to these lengths to persuade a subcontractor that he is not indispensable. In this case, HRH were aiming their ruse at La Sala, the masonry contractors, and the strategic placing of a pre-cast panel on the site—where it couldn't escape the notice of the La Sala people—would emphasize that HRH were willing to consider alternatives if the masonry quotation didn't come down.

One evening in February 1987 Schubert sat in his office contemplating the pressures being placed on the architects to accept design changes that would lower the cost of some of the bigger contracts:

> The reason I'm here late tonight is that I ran up to HRH for a spur-of-the-moment meeting to review a particular item that HRH thinks they might be able to make a saving on. "Why did we put the insulation in this wall in the particular place that we did?" And you go through it and you explain it, because it's been identified as a potential area for saving money. We feel very strongly, technically, that there were very logical reasons to do it. HRH listens, and they go through it, and they say, "Oh yeah, well, it starts to make sense. We want to do some more exploration." But this exploration and challenging and pushing is part of this process. You've got to make sure that what you've done is correct.

But the combination of dirty tricks and a line-by-line scrutiny of the plans failed to reduce the masonry price as much as everyone would have liked, and Schuster watched the negotiations with some dismay:

> The brick supplier knew he had a captive audience, and his price was just as he had quoted us. Drawings were issued and were bid by five of the major brick subcontractors in the city of New York. The spread in price was very substantial, but in all cases very, very much higher than our budget, principally because of some design features. Also, the city of New York is in a brick frenzy, so that the competition was really not as good as it will

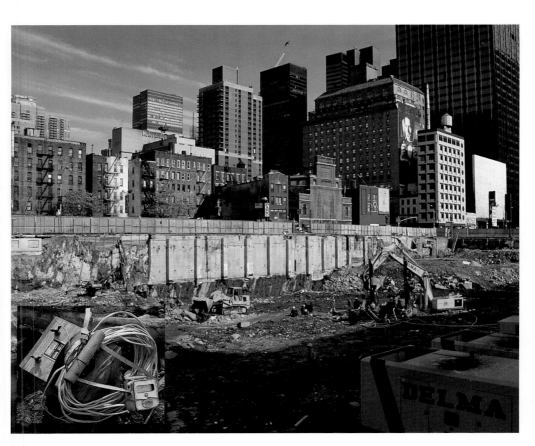

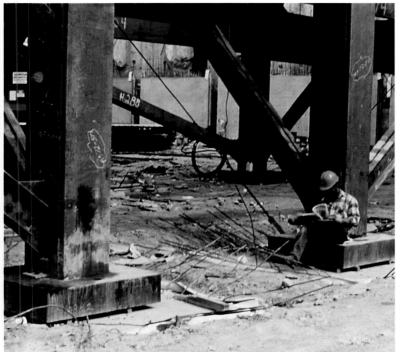

Rock has to be
blasted to a
depth of 30 feet
for the founda-
tions.

The lowest
columns in the
steel frame-
work must bear
a load of 3,500
tons.

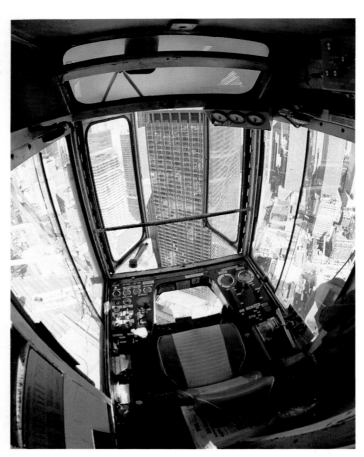

The view from the
crane operator's cab.

Craning to see what's
happening.

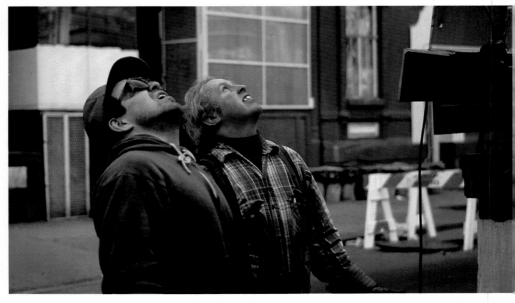

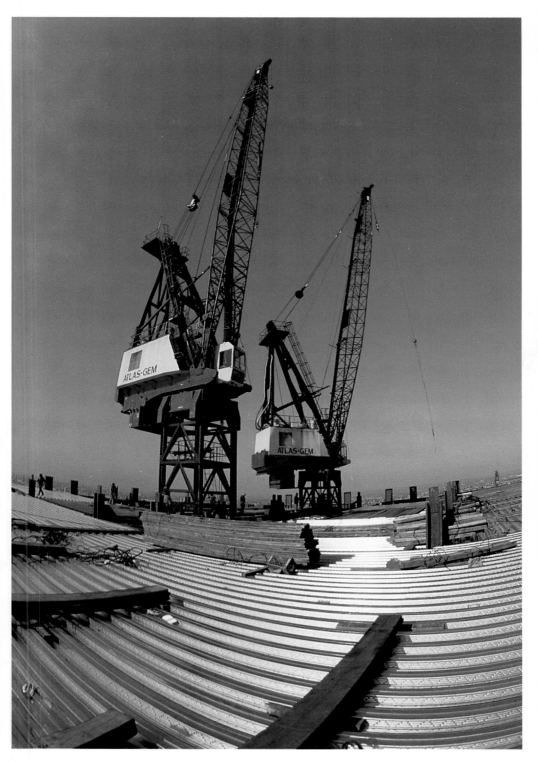

In the confined space of Manhattan, the cranes are fixed to the top of the skyscraper and rise with it.

Concrete is piped
under high pressure to
the upper floors.

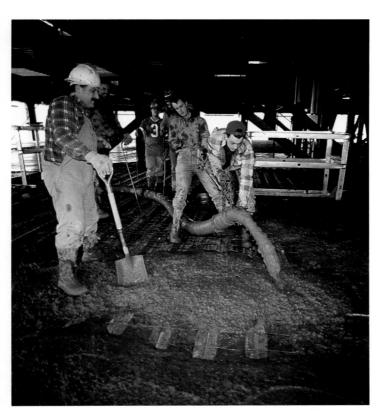

While the concrete is
still wet, the surface
is polished to a smooth
finish.

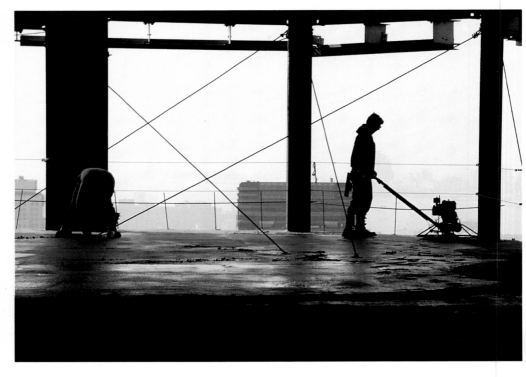

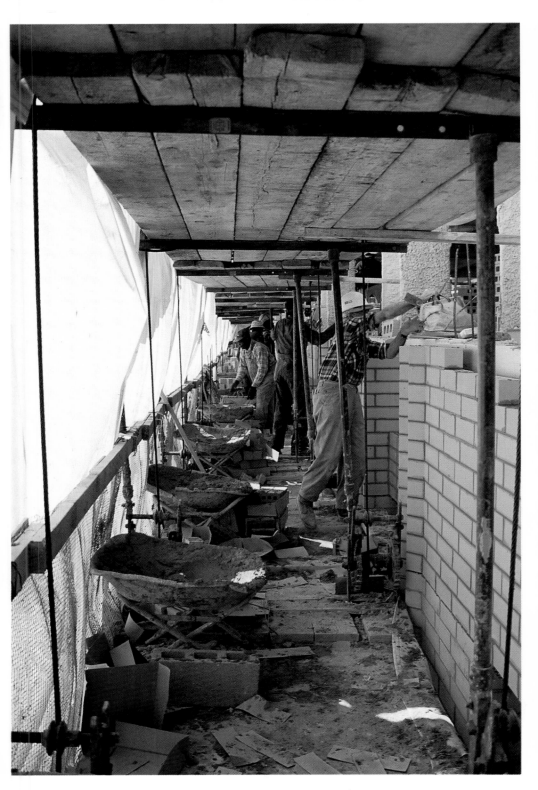

Worldwide Plaza was the biggest brick job in New York for some time.

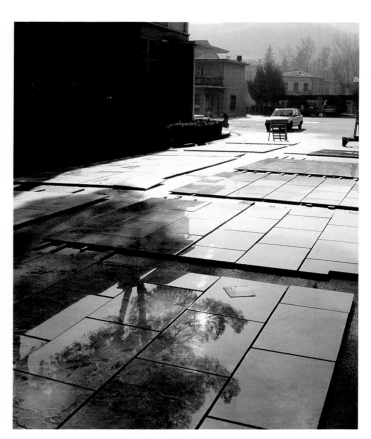

Marble samples for the lobby floors, laid out in Italy for the architects to inspect.

Granite slabs arrive in New Jersey from Italy.

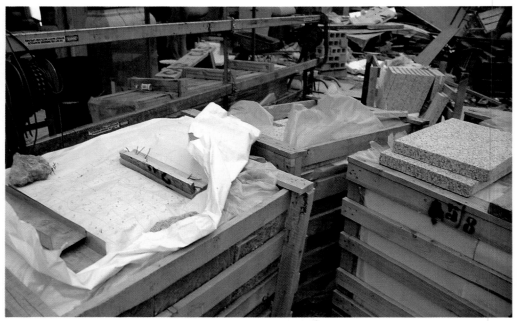

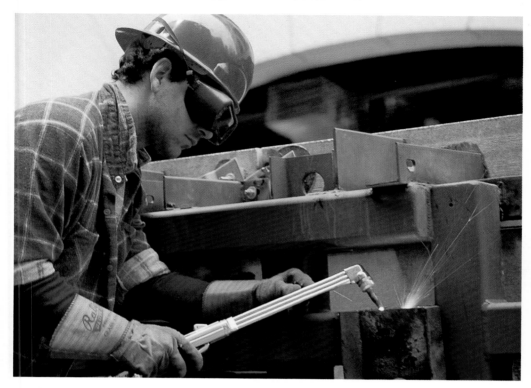

Steel trusses hold several slabs of granite to make large panels for the exterior of the skyscraper.

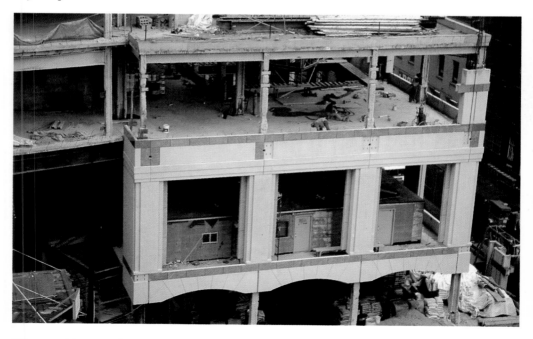

The troublesome façade of the lower floors, covered with granite and precast concrete.

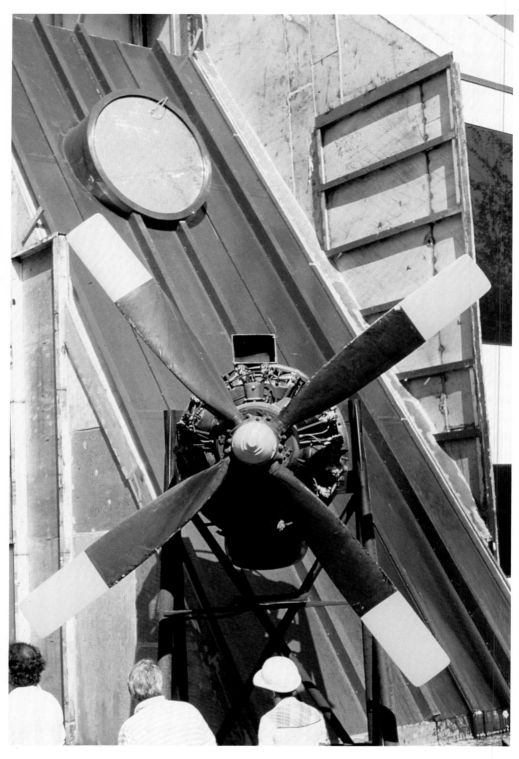

An aircraft engine is used to test the roof's behavior in a high wind.

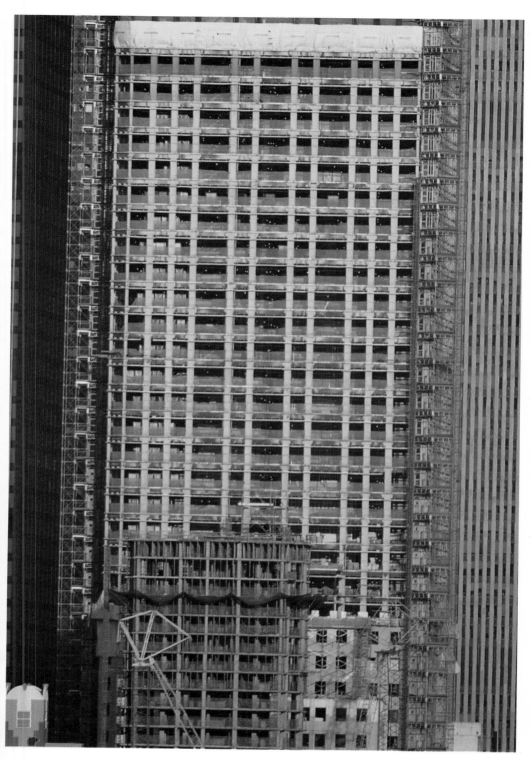

During the peak of construction activity, more than a thousand people are at work on the site, hidden from view.

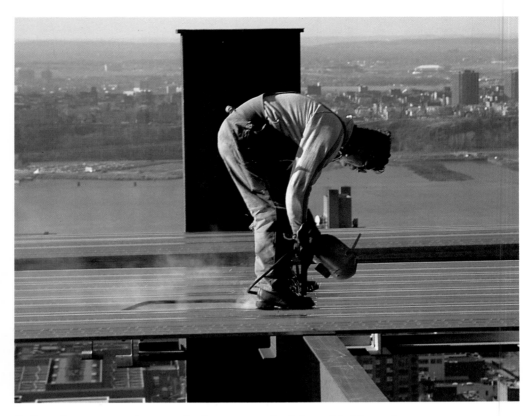

Before the concrete is poured, the support deck is welded into place.

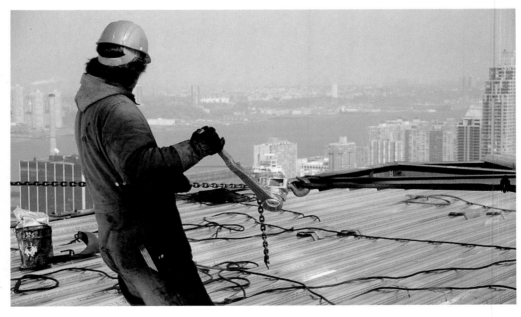

Tensioning the cables so that the steel skeleton is plumbed up square before welding or bolting.

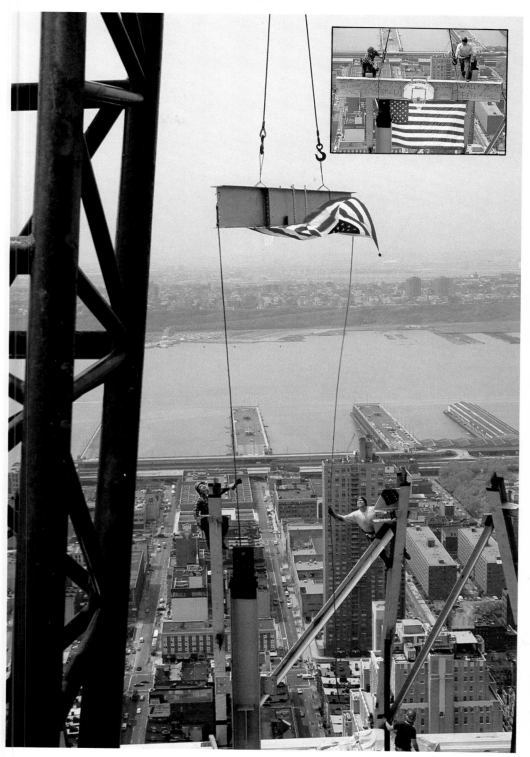

The last girder—ceremoniously hoisted into place at the topping-out on Friday,
May 20, 1988.

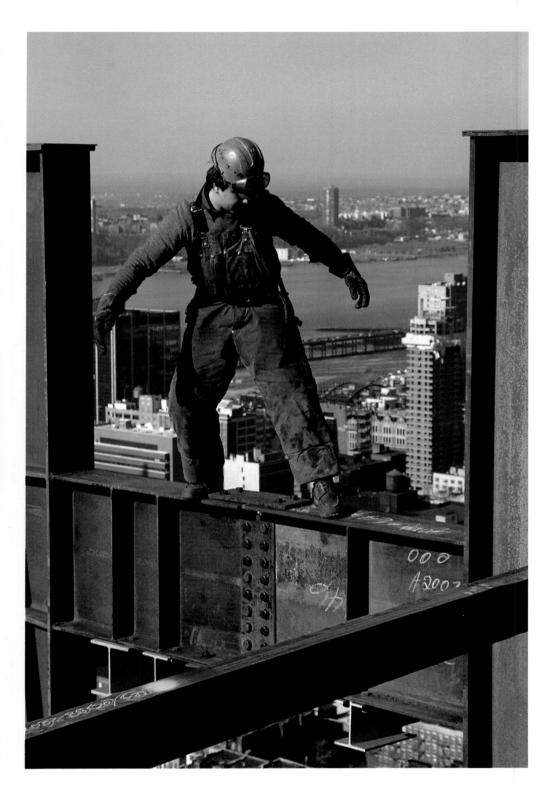

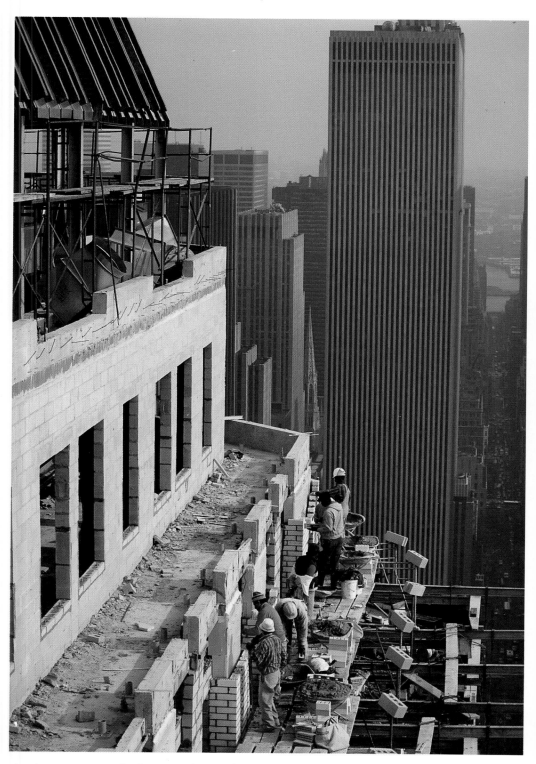

As the masonry is laid out on the top floors, no one yet realizes that some of the walls are in the wrong position.

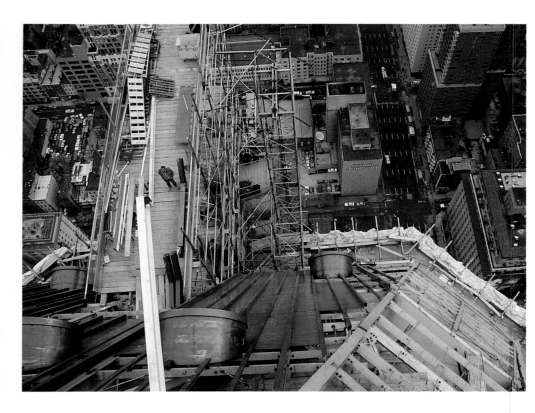

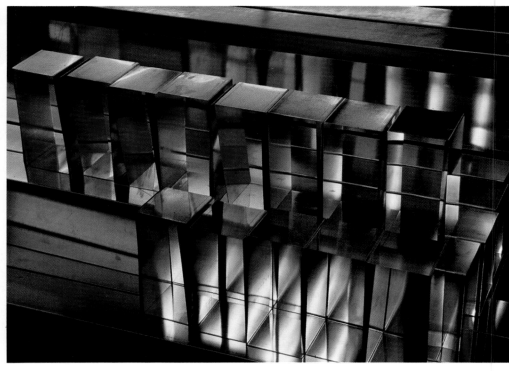

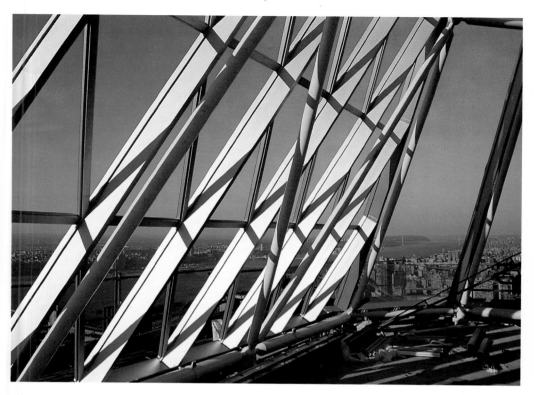

The glazed pyramid at the top of the building will house a beacon to shine over New York.

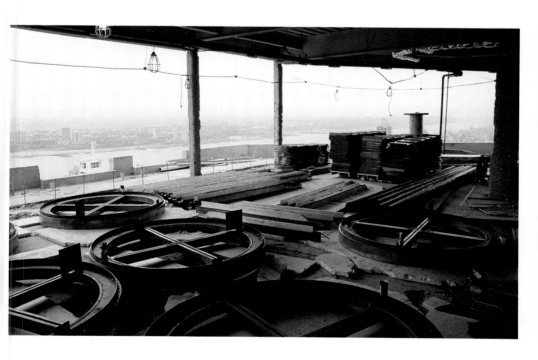

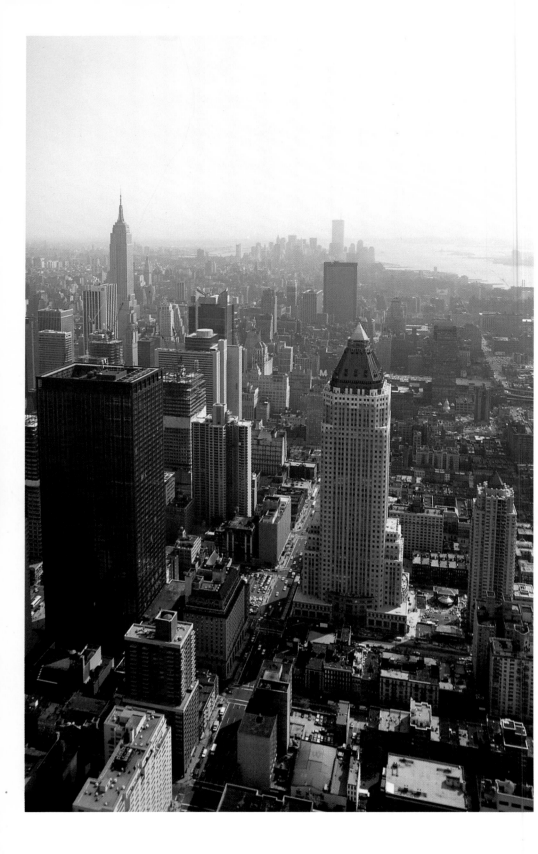

be a couple of years from now or as it was a few years back. When the prices were in, we then started calling the subcontractors in to try to get them to moderate their prices a bit. We were successful in getting some of the prices down without sacrificing either the quality or basic design, because had we tried to do that we would have had the design team from Skidmore down on us like a ton of bricks. But we did end up by awarding a contract $1 million above our budget. You can't win every battle, but so far our budget looks fairly decent, so we hope to win the war. But we sure lost that battle.

When a hundred sticks of dynamite, nine hundred pounds in all, exploded in a clay pit in western Pennsylvania, it marked the birth of the bricks for Worldwide Plaza. The pit was the source of the clay for the bricks made at the Hanley plant of the Glen-Gery brick company. The explosive sent tons of clay soaring two hundred feet into the air, and when the dust had settled two minutes later, there were piles of gray powdery clay lying around to be picked up and trucked to the plant, eight miles away.

This part of Pennsylvania is a seven-hour drive from Manhattan, but a world away from the bustle and pressure in the offices of the Zeckendorf Company, SOM, and HRH. The town of Brookville has a main street straight out of a 1950s movie, right down to the lettering of its shopfronts. This is the boondocks, that mixture of the appealing and the tedious, where the city visitor marvels at the tranquillity and the rustic simplicity, while champing at the bit to be back in the big city. Certainly little awareness of Manhattan and its skyscrapers seemed to impinge on the people working on the Worldwide Plaza brick. That's not to say they weren't interested in what they were doing or that they took no pride in it, just that their goals were more immediate—to nurse the clay aggregate through the chain of dusty machinery turning it into almond- or pink-colored bricks.

In September 1987 the plant began making the 1.2 million

bricks that would be laid by hand all the way up the six-hundred-foot-high walls. It was a complex job: there were three colors of brick and over fifty different shapes. Essentially, bricks have to be shaped, colored, dried, and baked. The basic shape for Worldwide Plaza was produced by a mechanized conveyor-belt method called the "stiff-mud" process. The clay was pulverized and mixed with water to produce a stiff paste. This was passed through a vacuum and then extruded through a rectangular die to produce a long strip of gray clay that went through a rotating wire cutter which chopped it up into batches of twenty or thirty bricks. The extruder produced twelve holes in each brick, which had two useful effects: they helped to speed up the process of drying by allowing the heat to penetrate more quickly to the center of the bricks, and they provided finger holes for the masons to use when laying the bricks.

After they had been chopped into the right shapes, the bricks passed through a spray that coated them with the contentious colors selected for Worldwide Plaza. Some bricks take their color from the clay they are made of, combined with the method of firing them in a kiln. To produce a dark brick, for example, it is baked at a higher temperature. Depending on the type of firing process—how much oxygen is in the kiln atmosphere, for example—the iron

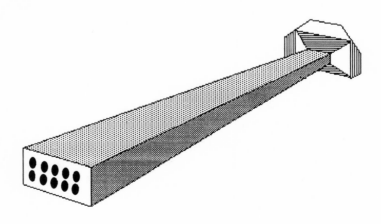

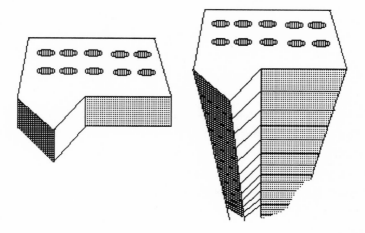

found in most clays will turn red or purple, and other chemicals in the clay can interact with the atmosphere in the kiln to produce other colors and shades. But because of the subtlety and lightness of the colors required by SOM, these bricks were glazed with a ceramic coating. Like uncoated bricks, these acquired their correct tints only after they had been baked.

Twenty-nine thousand bricks had to be shaped and finished by hand. Many of these would produce the vertical projecting stripes that ran down the four faces of the building. Each of these bricks was cut out by hand and hand-smoothed on a tabletop in a corner of the plant. Of all the elements in the skyscraper, these bricks most brought home the fact that this building was hand-made. And the care that was lavished on producing a smooth face on the front surfaces of the brick would be evident only to pigeons and window cleaners.

The kiln at Glen-Gery was a five-hundred-foot tunnel running along one side of the plant. The dried bricks were stacked on railroad cars and moved slowly from one end of the kiln to the other at a speed of .0025 mile an hour. On a thirty-hour journey they passed through a maximum temperature of over two thousand degrees

Fahrenheit. The kilns were surrounded with a bulky layer of insulation in which pipes were embedded to carry away some of the waste heat, which was used to dry bricks that were waiting to be baked. Bays were cut at intervals into the side of the insulating layer of the kiln, with tiny peepholes opening straight into the kiln. Once an hour, for a few seconds, a man would step into this infernal gap and, holding a mask with a mica window, inspect the trucks of brick to check that they were moving correctly through the heat. At the other end of the kiln, the cars crept out with their loads of baked bricks, now with the correct color.

The final act in making the bricks is called "mingling." Each carload of bricks will come out of the kiln with the same colored coating. But however carefully the coating is mixed, and however accurately the temperature of the kiln is controlled, there will be variations in shade from one carload to the next. These variations are very slight but can create large, slightly contrasting patches in the curtain wall if the bricks are laid carload by carload. "Mingling" avoids this problem: bricks from two or more batches baked at different times and with different shades are placed at random in a third pile. When this pile is laid, the different shades are mixed, and from a distance they merge into one shade, which has the pleasing property of homogeneity and variety combined.

In late 1987, after all the discussions about color and coating and prices had been concluded satisfactorily, or at least reached a point where no further change would be allowed, Fonti sat in the site office awaiting the arrival of the first of the 1.2 million bricks HRH had ordered. But the bricks never arrived. Steve George had decided that because the site wasn't nearly ready for the bricks he would not start making them, whatever Fonti said. This led to a continuing source of strife in November and December as Fonti tried his best to get the skyscraper built—and the world appeared to conspire against him to prevent it.

9

CURTAIN WALL

For someone who is not involved in the construction of large buildings there are two surprises: some aspects of the process are *simpler* than one might have thought—the steel framework is almost as simple to construct as a Meccano set—while others are far more complex. The walls of the building come under the second category; indeed, in some respects they are the most complex part of the building. To take the anatomical analogy used by Marvin Mass, the mechanical engineer, the walls of the building are its skin in the same active and complex way as our own skin. Ostensibly just a thin outer covering, in fact both types of skin have functions of protection, aesthetics, transport, flexibility, and separation.

The evolution of the curtain wall went hand in hand with the invention of the steel framework. Buildings like the Monadnock could reach sixteen stories only by placing one solid unit on top of another to attain the desired height. To let in light, the architects left a few gaps—windows—in the essentially monolithic exterior walls. With the steel frame, the situation is the reverse; almost any height is possible with linked steel members, but it isn't at all useful as a building until the gaps between the beams and columns are filled in. The means of filling in those gaps is the curtain wall.

The main functions of a curtain wall are to keep water out, prevent air leaks, and insulate the building, but it is also the public face of the building: striking buildings are remembered for their curtain walls. Unlike the more traditional methods of construction, however, a curtain wall does not bear any of the weight of the building. Once it was no longer necessary for one wall component to rest upon another all the way to the top of the building, as had been done with brick or stone, a new range of possibilities opened out for architects to enclose their buildings with a wider variety of materials. The floors themselves were strong enough to support the weight of the materials used to fill in the gaps. Although architects talk about "hanging" a curtain wall, it doesn't really hang but sits on a shelf, something like partitions resting on the floor. Often, a curtain wall consists of prefabricated metal and glass, made up in panels away from the site and brought in to be fixed in position.

The brick story that dominated 1986 and 1987 was essentially motivated by concern about how the exterior would look. How the exterior would *function* was an entirely different concern. The brick was only the outermost layer of the skin and, like human skin, it would be backed up by a complex series of layers, each element of which would have to be designed, manufactured, and put in position. This task fell to Ed Narbutas and his team, after they had been handed the designs produced by Childs, Jim Bodnar, and their colleagues.

Narbutas's team used as a starting point a drawing like the diagram on page 188, supplied by Bodnar. To the informed eye, these simple orthogonal lines concealed a wealth of meaning. For the structural engineer considering how to design a steel skeleton for the skyscraper, there were certain important implications. For a start, masonry walls are heavier than conventional glass-and-aluminum curtain walls. The components that surround the windows—concrete and brick—are much heavier than aluminum. Then, a brick curtain wall will be supported differently: it will rest on the beams, which must therefore carry the weight before passing it on to the columns at their attachment points. All this affects the weight and thickness of steel that the designer instructs the steel fabricators to supply for the beams. And the weight of the wall is not the only force to be dealt with: the curtain wall takes the brunt of the wind pressure on a building. Like the sails of a ship, the four walls of Worldwide Plaza would present a large surface area to the winds that blow through mid-Manhattan. And the pressure on a single square yard of the wall varies with the height and orientation of the wall. The wind-tunnel tests had given useful information about the high-pressure areas and the maximum wind force to be expected. The engineers now had to find how those forces would behave once the brunt of the wind had been received by the walls and passed on to the structure.

When Narbutas and his colleagues were first thinking about how to make an effective wall—in the design phase, back in 1986— they were told that no one had ever built their type of masonry wall to withstand more than about forty pounds per square foot. But the wind tunnel specifications called for this wall to be able to withstand seventy-five pounds a square foot. This was derived from figures for the likely maximum pressure to be experienced from a hundred-mile-an-hour wind, a wind New York might experience once every

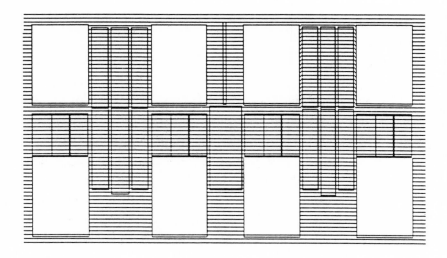

fifty years. Under such a wind each square foot of the wall would experience a pressure of fifty pounds. The safety code specified that the wall should be able to withstand that pressure plus 50 percent—i.e., seventy-five pounds per square foot. The significance of these wind loads was twofold: first, of course, the wall must be designed and built in such a way that it wouldn't crumble or crack up under this kind of pressure; second, the total wind load will make the whole building move, as Narbutas described: "Buildings are a little bit lighter than they were fifty years ago, and so they move a little bit more. The building sways about sixteen inches off center at the top. Now you've got this relatively thin skin on a building that's moving, so you have to find a way of allowing for this building not to come apart on itself. That's the trick."

Performing this "trick" was only one of the tasks that the SOM group achieved in their design of the curtain wall. They came up with a layered structure that had several different elements. The outermost layer was the all-too-familiar brick. Its contribution to the functioning of the wall was simply to sit there and look beautiful. It was not expected to be waterproof, although obviously in combination with the mortar it should present a united front. Behind the brick was an air gap to allow water penetrating the brick to evaporate, and then a layer of Styrofoam, a lightweight insulating material. This was fixed to a wall of concrete blocks with a sticky substance called "mastic," which waterproofed the wall. On the outer side of the mastic, it didn't really matter if water penetrated— as it inevitably would through the porous brick and through various small gaps around the windows. But everything on the inner side of the mastic had to be kept dry. Beyond the concrete blocks there was the steel column, on the other side of which was a rigid frame using metal uprights, called "studs," that held the plasterboard panels forming the inside walls of the building. These walls would be painted or wallpapered to provide the interior finishes.

Each of these layers had a specific job to do. But one other element in the curtain wall had to be fitted in somewhere: the windows. They had to be designed and manufactured to be water-proof, airtight, wind-resistant, and insulating, as well as trans-parent.

Having decided on the materials and the detailed specifications for each of these elements in the curtain wall, Narbutas and his team had to decide how to fit them all together and preserve the overall effectiveness of the wall. Seamless walls and seamless win-dows would be no good if there were gaps between the two. And the task of avoiding gaps was not simple: two factors could distort the wall vertically and open up gaps. First, in high winds the build-ing could twist and turn and pull sections of the walls or windows apart. Second, once the building was fully loaded with people, fur-niture, and the other heavy objects found in offices, the beams would deflect under the load and could push down on the tops of the lower walls. Because of these two factors, there had to be some "give" in the construction method to allow for small movements of windows in relation to walls, or one part of the wall in relation to another. What the SOM team did was to incorporate a gap all the way around the building at each level, filled with flexible sealant instead of mortar. This would allow for a vertical movement of a

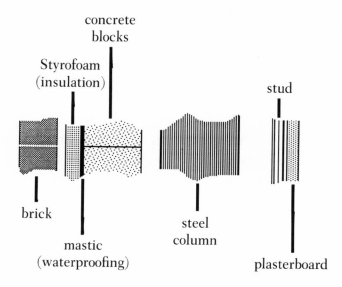

fraction of an inch at each level without breaking the seal. The sealant would expand or contract by that amount as the building shifted. In effect, the several inches of movement over the whole building were shared among the forty-odd floors to make it manageable.

Each section of wall—the strip between the two layers of sealant—would be attached to the floor so that, as the building moved, the section would move as a unit. This meant that the window also needed a little room for maneuver at the top, some kind of joint that would widen and narrow but not let in air or water.

The work that went into sorting out the details of the skyscraper's curtain wall was prodigious. The first, neat design drawings showing a section of wall with some windows in it were really a shorthand way for Bodnar to say to Narbutas and his team: "Draw up plans for a two-layer wall consisting of concrete blocks behind and bricks laid in front, holding windows safely and connected to the floors above and below. Make the wall waterproof, airproof, and thermally insulated. Specify how the brick walls are to be connected to the block walls and the windows connected to both. Make allowance for water that gets through the brick walls to get out again

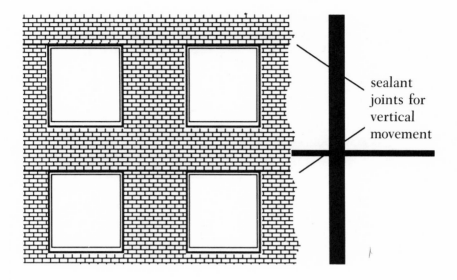

sealant
joints for
vertical
movement

without building up"—and a few other things. The drawings that finally emerged were half life-size in their scale, specifying down to the tiniest detail what all the components should be made of and how they should fit together. At this level of detail a drawing of the whole building would have been about a hundred yards long.

The complexity of the curtain walls on Worldwide Plaza was, of course, nothing new in the world of building skyscrapers. Nevertheless, there was a degree of innovation in one aspect of this design: its ability to resist high wind. People *had* built masonry walls to resist seventy-five pounds per square foot before, but there was much more bracing behind the brick and the concrete than Worldwide Plaza would have. With Worldwide Plaza, the ten-foot-wide spacing between the columns meant that a larger-than-average area of wall had to bear the wind load without buckling or cracking, and without having any structural bracing behind it.

The SOM team solved this problem by designing a system of steel reinforcing rods embedded in the concrete floors and then turned through a right angle to thread their way through the block wall. They *thought* that this would enable the wall to sustain the

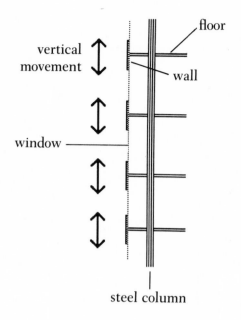

wind loads expected of it. They also *thought* that the various layers of waterproofing, insulation, and sealants they had designed would supply the necessary weather protection. But *thinking* things will work is not enough, particularly in a situation where this exact combination of elements has never been built. They needed to *know*, with enough certainty to avoid embarrassment, inconvenience, and lawsuits when the building was completed.

The windows of the John Hancock Building in Boston provide one example of the unpleasant surprises lying in wait for the best of architects and construction managers. One November day in 1972 a pane of glass fell out of the newly completed sixty-story building. It was the first of hundreds of panes that were to shower down on the Boston passers-by until they were wise enough not to pass by. Each pane that fell out was replaced by a sheet of plywood, and this led to the nickname "plywood palace" for the award-winning building. It took four years of falling glass for the architects and construction company to decide what to do. At times, in one of the less interesting employment opportunities on offer, men were

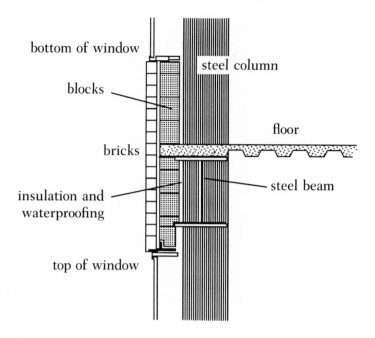

paid to watch the windows from six in the morning till midnight, looking for panels that were about to fall. Apparently about five minutes before a sheet of glass fell out it gave some warning of its intentions by losing its reflectivity and fracturing.

Due to conditions imposed on the parties to the subsequent legal settlement, the true cause of the failure was never made

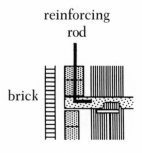

public. But hints as well as windows have been dropped from time to time. The most likely explanation now seems to be that it was a problem caused by combining in the curtain wall several different elements that had never been combined before. The double glazing had a metal layer that helped to create the reflective view from outside and cut down bright light inside. This metal-coated glass was sealed into the window frames with a type of sealant that had been used before on ordinary glass but never on glass with that particular coating. Somehow the bond between the two chemical layers was not as strong as it should have been. Under the normal stresses and strains of a tall building under wind load, the incompatibility of the sealant and the coating led to a parting of the ways on some panes of glass—with the notorious results.

Such mistakes can be expensive. It has been estimated that the total cost of the John Hancock problem, including replacing all 10,344 panes of glass, was more than the original cost of the building, $95 million.* Such events provide an awful warning for architects and construction companies, and make them willing to spend a lot of money at the design stage to ensure that the design of *their* building will not hold unpleasant surprises.

Building owners like to carry out tests on curtain walls to make sure that a particular design meets the criteria devised for it. The tests are not compulsory—but someone who didn't make them would be in a difficult legal position if a wall failed later. These tests involve building a replica of one section of the curtain wall, containing all the main elements—the brick, the insulation, the waterproofing, the windows and their connections, and the reinforcing steel—and subjecting it to a simulation of the worst environmental conditions New York could be expected to provide. These mockups are detailed and sophisticated constructions, and the one for the Worldwide Plaza curtain wall cost nearly $40,000. It was built at a specialized laboratory, and the tests took place when all the

---

* Steven S. Ross, *Construction Disasters*, McGraw-Hill, New York, 1984.

contracts for the curtain-wall components had been awarded. This was because both the method of assembly and the design were under test, and any mistake or change in the way things were put together could easily have introduced a fault in the integrity of the wall. As if people were tunneling through a mountain from opposite sides, when different contractors are involved even the architects find it difficult to make sure that steel, stone, and brick meet at a secure and accurately aligned joint.

Although large areas of the wall seem identical from the outside, they may vary in underlying structure, depending on the expected forces at that area of the building. SOM selected a specific area that would experience the highest pressures in a high wind.

Two main sites in the United States are used by SOM for curtain-wall testing. The one chosen by HRH was Construction Research Laboratory in Miami. In late June 1987, under the supervision of Dr. A. A. "Zak" Sakhnovski, a team started erecting a replica of the steel framework of part of the thirty-fifth floor of the building. On this framework they constructed an air- and watertight chamber, with the curtain wall as one of its sides. In this way the testers created a chamber from which all the air could be sucked out, thus encouraging any water outside to penetrate the smallest holes there might be in the wall.

Such mock-ups have sometimes had one other use, for the architects particularly. This can be the first time they see how the wall will look with its various components life-size. The Worldwide Plaza mock-up was not a truly *visual* one—it didn't have all the correctly shaped bricks, and a shortage of one color led to odd stripes of darker brick which wouldn't appear in the final building. Nevertheless, there was a sufficient area of correctly colored brick to give the architects *some* visual impression of what it would be like. Since the brick color continued to be a thorny topic, the mock-up would enable those who hated it to say, "I told you so," and those who liked it to confirm *their* prejudices.

Until the curtain wall had passed its test, none of the work on the walls could start. HRH were becoming impatient because the curtain-wall tests hadn't started; on the other hand, SOM feared they might be started too soon, before the most accurate mock-up could be built. One of the SOM people said resignedly, "HRH has a bad habit of rushing mock-ups." A date in late July was set—and went by. But by mid-August it looked as though the tests really would take place in the next couple of weeks. Sakhnovski and his team had built the mock-up under Dominic Fonti's supervision, and if all went smoothly, an SOM team would head for Miami on the last Sunday in August.

As the summer wore on, Fonti began to get a little frazzled. Unexpected events in New York added to his worries. He had to deal with the aftermath of a strike which had delayed the erection of the steel and had a domino effect on several other deadlines. A three-week strike meant a four-week delay by the time everybody was geared up to return to work. And there were other problems with the steel: Atlas Gem, the erectors, had decided to change the order in which they erected it. That would have been all right had it not been for the fact that, at A. J. Ross's marshaling yard, all the pieces were laid out very carefully in the original order. So when the daily pickups were ordered from the site by phone, the required beams and columns were in a number of different piles. Before long there was unutterable confusion in the marshaling yard, and work on site dropped behind schedule as everyone looked for the right pieces, and failed to find them.

As a contribution to HRH's anxieties, an incident on another of their sites served as a reminder of the need for constant vigilance over the safety of a large and complex construction site. Artie Nusbaum and other senior managers at HRH were having to deal with the aftermath of an accident in which an eight-foot-long piece of wood fell six hundred feet and decapitated a pedestrian. Although nothing to do with Worldwide Plaza, it led Fonti to take another look at the protective screens around each floor that were intended to stop such incidents.

So Fonti and his family were ready for the vacation they had planned, although there was one minor drawback: they were going to Florida, where Fonti might be tempted to become embroiled in the curtain-wall tests, now scheduled for the last week of their vacation. Late August had become both the best and the worst time to go away: the best because Fonti needed the vacation; the worst because the work could not stop—the owner still wanted the project to stay on schedule, and the curtain wall was a major concern of HRH and therefore of Fonti. In a triumph of optimism over realism, the Fontis left New York for their vacation.

For the first two days, the Fontis were like any other American family on vacation. They went to Disney World; Fonti spent quite a lot of time teaching his son to swim; Elena Fonti lay on the beach soaking up the sun. And in the evenings Fonti tried not to think about what might be going on in New York or at the test site. But two days into the vacation the phone started ringing and he started covering pages of his little yellow notepad. Then a telegram arrived from the office, suggesting that Fonti was needed in New York *as well as* at the curtain-wall test, since a major scheduling exercise was in progress to see what dates could be guaranteed to the owner and to the tenants for the completion of the office tower.

By the fourth day of that week, it had become clear that the job was occupying more of Fonti's mind than his family vacation. Elena had expected, or at least wanted, him to have a few stress-free days away from Worldwide Plaza. It seemed a reasonable desire. But when she asked her husband if it wasn't possible, just for once, to cut himself off from this stream of importuning phone calls and telegrams, she received the classic answer given by many husbands in high-stress, high-paid jobs: "Do you *really* want me to get a less responsible job, where they may not require my input as much, where they won't call me during my private hours? In the type of position I have, I'm on call. Whenever they need me, they can call me."

Well, they called him, and Fonti responded. Before heading

back to New York, he planned to drop in at the test laboratory on NW 79th Street in Miami for a few hours, to see how well the preparations for the test were going. Then he would catch an afternoon plane to New York, missing the architects from SOM on the eight o'clock evening flight.

On Monday morning, August 31, Fonti walked up the drive of Construction Research's Miami laboratory to see the twelve-foot-high mock-up for the first time. The telephone messages had already prepared him for some of the problems. The one he was most irritated about—"irate" was his word—was the fact that the wrong caulking had been used to seal the various joints in the mock-up. "Caulking" is a gooey, viscous liquid that is squirted into gaps in the structure to seal every last chink in the face of the building. Before the test could be started, the mock-up had to be sealed in the way the architects specified, since that method was one of the aspects under test. The trouble was that the company that would *eventually* caulk and waterproof the building had not yet been appointed. HRH hadn't quite gotten around to it yet, but the test couldn't be delayed any further because of the schedule pressures to start building the curtain wall on the site. As a favor, the masons at the test site had said they would do the caulking of the mock-up. They also said they would do the flashing, another aspect of the waterproofing of the building. Flashing is a plastic or rubber sheeting material that makes a waterproof layer between certain surfaces in the wall.

Unfortunately, as it turned out, Fonti could have done without such favors. First, the wrong caulking had been used. Although a two-component sealant had been specified, the masons had decided to use ready-mixed sealant that saved them from having to prepare a new mixture each time they refilled the caulking gun. In the architects' view, this simple labor-saving measure—had it been allowed to stand—would have rendered the whole test meaningless. The important thing was that the mock-up *had* to be as near as possible to the specifications of the building.

When the architects discovered this, they left HRH in no doubt that something had to be done about it, and fast, so that the test was delayed as little as possible. So the wrong sealant was picked out of all the crevices and the correct, two-component mixture squeezed into place. Working flat out, the testers completed the work by about ten-thirty on Saturday morning.

If one listened to Fonti at times like this, he seemed to be wondering whether architects weren't a little overfussy about the minutiae of their projects: "We've gotten a lot of grief from everyone—architects, consultants, subcontractors. The difference between us and them lies in the fact that an architect feels that this is a monument to the world, whereas we think it's a masonry wall, and there's been thousands of masonry walls built in this city. We felt that the normal standard of construction would suffice and there would be no need for this, but he has other ideas."

This cynicism was shared by others on the test site, including Steve Brasecker, supervisor of the test:

In this particular building you have a pretty characteristic group. You have the architect, who has design as his main consideration. He wants to put up a monumental building, something everybody is going to see and say, "Hey, wow! That's great!" It's his entry into posterity. The construction manager, HRH, they're interested in having a building up that they don't get sued over, that's going to stay in place. Each of the individual trades have the same interest as the construction company. The only difference is, each of the trades says, "I'm only going to do so much. The rest is someone else's responsibility." So then you have to argue out who's actually doing what part of the interface between the various trades. The consultant is working to represent the interest of the owner. Again, he's after a viable building, something the guy can make money with. He's not investing money to lose it. He also wants to make sure it's sound. I tell you, he has about the same interest as the construction manager.

As soon as Fonti arrived at the test site, he was briefed on the state of the curtain wall by Al Bianchi, the representative of an independent consulting company, Gordon Smith, Inc., which had been appointed to advise the owner directly on the quality and efficiency of the testing procedure. The test couldn't start until Tuesday, because there had to be a seventy-two-hour period after the caulking was in place till it became "tack-free" and lost its stickiness. But the pre-test had already revealed a possible problem with the windows. Fonti clambered inside the mock-up to have a look. When the mock-up was constructed, the builders had only just managed to squeeze one of the windows into the gap in the wall. The architects had designed the windows with a tolerance of half an inch, but it seemed that might be insufficient to guarantee that all the windows would be easy to fit on site; perhaps they should be made half an inch shorter.

Discoveries like this justified making a mock-up in the first place. With a factory in Wisconsin standing by to make over three thousand windows, it was important to ensure they were the right size. And since it took three to four months to make the windows and get them on site, the sooner the decision could be made the better.

After a brief handover discussion with Jack Leahy, his assistant, Fonti set off to collect wife and children and take them to the airport. At the test laboratory, a couple of pre-tests were organized to make sure that everything was in working order for the full test the following day.

The first test was for watertightness. A large framework of waterpipes was wheeled in front of the wall, and the water switched on. Almost immediately water from outside poured underneath one of the windows and flooded the floor of the test chamber. Six minutes later more water started leaking through the top right-hand corner of another window. Something seemed to be wrong with the flashing—instead of deflecting water and sending it out again through small "weep" holes in the mortar, it seemed to be letting water right through into the interior.

A downcast Leahy headed for the telephone to report back to New York. It wasn't only the leaks that upset him, but also the fact that one of the testers was insisting that they wait for the architects to decide how to seal the flashing rather than setting to work there and then to rectify the holes. "It'll kill us," said Leahy to Bob Sanna, in Fonti's office. The architects, who were arriving on the evening flight, wouldn't be at the test site till the next day, and waiting for their decision could delay the test for a day or more, by the time the modifications to the windows were completed.

The next pre-test was for airtightness. A smoke candle was lit inside the test chamber. The watching team could see through the windows that the interior of the chamber quickly filled with smoke. It wasn't long before the team could also see smoke *outside* the test chamber, as a steady stream issued from one of the corners of the mock-up. With an expletive or two, Bianchi and Leahy ran to the corner to see where the leak was. It could have been another weakness in the design of the curtain wall, or the test chamber itself might have been at fault. Even as they stared up toward the top of the mock-up, more smoke was seeping beneath the lowest layer of brick, to curl insidiously around their feet. Obviously there was a lot to talk to the architects about.

The following morning was not a pleasant time for anyone at Construction Research in Miami. Three pre-tests on Monday had revealed a degree of leakiness to air and water that nobody could be happy with. Some patching work was carried out on the chamber, but everybody realized that the way the mock-up had been constructed was the real source of the problem. Now, as the water-spraying rig was pushed against the mock-up and the jets switched on, it became clear that the flashing and sealing between windows, brick, and block simply were not doing their job. Three SOM people had flown down from New York and arrived at the site—Ed Narbutas, Dick Rowe, and Gary Steficek.

Since everyone's workmanship was potentially on the line, an air of concentration surrounded the proceedings. Narbutas took close-up photographs of the windows from the outside of the mock-up; Rowe and Steficek stood back contemplating the overall structure; a man from Wausau Metals in Wisconsin, who had flown in that morning, stood by a desk in the open air and pored over the shop drawings of the window, looking at the detailing for possible areas of leakage. Each participant hoped it wouldn't be his workmanship at fault, and found reasons for suspecting the others.

The architects were fairly confident that it wasn't a design fault. The masons were pretty sure they had built the wall to specifications, two courses of block for every four courses of brick, ties across the gap to keep the two layers together and pinned to the steel framework. The window manufacturer was fairly happy with the windows he had fabricated and shipped to Florida for the mockup. The testing company, which had supervised building the mockup, seemed confident that all the instructions had been followed as closely as possible. As they talked among themselves, rumors spread. It was all the fault of the new sealant, wrongly applied after the mistake with the old sealant; it was scrappy flashing, put in piecemeal instead of the method specified; it was faulty design around the window-washer buttons, the anchor point for a cradle that would enable window cleaning and maintenance to be carried out all over the finished building; and there was one other candidate—as Bianchi put it, "the way the flashing was put in didn't allow the window to weep under pressure."

As the day wore on, the architects began to wear out. The water test was rerun four times, and on each occasion water continued to leak through the wall, even after more gaps were plugged. There was much waiting around between tests, and a lot of guesswork went into discussing what was really going wrong.

As the architects sat around their hotel pool that evening, they discussed what they thought was the real problem. All along they had known that the one contractor who would not be at the test was the waterproofing contractor, for the simple reason that he had not yet been appointed. It had seemed madness to SOM to go ahead and test the watertightness of the curtain wall without having the proper waterproofing team to prepare it. But they were overruled by HRH and the owners, eager to proceed to the next stage and give the go-ahead for window manufacture and to schedule brick-laying. In fact, once Narbutas and the others started looking closely at the points where water was penetrating, it was clear that the rubber flashing strip had not been laid in the most effective way. If you push a strip of rubberized material into a crevice to waterproof it, you don't generally use a sharp steel trowel to push it, since the probability of making holes in the strip is fairly high. That appeared to be what had happened.

The following day, Wednesday, would see the severest test of all: the dynamic test to simulate the buffeting of wind and rain in a storm. If today's tests had been anything to go by, tomorrow's would be worse. They went to bed in a somber mood. Ominously, at about one in the morning, their hotel's curtain wall failed as Steficek's bedroom window was blown in by a gust of wind.

The dynamic test was related to the wind-tunnel tests in Ontario a year before. Those tests had put a model of the building in the path of a scaled-down New York wind to measure the forces each of the faces would be subjected to. Now the mock-up was to be put under 50 percent higher than the maximum wind force to see whether the brickwork cracked or the windows fell in or out. To produce this wind, an airplane propeller and engine were wheeled in front of the mock-up and started up. For a deafening few minutes air and water were flung at the wall and windows while the anxious spectators stood inside waiting for the inevitable water to start seeping through. Bianchi improvised a draft detector with his cigarette up near the top left-hand corner of the window; the man from Wausau mopped the inside windowsill ineffectually with a cloth; Steve Brasecker inspected the "buffet-meter" that showed the vibration of the glass three feet away from the nose of the rotating propeller. At least the mock-up was holding up *structurally*. The one consolation of a dismal three days in Florida was the news that the curtain wall wouldn't crack up in a big storm, even if the office workers found themselves standing ankle deep in water.

In retrospect, it seemed clear that the Florida tests shouldn't have happened. Of course it was faintly possible that masons unused to waterproofing could nevertheless carry out the architects' detailed instructions effectively. Had they done so, and had the flashing and caulking worked, the tests would have been a realistic simulation of one section of the curtain wall under air and water. But they weren't. Two months later waterproofing contractors were finally appointed and went to Florida to set the bedraggled mock-up to rights. They replaced the flashing correctly and made new seals to overcome the leaky patches at the top and bottom of the windows. Then the mock-up was once more subjected to the sort of wind and rain that New York gets once every fifty years—and came through as dry as a bone.

10
COMINGS
AND GOINGS

When David Schwartz of Cravath, Swaine and Moore tried to convince his partners that it made sense to move to Worldwide Plaza, he had to marshal some persuasive arguments. Cravath— as everyone called it—was an old, established New York law firm, tracing its ancestry back to Abraham Lincoln's Secretary of State, William H. Seward, and it was not known for making dramatic gestures. It didn't seek publicity, it didn't expand aggressively, and because of its quiet conservatism it seemed to make steady progress in a climate where only the previous year another multi-partner American law firm had disappeared almost overnight with major financial problems. But although not aggressively expansive, Cravath did need more space: its total staff of over a thousand was becoming cramped in its downtown offices in the Chase Manhattan building near Wall Street. Also, its lease on those premises would run out in 1993 and the renewal terms would be significantly more expensive. So the firm decided to ask a real-estate broker, Julian Studley, to locate every single site that might have between three and four hundred thousand square feet of space available.

One day, while on business in Chicago, Studley opened his *New York Times* to see a full-page advertisement for Worldwide Plaza. He rang the Zeckendorf Company and spoke to Bill Zeckendorf, who was in his office with Terry Soderberg. "Would Worldwide be able to supply Cravath's needs?" he asked. Neither Zeckendorf nor Soderberg dared to believe that such a plum deal would come to them, but they started discussions anyway.

One of the factors that inclined Cravath toward Worldwide was the need—or, rather, the desire—for a view. Schwartz was emphatic that the company wanted good views from its windows, and he was keen to find a building in which the firm could occupy high floors. When you see the premises Cravath was leaving behind, you realize why this somewhat sentimental, or at least uncommercial, factor weighed so heavily. The views from the fifty-seventh floor of the Chase building are stunning: Schwartz's office, on the south side of the building, has a wide-screen view of the southernmost tip of Manhattan, with the Statue of Liberty in mid-distance, ships at anchor in the Upper Bay, and helicopters buzzing back and forth several hundred feet beneath the windows. In fact, the only better view was from the north side of the same building, from some of the other Cravath offices. There you could see the rest of Manhattan, from the Wall Street area north toward Central Park. So, whatever the needs of the company for more space and an affordable rent, that space had to be at the top of a sizable building to give the partners and the company the views they had become used to.

Certainly Worldwide Plaza offered what Cravath wanted. A view from seven hundred feet above the old Madison Square Garden site went some way toward meeting their desires, although, in Schwartz's words, the neighborhoods had different merits: "North was acceptable, south frightened us, and the west was a fine, decent area." There were of course other ways in which Worldwide Plaza fit the bill very well. There were thirteen floors to give them the 370,000 square feet they needed; the rent they felt they could agree was reasonable; and they could argue for an equity share in the building as well.

But there were a number of disadvantages to the site that Schwartz had to put before his partners to give them the full picture. The main disadvantage was the current state of the area. However good a face was put on it, Clinton was not as salubrious as Wall Street. In fact, the memo to all staff telling them the news didn't even mention the name of the area, but related the site to all the surrounding landmarks and amenities, most of which were several blocks away. Some of Schwartz's colleagues reacted predictably to their image of the area: "Don't you realize what you're doing? You're like the Pied Piper leading this firm into the sea," said one somewhat inaccurately, and another complained: "I didn't practice law for some thirty-odd years to wind up in Hell's Kitchen." But Schwartz was undeterred in his efforts to keep Worldwide Plaza on a shortlist of three possible buildings to move to.

In early February 1987, at a meeting of the development partners, Zeckendorf was relaying his general pleasure at the interest shown by Cravath in the building:

The biggest question they have is, will they be the only commercial structure on Eighth Avenue? Actually, if you go up Eighth Avenue from 42nd Street, there are probably only three or four office sites. There's one directly across the street. There's a site directly to our north which is a porno house. There's Morgan Stanley, who will go ahead with a block between 48th and 49th Streets.

So, with Broadway also becoming an investment and banking center, we're suddenly seeing the thing I never thought we'd see, the West Side becoming the financial center of New York. I mean, I just never would have believed that Morgan Stanley would wind up on Broadway.

A symbol of Cravath's concern was the Adonis Theater—"the porno house," in Zeckendorf's words—that formed part of the block to the north of Worldwide Plaza. Cravath felt that the proximity of the theater, which showed only films with a homosexual theme, was "somewhat incompatible with our presence." This was a point on which a developer like Zeckendorf could offer some assurance. Since his whole intention was to raise the tone of the area and, as one consequence, to raise property prices, it would have been surprising if the partners had not cast an eye on surrounding blocks to see what else was available for sale. Indeed, the matter was in hand, as Arthur Cohen, one of the partners, explained: "We have acquired the total block front just north of this property, to build a very top-flight building there. If you develop an area it's foolish not to maximize by purchasing the properties around it." And, as Soderberg joked: "We have an understanding with the partners of Cravath that the Adonis Theater will be gone by the time they occupy. Whether we buy it, someone else buys it, or it's a midnight raid, it will be down before October 1, '89."

The partnership was clearly very keen to get Cravath into the building. The deal could have many repercussions on the way in which other potential tenants—and the community—perceived the building. Everybody connected with the leasing of Worldwide Plaza believed that the project could actually transform the area for many city blocks around it. This argument was good for the perception of other potential tenants, for shops and restaurants that might rent space on the lower floors, for the city authorities who would look more kindly on the development, and for those members of the

community who wanted a changed environment rather than a pre-
served one. In the early period of the project the argument was a
hope rather than a reality, but as the project progressed, it was as
though saying it often enough would make the belief come true.

In an attempt to deal with Cravath's concerns about the area,
the Worldwide partnership arranged a meeting at which senior
figures from O&M could try to persuade Cravath's executive committee that it wouldn't be so bad out that far west. Like pioneers
pulling their wagons in a circle, they implied that the combined
presence of the two prestigious companies would fend off the ma-
rauding tribes. In fact, it might even provide an opportunity to
convert them.

One particular concern related to public transportation. Many
of the more highly paid lawyers lived on the East Side of Manhattan
and were used to a reasonably quick and easy subway trip to the
Wall Street area. Now they were faced with a journey to a different
and unfamiliar part of town. How would they cope? Schwartz described how Zeckendorf resolved that problem, in a move that might
seem a little obvious but which did the trick: "We told Mr. Zeckendorf, 'Look, we'd really like to go to the building, but you can't
get there from where we live.' He said, 'Oh, nonsense, the whole
New York City transportation network leads right to the building.'
I said, 'Well, you'll have to show me that.' And he came up with a
map in rather short order. And we could see immediately that, quite
frankly, you can get there from almost anywhere."

Armed with a subway map, Schwartz and the others who supported the move influenced enough of their partners to make it
look increasingly likely to happen. At one stage in the discussions,
Zeckendorf said to Schwartz, "Is there anything else I can do to
help make up your minds?"

"There's only one thing, but I don't think you'd do it."

"Go on, tell me, and I'll see if I can."

"Move the building two blocks to the east," said Schwartz.

One major advantage the development partnership had was the perception of Zeckendorf as different from other potential landlords. In Schwartz's words, he was "honest, decent, and pragmatic":

> You don't feel like you're at the dentist's office with him pulling every last tooth out. You sort of come in, you sit down, you're very comfortable, and you explain what you need. He then explains what he needs, and a deal can be put together fairly rapidly with him. We would not go to a building where we felt we were eventually going to be harassed by someone who just was looking solely at the economics of things. We wanted someone who had a long-range view.

Perhaps this, more than any other factor, kept Cravath interested in the building. Zeckendorf's openness and his skill in seeing what the tenants needed and giving it to them disarmed Cravath whenever they came to a sticking point in the deal.

It wasn't all clear sailing. Both sides had a lot invested in making the deal work, but Cravath had the upper hand. The firm knew its value to the project and pressed for every advantage it could. Much of that pressure was put on Bob Salomon, who would take a considerable amount of credit for the deal if it happened, and blame if it didn't.

While discussions were still going on and before any deal was signed, vague attempts were made to keep the negotiations secret, although, with more than a hundred Cravath partners in the know, the real-estate community were bound to discover what was going on. When Cravath did eventually reveal its interest in the site, the *Wall Street Journal* left no one in any doubt about the unusual nature of the proposed move: "Cravath, Swaine and Moore stunned some local real estate executives by disclosing it is considering a move to Eighth Avenue, a less desirable area two blocks from what is generally considered as midtown. . . . 'It blows my mind,' one developer said of Cravath's disclosure. 'They represent the ultimate white shoe firm.' " But another broker commented, "Well, Cravath's an elephant, it can sit wherever it wishes."

Within the Zeckendorf Company, there was a general air of excitement that a large and prestigious tenant was negotiating. But with so many areas of potential give and take, the discussions did not run smoothly. Salomon shared both the excitement and the worry about whether the deal could ever be completed:

> The excitement is so great. Nobody could conceive that this tenant would move to the West Side. I can't think of a tenant who would do more for our building than this particular tenant, and I've worked with the largest industrial tenants and so on. There's something about them, an aura, which would create such an impression that my worries would be over. There's no question about it.
>
> First I was a so-called hero. Everybody said, "Well, Bob, you're really doing so great with that deal," and then all of a sudden we got reverberations—the tenant may need more space, they're exceeding their budget, and so on, and there was a lot of negative feedback. We became very unsettled. We had turned down other tenants because of this deal. We had told them that we had a lease outstanding, which we did—we were in heavy negotiation and about to consummate it.

One of the sticking points was Cravath's cunning argument that it should qualify for a rental figure *below* market value, below even the lower rents expected in that area of Manhattan: "We understood that it was a significant feather in Mr. Zeckendorf's cap if the Cravath firm would move to his building. And we let him know we understood that and that we expected to receive a comparable benefit for ourselves in that regard. We felt we were improving the neighborhood by our very presence, by taking the Cravath firm and moving it to an address that other firms might not be willing to move to. If we paid market value we would be paying for our own prestige."

All through 1987 the negotiations with Cravath continued. Although it seemed highly likely that the firm would complete a deal, Zeckendorf was talking to other clients while Cravath was still considering. Some were competing tenants in the sense that they might occupy the space Cravath had earmarked; others were companies considering taking floors in the middle of the building. At one stage in the search for a tenant a major company turned up wanting 1.1 million square feet—thirty-six floors—too much to accommodate in light of the lease that had already been signed with O&M. As the year progressed, two other companies showed serious interest in the building: N. W. Ayer, another public-relations company, and Polygram, one of the six largest record companies in the United States. They were interested in three floors and ten floors, respectively—not such large deals, but still important to nurse along and bring to a successful conclusion.

Another high-quality client was Viacom, the giant American communications corporation. They were after a lot of space—fourteen floors, the ones Cravath were after—and were initially no easier to pin down. They were on, then off, then on again; then they were taken over, and it looked as if they had dropped out; then they came back in. Soderberg had a nerve-racking time, which seemed to be over by late 1987. If negotiations could be successfully concluded with Ayer and Polygram and with Viacom or with Cravath during 1987 and early 1988, Soderberg would have a virtually fully leased building almost a year before a target date of January 1989, an enviable feat in the volatile New York real-estate market.

On Monday, October 19, 1987, two unexpected events occurred that could have had serious consequences for Worldwide Plaza, if on a rather different scale. First, the Dow Jones Average on the New York Stock Exchange fell by over five hundred points. Overnight, the fortunes of big companies changed and any plans for the future had to be reconsidered. In spite of the general optimism about both Cravath and Viacom, no deal had been signed with either. But Soderberg, in spite of his reputation as "Dr. Gloom," was continuing to be hopeful. Discussions with Viacom seemed to be continuing: "We made Viacom a proposal that we thought was fair and in a matter of three days we had a handshake on approximately 421,000 square feet in the middle of the building. We have a first draft of the leases out now, and we've had some technical meetings in the past week, so things are moving ahead very smoothly, we feel."

On the day of the handshake, Soderberg told Cravath about the Viacom deal. Cravath was disappointed but asked to be kept in touch. Soderberg could begin to relax—with two major tenants, it would be easy to rent the rest.

The second event on "Black Monday" was a career change for Rob Schubert. His position in SOM was responsible but, in his eyes, not overpaid. And the company had qualities that were both admirable and at the same time constricting:

> There are two things working against Skidmore: it's both an institution and a partnership—the most conservative form of business that you can have. There are certain rules that that partnership has to operate under. Being a Chicago firm, it doesn't necessarily recognize to the full extent the economic realities of living in New York—it's an expensive place to live. I keep thinking: Where am I gonna be in five years? Will I be promoted to a partner? I don't know.

When Schubert was not promoted to associate partner in 1986, he began to consider the possibility that he might not spend the rest of his working life at SOM, although he didn't do much about it. Worldwide Plaza took up a great deal of time and emotional energy and provided a distraction from personal worries about money and status. Then two things happened almost at the same time: in 1987 Rob was made an associate partner, not before time, but it was gratifying; and a headhunter approached him on behalf of a leading real-estate broker called Cushman and Wakefield. One section of this company specializes in finding premises for large companies and helping to make them ready to move into. This often requires a large amount of architectural design and construction work. With a new building this could involve changes to the basic building, not unlike the work Schubert had helped to monitor when O&M were planning how they would use Worldwide Plaza. So a project manager like Schubert, with experience in running an operation as complex as Worldwide Plaza, would be very useful to Cushman and Wakefield as they helped their clients move into office premises that the brokering side of the company had found.

On August 26 Rob had the first of five interviews with Cushman and Wakefield. By the end of the interviews he felt that Cushman and Wakefield were selling themselves to him as much as he to them. With the salary they were offering, he didn't need much persuasion to accept their offer of a job.

All this was unknown to the rest of the team at SOM, although Leon Moed, Schubert's immediate boss, sensed that something was up. "Why don't you take a vacation?" he suggested at one stage. It was in fact while Moed himself was on vacation that Schubert resigned. He would have preferred to do it face to face but the need to give notice forced the timing.

SOM's reaction was muted. There was no attempt to persuade him to reconsider. As Schubert himself put it: "It was just like they knew that they couldn't get into bidding more than Cushman and Wakefield were offering and so they didn't even try." David Childs was unruffled, although he claimed to be surprised that recent events hadn't kept Schubert in the company:

> We had just given him an enormously large step by making him an associate partner, which was something that people struggle for many years before getting. And along with it comes a substantial raise in income. So the timing was surprising to me. But this often happens in the project-management side of our work—

very rarely in the design side. And that's because the other professions pay much better than architectural design. So someone who is trained in management, in financial matters and in organizational skills, in the real-estate world is tremendously valuable to a construction firm or to a real-estate firm. And so we have decided that when somebody leaves to change professions there's nothing we can do about it. We can't offer him double the salary, which is literally what it would take to keep him. We just can't afford it in the profession that we've chosen. The only thing that was really surprising was the timing for Rob. But he got an offer that he couldn't refuse, and it was a wonderful step for him. He's essentially doing exactly what he was doing here in SOM except he's being paid a lot more for it, and with a great career path ahead of him. So I felt wonderful for him, and sad to lose him.

But Childs found some small potential consolation for his sadness: "You know, there's a good side too, because these people often come back to be our clients. And I expect that'll be the case for Rob."

There were things Schubert was also sad about. He acknowledged that he was moving out of the gentlemanly world of architecture into a different working environment: "Skidmore has got down to a fine art the breeding in its employees of a dedication to the profession and to the excellence that they bring. I think one of the things with this job that I'm astounded by is the degree of incompetency in the world, and I'm heartened by the fact that I come from a Skidmore way of doing things, a dedication to excellence. I may not find that again. Abandoning that was the scary part, like jumping off a cliff."

His other regret was the friends and colleagues he would be leaving behind him. Only Schubert had appreciated the irony when, on April 15, 1987, a small group of Worldwide Plaza people had gathered for lunch in the Seeda II Thai restaurant opposite the site. Such informal lunches took place from time to time, but besides providing an opportunity for the informal exchange of information, this lunch had had an extra function: a chance for the group to celebrate Schubert's appointment as an associate partner in SOM. Present were Dominic Fonti and Tony Raffiniello from HRH, and Schubert, Ed Narbutas, and Gary Steficek from SOM. At the end of the meal, Janet, the pretty Thai manager of the restaurant, arrived at the table with a bottle of American champagne and a rather ornate ice-cream dessert with candles stuck in it. As a mark of their respect and liking, Schubert's friends had organized this celebration. "The candles are edible, by the way," Fonti joked. "Go ahead," said Narbutas, "trust the contractor." They all burst out laughing.

The group building the Worldwide Plaza had, on the whole, managed to separate personal feelings from the kind of creative animosity that people like Jack Schuster used as a management tool. Schubert himself confessed to a degree of overreaction to the inevitable snarl-ups of daily life, in order to help him run the project team: "Sometimes it's much easier to be screaming and shouting and railing against the illogical nature and futility of it all. It diffuses some things. Instead of people going off and going, 'Unnn gngn umm,'' and mumbling and letting it fester, here's somebody who's screaming about it. 'Don't worry about it, it's just nonsense. We'll get it taken care of. Don't worry, it's going to work itself out.' It's part of my job of communicating what's going on."

It's carefully considered maneuvers like this that led to Schubert's being considered a "bullshitter"—a word that contains an element of affection in its scatology. As Schubert himself remarked on another occasion, there was value in this approach: "You can't bullshit a bullshitter."

At an early stage in the project, before he decided to leave, Schubert privately summed up his opinion of Fonti in a way that reflected the best aspects of relationships between SOM and HRH as a whole:

I like Dominic as a person. I think he's pretty straightforward. He doesn't BS [bullshit] you. I think he's a very proud man and I respect him a lot. I think he's smart. We're still working—we do a dance. It's like the birds that dance, at times. Everybody's dancing around each other. Not in a posturing way, but just starting to get comfortable with each other. Dominic's not really a hothead. Well, correction, he *is* a hothead in that, if something needs to be done, he will climb all over you. Fine, but he doesn't climb all over you unnecessarily, for the sheer joy of it. There are a lot of people in the construction business who love to do that. They just love beating up on architects. I think that we're remarkably free of architect beaters here.

Fonti, for his part, was fond of Schubert, and sorry to hear of his imminent departure: "I was surprised, very surprised, because Rob was involved with this project from the inception. And when he called up, he says, 'I'm leaving, I want to introduce you to Jim Parker.' I said, 'Who is Jim Parker?' He said, 'Oh, he's my replacement.' And then I got really forlorn. But he tells me that he was coaxed away, he did not look for it, and I said, 'Good luck and God bless.' "

When SOM decided to close down their office in Denver, Colorado, an architect named Jim Parker was the last man out. He had been offered a job in the New York office, and on the day of his arrival at SOM, the place was buzzing with a piece of news that meant more to everyone else than to him. Someone named Rob Schubert had resigned from SOM to go to a better-paid and more responsible job.

While SOM chewed over the significance of Schubert's departure (and while the partners studiously didn't try to persuade him to stay), Parker tackled the three or four projects he had been given to get on with: one in New Jersey, another in Manhattan. Ten days after he joined the New York office, he was asked to take on Worldwide Plaza. It was a daunting task, as he found out within a few days of immersing himself in the project: "Many of the things that are going on on this project are similar to projects I've worked on in the past. So there's a ring of familiarity, but there are different people doing everything, and different subjects being discussed. Everything seems very familiar but I can't quite put my hand on what it is they're talking about or what the decision is that they're reaching."

Within three days of being appointed project manager, Parker tendered his resignation, in what some interpreted as a realization that the task before him was too enormous. A day later, with an increased salary, he was back on the job, in charge of a project that had been running for three years with a team and plans and subcontractors and developers and a schedule that he knew very little about. For the time being, at any rate, there was no possibility of his taking over the reins Schubert had controlled since the beginning. All he could do was let the project run, chair some meetings, and bow to the greater wisdom of the other members of the team. And although Parker was the *formally* appointed project manager, they were likely to look to an informal leader from among themselves, someone who had lived through the project. In terms of seniority this meant Bodnar or Narbutas. But Bodnar's aloof inscrutability worked against him. Somehow his clipped, economically worded interventions at meetings, delivered with a tight-lipped smile, wouldn't have held the team together. Narbutas's more open, self-aware approach seemed to work well, filling out the picture for Parker and generally getting things done.

Meanwhile, Schubert was gone but not forgotten. One of his first projects at Cushman and Wakefield was to help a large communications company plan its move to a new skyscraper on the West Side—the company was Viacom, the skyscraper Worldwide Plaza. On November 16 Soderberg met Schubert in his new capacity to discuss Viacom's needs for the building. He found it an interesting experience:

We had a meeting Monday, with Rob wearing the black hat instead of the white hat. Rob knows the building well and he's going to be advising Viacom on what the building can and cannot do for them. And Rob has also to remember that he was on the design team, so he can't really walk away from issues. It's going to be fun.

In fact, there's not a lot his client could do to the building. We made the important decisions years ago. They may not be the right decisions for this tenant, but we did what was right, and if the tenant can deal with them, fine, because we aren't going to change the building. We're at the twenty-fifth floor now with steel—it's too late. If it works, it works—if it doesn't, it doesn't. If it doesn't work, Rob is going to tell his tenants why it doesn't work. *I'm* not going to.

Schubert seemed untroubled by the switch in loyalties. One place where this was perhaps most an issue was the fact that Viacom wanted to put a large dish antenna plumb on top of "David's diamond," a suggestion guaranteed to have appalled Schubert when he was at SOM. Now it seemed to matter less:

You take your lead from the client. In the case of being project manager for Skidmore, I was taking my lead from the Zeckendorfs, obviously, and I didn't want to crap up the building. As architects we didn't want to mess up the building either. The problem is that the technologies are changing, with the microwave antennas and the satellite dishes, they don't quite fit into the design of this roof easily. Satellite dishes sort of stick out like pimples—you can see them all over Manhattan. There are plenty of instances where they look like a mistake. The intent here is to make it look like it was thought about, to make it disappear because it looks like it belongs there.

I've talked to Terry just briefly to see what kind of leeway there is. The logical place to put an FM antenna is right up on

the peak. City planning won't let us do that—there's a legal re-
striction as to the height of the building—so now we have to go
back to our client, Viacom, and say, "Well, maybe there's another
way to get this done," and see how we can integrate it into the
building for the best of both parties.

As it happened, this issue was soon of little concern to either
Schubert or Soderberg. In the world of corporate real estate, things
changed at a bewildering pace. Viacom had committed themselves
to the project with Terry's "handshake" on 421,000 square feet in
early October. Schubert had joined Cushman and Wakefield on
October 19—Black Monday—and taken over Viacom's tenant work.
By early December, Black Monday had wrought its worst and Viacom decided that they could not after all afford to move into Worldwide Plaza. It was a worrying time for Soderberg, with several deals
out but none of them signed, apart from O&M:

> You have to be very worried, very concerned. You have to look
> at each of our tenants and see how they're affected. Unfortu-
> nately, when you're in the middle of a project there's no stopping.
> You can worry like hell but you can't stop. So you have to really
> see: What do I do as the next stop? How do we pull this thing
> around? Where's the good in it? One thing that's good appears
> to be happening: interest rates are coming down. So we might
> have a window at this point to go out and do our permanent
> financing. The bad side is obvious. You've made a certain com-
> mitment but you haven't gone all the way, and so you could pull
> back at that point and say, "I will not proceed." And then, thirty
> days later, you could change your mind and proceed again. No-
> body really knows.

Faced with Viacom's wanting to pull out, Soderberg's first reaction was to see if they could be persuaded to stay in on a different
basis: "Sweetening the pot," he called it. But it was no good—
Viacom were permanently out of the picture. Soderberg allowed his

Dr. Gloom side to show even more than usual: "We went so far so quickly and we were all so elated and we watched the bubble burst. It's sort of sad. You know, after spending three and a half years on the project, we're talking about permanent takeouts one day; then the next day you've got a half-empty building. It's sort of hard to take."

The obvious next step was to turn back to Cravath, but the firm was in no better position than Viacom, as Schwartz explained: "During the October crash we stopped everything. We simply didn't know what was going to happen next—I guess no one really did—and so we ended all negotiations with everyone."

But then Bill Zeckendorf intervened. "Sometime around Christmastime," Schwartz recalled later, "Bill Zeckendorf called me up and said, 'Listen, Dave, I've been negotiating with a variety of people, and if I'm going to be Santa Claus I might as well pick who I want to be Santa Claus to.' And he then sweetened the offer that we had been considering prior to the crash." There was now one key difference. Throughout the property market, deals that had been nearly completed were called off. There was a great deal of property on the market. Cravath could drive an even harder bargain than it had been able to before.

There were two areas of bargaining: rent and work letter. Cravath wanted to spend a considerable amount of money on the interiors and would try to get as much as possible back from Worldwide. Before the deal had been called off, the Zeckendorf partners were talking gloomily about the large gap between the work-letter figure they would try to offer—$25 per square foot—and what Cravath would undoubtedly want to spend—$70 or more a square foot. When you consider that the whole building cost about $90 a square foot to build, that gives an idea of the amount of work still to be carried out before a major tenant moves in.

After Black Monday and the collapse of the Viacom deal, there could be little argument. Although neither party will confirm the final work-letter figure, it is believed that Cravath obtained most of what it wanted. When this was combined with the lower rent it could also argue for, the finally agreed deal had quite an effect. According to Soderberg: "Black Monday probably had a 10–15 percent effect on our package. With the rent and the work letter, we probably took about a $25-million hit."

But the real-estate world seems to specialize in clouds with silver linings. No disaster is quite what it seems. The inexorable rise in rents meant that, even at the reduced rate, Cravath was probably paying more than if it had come in at the same time as O&M. And since it was such a classy tenant, some of the losses caused by Black Monday could be recouped by the very factor Cravath had used to its own advantage: its prestige would make the whole building more attractive, and allow Zeckendorf to charge more to other tenants.

Salomon was his usual buoyant self:

> We had to pick up our teeth, so to speak, after the Viacom deal fell through. But we said, "This building is great, we'll find other tenants." And we will. And if we consummate the lease for Cravath, our worries are over, because we'll get higher rental if the other people [Ayer and Polygram] decide that they don't want our building. We would not renege on a deal, we would not turn around and say, "Your rent's going up," but if the negotiation breaks off and they decide that they don't want our lease anymore for the mid-rise, we'd be in a position to probably get $2–3 a square foot higher because of Cravath.

In fact, he felt he could obtain $32 net a square foot instead of the $29 under the current deals. But of course, until a signed contract was in their hands, all three deals could fail, as had happened with Viacom, so in conversation Salomon and Zeckendorf lowered their voices whenever they mentioned Cravath, as if the fates might overhear and punish them again for presuming on a contract that wasn't yet signed.

While the Zeckendorf Company were preoccupied with the leasing, and SOM dealt with the comings and goings of its project managers, HRH were getting on with the building. Or, rather, they were trying to, in the face of some provocation from the brick manufacturers. With the steel more than halfway up, it was time to start constructing the stone and pre-cast walls around the base of the building, and the curtain wall from the sixth floor up. To build the curtain wall, they needed the bricks on site. In fact, Dominic Fonti wanted bricks on site before the bricklayers were quite ready to lay them, just to be sure that things would get off to a quick, smooth start.

There was probably a further factor in Fonti's mind. If he could see the bricks in their piles on the site, he would know that they had actually been manufactured. If he delayed ordering them until the day before the bricklayers were ready to start work, there was the tiniest possibility that, due to some unforeseen hiccup at the Pennsylvania plant, the bricks might not be ready, and Fonti's whole schedule would grind to a halt. Steve George of Glen-Gery had reassured HRH that there was no problem: all the bricks they needed would be delivered when they were ready for them. But one or two uncharitable people in HRH were not 100 percent convinced—Arnie Kriegel, for one:

Contractors lie all the time. They don't really mean to lie, they just don't want to tell the truth in the sense they don't want to say to all their clients, "I'm not working on your project." Every client calls the contractor up and says, "Are you making my brick?" or "Are you making my windows?" and the contractor says, "Absolutely." Now, the fact is, he's not. He can't possibly be making everybody's bricks or windows. So he lies a little bit and he tries to get the ones out that he has to get out. He takes a look at his manufacturing schedule, and when he thinks that the people out there really need it, he makes them. One of the things that we have to continually do is to send people out there to make sure that, when he says he's making brick for us, he's making brick for us and not for somebody else.

But spying can be a two-way process. Just as the builder can visit the plant to check that his bricks are being manufactured, the brick contractor can visit the site and see whether the builder really needs the bricks or is just panicking. Steve George was confident that he could judge when HRH needed the bricks and was unmoved by the increasingly urgent inquiries from the Worldwide Plaza people:

Arnold Kriegel's first statement to us about when they wanted the brick was September 1. When Dominic Fonti got involved, it changed a little bit, to October 1. At that point there was very little construction going on on the site. We've been in business for a long time. We know about how fast projects go up. We knew for a fact they could not possibly require brick physically on that site so that the mason could start laying it prior to November. It was an impossibility. Regardless of how many people they put on there, how fast the steel went up, or anything else, they could not use the brick faster than that. There was a time in Dominic Fonti's office where he kept saying, "I need brick the beginning of October and I said, "Dominic, right behind you your bar graph says you need it mid-November; why are you telling me October?" He said, "Well, that's wrong, ignore it." "OK, fine," I said. "Well," he said, "probably mid-November's OK." We're mid-November now and they still don't need it. Our earliest estimate now is around mid-December. We're looking at starting to manufacture in the beginning of December for availability around that time, and in all sincerity I don't think they're going to need brick in mid-December. It's probably going to go a week or so beyond that point.

It's a game that construction managers play, and I have to admit they play very well. They try to apply pressure on both the masons and the material suppliers. Any material supplier or mason that has been in the business for any period of time knows that they're playing a game.

There was another player in the game: the masons, a company hired and paid by Zeckendorf, which, in turn, hired and paid Glen-Gery. It was therefore a subject of some concern to George in the autumn of 1987 when the masons appeared to be about to go bankrupt. He was not very enthusiastic about setting the wheels in motion for the manufacture of 1.2 million rose-colored bricks until the company knew someone would pay for them. But in a neat side-stepping maneuver the masons set up another company, La Sala, to carry out the Worldwide Plaza contract.*

Fonti was, of course, entirely unsympathetic to Glen-Gery's concerns. In mid-November, when, in spite of his insistence, there was not a brick on site, Fonti was discussing the situation with Artie Nusbaum on one of Nusbaum's visits to the site. Nusbaum reacted with ill-suppressed annoyance: "I don't consider it against my religion that we have the brick a week or two early and that we put up the hoist and start lifting the brick to the floor. It's very hard to get a contractor to take you seriously when there isn't a pile of material sitting there in front of them. What will you do if you have a hundred bricklayers on the job and Glen-Gery screws up—say 'I'm sorry'? So we say, 'Put it here' or, as they say in my language, *'Tuchis afn tish'*."†

Fonti chipped in: "Mr. Steve George should not really care what the status of the building is. That's not his job. His job is not to determine whether or not we need the brick and when we need the brick. It's strictly up to us to tell him when we need the brick. OK? I said to him, 'I want the brick, I will pay for the brick, and I will receive the brick, just bring it to the job.' "

---

* Their threatened bankruptcy was, in any case, part of their tactics in an argument with the U.S. government over allegedly unpaid taxes.

† Literally, "Buttocks on the table."

Nusbaum had strong views on what should be done if George continued to make up his own mind about when HRH needed the brick:

> Expletive, expletive, expletive. He has been put already on notice that further delays to this project caused by the brick will carry a tremendous financial burden and we intend to make it stick— that's about the only power that we really have. And in addition to that, Mr. Schuster is now in the midst of awarding a multi-million-dollar contract on masonry on another project that he's involved with, and Jack is making some phone calls. . . .

His threat of reprisals hung, unfinished, in the air.

In the event, it was early February before the actual physical business of bricklaying began, giving George the quiet satisfaction of believing that he was right not to commit his manufacturing plant to making the bricks months before they were needed. And the work got off to a very slow start. It was clear from Narbutas's complicated curtain-wall design that this would not be a simple job. For a start, three different trades would have to work on the curtain wall in order to complete each section. There were the masons to lay the cement blocks and the brick wall outside them; the waterproofers to put in the flashing and the caulking; and the ironworkers because of the way the brick wall was fixed to the steel frame. And this particular design feature led to a major problem that no one had really anticipated.

Each section of curtain wall was supported by a shelf called a "lintel." This shelf was attached to the steel columns, so that the weight of the masonry was carried across to the columns and down the columns to the ground. It had one extra, crucial feature. The lintel had to be adjustable in two planes: vertically, so that, as the brick courses came up from the level below, the lintel above could be raised or lowered to rest just above the bricks, without leaving a gap that was too large or too tight; and horizontally, so that, as the building rose, the walls didn't start bellying out or leaning in.

The lintels had been the responsibility of Mosher Steel. They had been required to attach them to the steelwork when it was fabricated. In 1986 it had become clear that Mosher were having problems with the lintels. As part of their contract, Mosher had offered to design a better way of supporting and adjusting the lintels than that suggested on SOM's original drawings. In SOM's design, the lintels were supported at four-foot intervals as well as at the ends. Mosher had the idea that, instead of having to make adjustments at four places along the lintel—both ends and two supports in between—they could design a means of supporting and adjusting the lintels from each end, where they were attached to the columns. After some months it became clear that Mosher's new way of doing things was fine, except that it contravened the New York Department of Buildings regulations, which the Texas-based Mosher were unfamiliar with. The New York code insisted that the lintels be supported at four-foot intervals, not just at each end.

So, after months of delay, Mosher had to resort to the more complex but legal way of supporting and adjusting the lintels. But

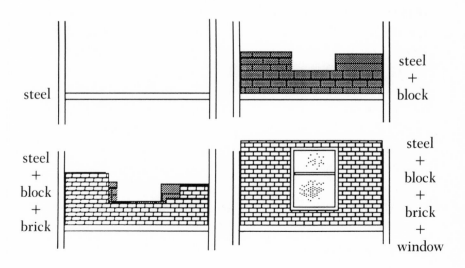

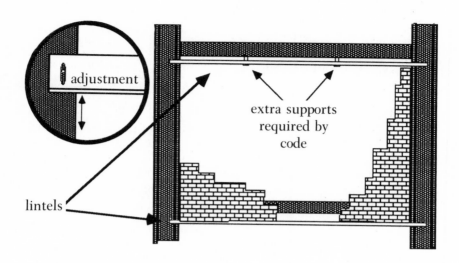

adjustment

extra supports
required by
code

lintels

this method posed a further problem, which became apparent only once bricklaying had started. The ironworkers are responsible for adjusting the lintels ahead of the other two trades involved, so that, as the bricklayers arrive and build the wall up to the correct height, they find a correctly adjusted lintel for the top course of brick to nestle against. The masons, waterproofers, and ironworkers usually work off the same scaffolding. On a well-organized and not-too-complex construction the three trades can carry out their tasks at the same pace, working their way in a spiral up the building. But it soon became clear that the work of adjusting the lintels on World-wide Plaza was far more time-consuming than had been expected. The main reason was the need to adjust at several points along the lintel, but the task wasn't made any easier by a mysterious union ruling that only one type of leveling device, a spirit level, was to be used rather than a plumb line, a more accurate tool for the job.

Since the ironworkers went first along the scaffold, if they adjusted the lintels at their pace the masons and the waterproofers would have to work more slowly than they needed. If the masons worked at their usual speed they would soon catch up with the ironworkers and everyone would be jostling for space on the same scaffold. Schuster considered the situation carefully:

We found that two things can't occupy the same place at the same time, that it was a horrendous scheduling situation. We tried to keep the steelman on the mason's scaffold but it was next to impossible. And the only way we could keep the schedule going was to have the steelman a couple of floors above the mason, pre-setting the lintels, measuring the correct dimension, and setting them in place, welding them in place, and going on so that when the mason got up to that floor he had no one on his scaffold other than the waterproofer, which was a slow enough chore as it is. The steelman felt that this type of operation was deserving of a rather substantial extra payment.

Pressed to reveal the amount, Schuster would say only, "It's in mid–six figures."

There was a certain amount of friction over this situation, among SOM, Mosher, HRH, and the Zeckendorf Company. No one accepted responsibility for the extra cost, and so the steel contractor set to work adjusting lintels on an oral promise of payment from HRH. With ten floors completed and no sign of payment, he began to get nervous. At the beginning of May 1988, since there was still no sign of a check, the contractor told his men to stop work and said that they could go back to the old method, from the scaffolding, and if that slowed things down, so be it. Within a few days he had his money, the lintel adjustment started up again, and the bricklayers worked their way up the building, delighted to come up against well-adjusted lintels on every floor.

There were about forty men in the team of bricklayers that built Worldwide Plaza. Their first task on each floor was to put up the block walls, lifting the heavy six-inch cement blocks into position and mortaring them into place. "We call these 'birth-control blocks,'" said a cheery, plump mason working on the sixth floor. "After lifting these all day you don't go home and make babies, you go home and go to sleep."

At any one time the masons were working all around the building on the same level, from a moving scaffold which was winched up by hand a few inches at a time, to keep each new course of bricks at hand height. They would start work on the northeast corner at the beginning of the day, so that the rising sun would "set up," or dry out, the wall faster. Then they would follow the sun around toward the south and west and finish toward the end of the day on the north side. The more skilled and experienced bricklayers—"corner men"—laid the bricks at each end of a row, with an accuracy of a quarter of an inch or so. The other masons then filled in the intervening bricks along a string stretched between the corner bricks.

At intervals, the masons would insert wire links across the gap between the block and the brick to hold the outer brick wall in place. In the gap itself was a layer of foam insulation, together with the waterproofing that had been tested so fruitlessly at the first curtain-wall test but had passed the second.

Of all the craftsmen on Worldwide Plaza, the masons had most to do with the appearance of the skyscraper. They took a keen interest in the color and the appearance of the brick-work on the building. On the basis of a sample of one, consulted while he was laying the top course of brick on the east corner of the building, this building was something the bricklayers were proud to be associated with. "I think it's magnificent, beautiful," he said. "The guy [the architect] certainly has a head on his shoulders."

The first brick had been laid early in February 1988, but it actually took six weeks to lay just that one floor, the sixth, because of the unanticipated complexities. George's cockiness over the late starting date was not entirely vindicated as the brickwork got seriously under way. In spite of his confidence about Glen-Gery's ability to supply the bricks as and when required, some of the special shapes that would create the sculpted details in the wall were not ready in time. But George brushed aside the possibility that this might have caused a few problems.

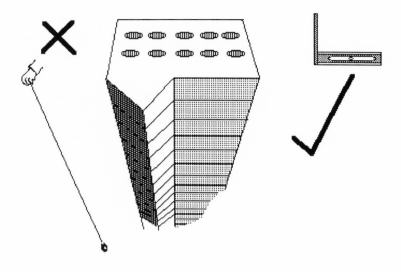

Once the shapes did reach the site, they put unusual demands on the alignment abilities of the masons. A normal type of brick pattern affords some latitude in the position of each brick along the horizontal row. Since the eye looks more at the broad texture of an area of brick laid in a conventional way, it doesn't really matter if a brick is not *exactly* above its counterpart two rows down.

With some of the hand-shaped bricks, however, especially the points that formed the ridges running down the building, each brick had to be exactly above the corresponding brick below. The smallest deviation might snowball and produce a wobbly vertical ridge when the whole wall was complete. There were two ways to ensure that the ridge would be vertical: to use a plumb line, a small weight on a string that could be hung from the point of a brick being laid and lined up with the points of the bricks in the lower courses; or to use a spirit level, which could ensure that each brick lined up with the one below it, to a certain degree of accuracy, but could not give an indication of the alignment of all the bricks in a vertical line. But again, as with the lintels, the union did not allow the bricklayers to use a plumb line. Instead, they had to make do with a spirit level. Only when a sizable area of wall had been built would it be possible to tell whether the alignment was sufficiently accurate, and if it wasn't it would be too difficult to do anything about it.

As the biggest brick job in New York for some time, Worldwide Plaza attracted the attention of brick aficionados, including parties of architects in town for a big architectural convention. The decorative brickwork attracted the most attention. By the time whole areas up to the sixteenth floor were visible, David Childs's intentions could be seen clearly. Even though the walls were not cleaned— blobs of water and caulking were scattered over them—it was now possible to get a sense of the three colors, and of the effect of the vertical ridges created by the points of each of the special shapes laid one above the other. Also at this time, the full implications of all the decisions made about color became visible. The sheer square footage of brickwork that rose from the granite and pre-cast pediment displayed that undeniable pink color that Victor Elmaleh wanted. But his words, "I think we'll both be very happy with it," were far from the truth. Privately Childs was very *un*happy, now that he could see the mismatch of color between the base of the building and the brick walls. All he could do was to keep his feelings to himself and hope for a general reaction that was less critical than his own, as the building showed its true colors to Manhattan.

11

BETWEEN A ROCK AND A HARD PLACE

O f all the contracts on Worldwide Plaza, the one that caused most hand-wringing, nail-biting, and loss of temper was that for the stone and marble on the lower floors of the building. Worrying about whether the bricks would be on site on the day the bricklaying was due to start was nothing compared with worrying about whether the stone would arrive in the right *month* for the masons to put it in place. At least HRH knew the bricks were somewhere on the same subcontinent as Worldwide Plaza. They were never sure where the stone was—New Jersey, in mid-Atlantic, in Italy, or even still in Brazil, where much of the granite came from. But, then, the company supplying the stone had a few problems that the brick company didn't have. The president of the company was preoccupied with other matters, legal and medical, just when, in HRH's view, all his attention should have been directed toward seeing that their granite and marble was being cut, shaped, assembled, and delivered.

Although most of the curtain wall was brick, the base of the building, the pediment on which the brick tower stood, was to be clad in different materials. The lowest six stories formed the part of the building that would be seen most closely, and a lot of thought and care went into the design and the materials from the point of view of visual appearance and texture. It was David Childs's only chance to create an interior as well as an exterior, as he designed a self-contained world for the people who passed by the building or who stopped and went into its lower interior. Higher up, where those working in Worldwide Plaza would spend their time every day, the interior environment was designed by the architects appointed by the various tenants. Only at the base of the building would SOM be able to say, "Step in here and see what we have created for you, and react to it."

For they *were* looking for a reaction. No artist wishes to go unnoticed. To Childs and Bodnar their task, and their duty, was to add beauty or excitement or visual pleasure to the lives of visitors to the building. Inside their building they wanted to provide surroundings that would be different from Eighth Avenue or 49th Street, and the way in which they characterized that difference would say something about what they thought people would want or appreciate.

The outside of the base was a rectangular box and on it would stand the square-sided tower. The base was elongated along the main axis of the whole site, with one of the shorter sides along Eighth Avenue and the longer sides parallel with 49th and 50th Streets. One Sunday afternoon in 1985, Childs and Bodnar came up with the concept of an elliptical arcade running around the whole base of the building. They felt this would impart a pleasing curvature to an otherwise rectangular building. Childs compared it to a part of London he was familiar with:

> If you think about Regent Street coming down to Piccadilly Circus and how it is always constantly unfolding, it reflects the natural way that people walk. They don't walk in grids, they walk along cow paths, which curve and meander, and so there is something attractive about a space like this, because it's constantly revealing itself. It doesn't go on forever, like a straight street, but it's always constantly moving as you go through it. So it's a humane place but dramatic. It's like the side aisles in church—uplifting and disappearing into gloom at the top. It's all mysterious and wonderful.

This "circling the square" became a striking feature of the base of the building; it also led to a series of design and construction problems that wouldn't have occurred had the architects stuck to right angles. For Gary Steficek and his engineering colleagues it provided some big headaches, perhaps because, as he saw it, it hadn't really been thought through properly: "That was our biggest structural problem, because the arcade cuts through the tube we had designed and it was presented to us as an established fact. The architects came back from a City Planning meeting where they had suggested doing it, and City Planning thought it was a great idea, so we were stuck with it, even though it totally destroyed our tube at the base."

As Childs and Bodnar developed their ideas in the early drawings, they designed three entrance halls, or lobbies, within the ellipse. One would be for the exclusive use of O&M, and the use of the other two would be decided when the building was leased to other tenants. Doors would lead from the elliptical arcade into the lobbies on the first floor, with escalators up to the elevators departing from mezzanine floors.

In deciding on the overall appearance of these lower floors, the

50th St.

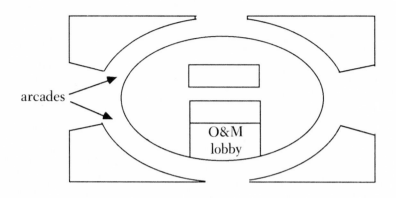

arcades

O&M
lobby

49th St.

architects matched the grandeur of their arcade with some splendid materials. To pick out the arches of the arcade and the doors and shopfronts within it, they chose granite, marble, and pre-cast concrete.

For Ed Narbutas, detailing and monitoring the fabrication of curved pieces of building in several different materials were bound to be trickier than dealing with entirely rectangular, three-dimensional spaces. He explained why each of the particular materials had been chosen: "What you try to do is to get the most bang for your dollar. The materials that are closer to street level, that people can touch and feel and walk right up to, you try to make them a little bit more expensive because you're in much more intimate contact with them."

At first, in fact, when the plan for an ellipse was revealed, the architects had been unsure whether they should use stone at all. To reproduce true curvature would have meant shaping every one of the pieces of granite that lined the arcade, a very expensive task. But they decided on a design that would allow them to use a lot of flat stone by dividing the ellipse into segments. Because the curvature was fairly shallow along the long sides of the ellipse, they thought they could get away with an appearance that would still emphasize the curvature of the arcade.

When Narbutas and his technical team looked at how to deal with the corners of the building, they were faced with a lot of in-and-out moldings, ledges, corners, and arches. This would be extremely expensive in stone, since many of the angles and variations would have to be achieved by assembling and fixing individual stones next to one another. "You'd have a nightmare as far as putting it all together and holding it up, and given today's technology and economics you just couldn't do it," Narbutas explained.

They opted for pre-cast concrete for the complicated parts, a high-quality smooth concrete, poured into shaped molds away from the site and brought in large pieces to be fixed in place. So whole pieces were designed to form the curved tops of bay windows and the corners of the lower floors, complete with molded parapets. An additional advantage of pre-cast concrete was that it could be colored to the shade the architect wanted. One way of doing this would have been to add a pigment to the concrete when it was wet, but Narbutas wasn't sure that this would last. "We were afraid that, if you add a tint, we'd get a variation in color, particularly as it ages. So we insisted on mixing in pink sands and aggregates to get the color we wanted. It's always do-able, you know—they sort of grumble about it but they'll certainly do it. At least we think they will. I suppose we'll find out in ten years."

Some of the complexity of the materials was a direct result of the decision to build in the ellipse as a basic ingredient of the lower floors. But this decision affected more than the cladding: it also forced certain changes in the structural-steel layout.

For Steficek, the elliptical area at the base of the building turned out to be just where he wanted to bring the columns down through to the foundations. With a largely rectangular building, the engineers can design a way to bring the columns all the way down the building from the top, through the ground floor into the

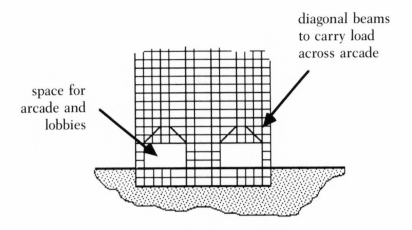

diagonal beams
to carry load
across arcade

space for
arcade and
lobbies

foundations, in a straight line. The only problem is usually to provide enough space between the colums at ground level to allow for
reasonably sizable lobbies. With a skyscraper whose base is considerably wider than the tower above it, the tower's steel skeleton
can continue right through the lower floors, and the lobbies can
be built out around the base, without being interrupted by huge
load-bearing columns. But the elliptical arcade actually snaked its
way through parts of the base of the tower—it was within the
"footprint" of the structural tube. So if the tube's columns were
carried through to the ground they would pierce the lobbies and
spoil Childs's and Bodnar's grand plan. The engineers had to find
a way of combining the loads that were carried on several parallel
columns higher up the building, into fewer columns at ground level.
This was done with diagonal connections between columns, which
went from the fifth to the third floor and "funneled" the load into
fewer, thicker columns at the base of the building.

Even with fewer columns at the base, however, the elegant
elliptical arcade still couldn't quite be made to work. Almost like a
slalom course, it wound its way through the structural columns—
but as originally designed it would have bumped into some of them.

Narbutas's team ended up changing the shape of the arcade from a single ellipse into a shape that combined parts of two ellipses with different curvatures. He described it as "massaging" the ellipse, but it was done in such a way that nobody would ever notice anything irregular about the shape.

One of the problems of coordinating all the components of a building as complex as Worldwide Plaza was the sheer difficulty of deciding, on the basis of two-dimensional drawings, where things would actually be in three-dimensional space. In any one area of the building, the details of many of the components were on many different drawings. SOM used a sophisticated computer-aided design system to simplify the task of understanding the plans for the building in three dimensions.

Day after day, Suzanne Smith sat at her terminal, calling up immensely detailed multi-colored images generated from the information that had been fed into the computer. The information was put into the computer at a scale that could be shown up to life-size on the screen—even down to keyholes—and this allowed architects to take a "fly-through" tour of the whole building before the first spade dug into the asphalt on the site. When Suzanne eventually went on site and explored the evolving interior on the ground floor of Worldwide Plaza, she had an oddly familiar sensation:

> Really, when I go out there and I see it on site it's a strange transition, because I feel I've actually had it in my hands in the computer. There is a lot of complication down on the ground floor which you can model on the computer and see if things fit or not. In some cases, when we were asked, "Is this going to fit?" we could look at the computer drawing and say "Yes" or "No" with very, very great accuracy. If it was just a hand drawing you could never really know whether you can get that piece of stone around that column, whether there's really four inches for the backup structure and the piece of stone or not, and so on.

The original idea for the lobbies was that whoever the eventual tenants were, their lobbies would have linked access so that there could be a mingling of different visitors to the building. A visitor to Ogilvy and Mather might bump into a lawyer or a record producer on the way, and this was seen as a valuable human factor in the architecture. And a valuable leasing factor was the combination of escalators and elevators that led people into the ground floor, up to the next floor, and past shops and restaurants before going farther up the building. Unfortunately, once O&M's views were made clear, both about the idea of linked lobbies and about the split-level journey to the elevators, the lobby concept had to change radically. Because there was still time to take O&M's views into account, and because they were such a prime tenant, the cost of changes they wanted in the lobby and elevator layout would be absorbed by the owners. There were the costs incurred by unnecessary work by subcontractors and the cost of new design work by SOM. There was also a cost in swallowed pride by the architects.

The cavalier dismissal of a major design feature of the building cannot have been easy to accept. But there was no place for preciousness or temperament when leases and tenants were at stake, and Childs, of all architects, was essentially a practical man. He appeared to accept with equanimity the abandonment of a carefully thought-through design feature: "Although this changes significant portions of the building, not only in terms of the design but in terms of the elevatoring and escalatoring and so forth, I wouldn't say there've been radical changes, compared to any other project. It's been an ongoing process of evolution for the design. Not revolution, but evolution."

Steficek, the engineer who had to deal with the implications of this change, preferred "revolutionary":

> The elevators had stopped at the second floor, and the elevation of the floor where they were now coming down to used to be three feet higher. So we had to lower all that steel; which in turn

impacts on bracing workpoints, and the columns that are now in this two-story-high space, where there used to be another second floor, are now thirty feet unbraced. So you have to do something to those columns so that they can sustain the load they were designed for. We ended up plating columns and reinforcing beams. Also, when you took out this mezzanine floor, it changed all the egressing requirements for the architects. Now they have stairs snaking around to avoid this space and coming down somewhere else, where we had no provision for openings. You have to reframe areas there. This, of course, upsets Mosher, the steel fabricator, because he's merrily going on his way, not knowing this is going to change. But you don't have any choices there; they're going to have to pay him to make the changes, and there'll be some delay in some areas.

Whatever grief these changes caused the engineers, the architects, and the subcontractors, Artie Nusbaum, on behalf of HRH, took them in his stride: "The owner is being reimbursed for it, we make a profit on it. I don't mind that kind of change."

Once the plans for the lower floors were sufficiently firm, Arnie Kriegel felt ready to look for a subcontractor. By April 1987 the SOM team had a reasonably exact idea of what they wanted the lower floors to look like—what should be stone and what should be pre-cast, what sizes and shapes of stone they needed, and a choice of color and texture: a salmon-pink granite from Brazil.

They were looking for a company to carry out several different but related tasks. As well as supplying the pieces of stone, cut to shape, the contractors would have to provide a method of fixing the stone to the steel. In planning how to clad the lower floors of the building, with its complex curvature, HRH had considered what was called "hand-setting," each piece of stone being attached on site directly to the steel framework. But this could be very expensive, and they decided on a type of pre-assembly system, away from the site, by which pieces of stone were fixed to giant steel frames, called "trusses," which would then be trucked in to the site. Stan Orr was a senior vice-president of HRH, involved in the complex discussions about how the stone should be fixed to the building:

> It's a very complicated system because of the elliptical shape of the building—if it was just a rectangle a lot of our difficulties would go away. The truss system requires a very long lead time. One, you have to prepare the structural drawings and have them approved by the architect and the building engineer and qualified to meet the codes of the city of New York. Once the truss system is developed, you now need the stone to go on it. While you're doing the truss system, you hope the contractor is slabbing the stone, cutting it, and polishing it.
>
> In order for it to be properly sized and shipped to the States to be applied to the trusses, the critical element is developing the drawings that allow it to be cut to the exact dimension to within an eighth or a sixteenth of an inch in each size. To complicate it a little further, we have a certain amount of pre-cast on the lower part of the building that also has granite embedded in it. So we have to have the information of the exact sizes to allow the pre-cast contractor, who's located in Canada, to make his necessary forms [i.e., molds] ready to receive the granite when it comes in from Italy.

It might well be asked why such a complex element of the building was left to a subcontractor to design rather than the architects. Dominic Fonti explained: "In an earlier world the architect got on with the drawings. In today's world it's left much more to vendors to produce documents which the architect checks. If you went back to the 1920s and 1910s, the architects made very complex drawings of every single part of the building but, in fairness to them, they don't get the fees to cover that. So they've passed on that work to the vendors, to make the more detailed, complicated drawings that they no longer make."

The front runner for the contract was a company called Hunts

Point. Its principal executive was Mr. Aniello "Neil" Migliore, of Italian origin. As would become public during 1987, Migliore was a *capo* of one of the well-known Mafia families, the Lucchese family.

If the general public knows anything about the construction industry, it knows that the Mafia have a role to play. This highly structured social group operate in various ways, from their links with organized labor to ensure tranquillity for the owner, to control of the concrete business enabling them to set their own prices, through to a more general influence on price rigging during the bidding process in some construction projects. The most charitable interpretation of the Mafia's role runs along lines like: It would really be nice if the Mafia weren't involved at all, because then a number of prices would be lower—for labor, for certain materials, and so on. But as long as they are involved and help buildings to get built without threats of violence or Mafia-generated strikes, why shouldn't we just let things be as they are?

From the point of view of an individual in the industry, torn between trying to keep his budget down and his legs unbroken, you can see why it's comparatively easy for construction to continue to be one of the many areas of American life where organized crime has little trouble making a living.

When it came to putting the stone and marble out for bids, Kriegel had several companies to choose from. When the bids were returned, the lowest estimate by far was from Hunts Point. In a contract whose total final cost was just over $6 million, Hunts Point bid nearly $2 million lower than the next bidder. Whether or not HRH were concerned that Migliore had Mafia connections, they had little choice about accepting his bid.

As an Italian-American. Fonti was understandably uneasy about answering questions relating to Mafia activities. Whatever he said, he was in a no-win situation. If he was publicly critical of their role in the construction business, he might attract unwelcome attention to himself; if he denied any such involvement, he might seem either naïve or deceptive. He did, however, point out that mere evidence of a lower bid in a construction auction did not justify jumping to hasty conclusions as to the reason:

> When someone bids work, they don't only do a takeoff on the quantities and takeoff on the materials. They look also at their workload and at the possibility of "How many extras am I able to get on this project?" If the design is very incomplete, then they tend to do one of two things, either price very high or price very low, and say, "This is what I did," knowing that the architect has to modify it. So you do get a great disparity in numbers, which is not necessarily indicative of any kind of setup. That happens across any trade, across any business.
>
> For example, I had some small work done in my house about a month ago and I told my wife. "Look, call up a few subcontractors and ask for a price." I had a man who quoted me $3,000. I told my wife, "That's crazy; call somebody else." A guy came in and says $2,000. Then someone comes in and says $400. And I asked my wife, "Are you sure it's $400 and not $4,000?" "No, $400." I say, "Fine, do it for $400." Now, if this was in a construction job, someone would say this is rigged, but again it depends on all sorts of factors, like who was more hungry, and who really wants to do the job.

In the case of the Worldwide stone, it soon became clear that, even at $2 million cheaper than the next bid, $6 million was much more than HRH's original estimates. The likely overspend first became apparent to an astonished Jack Schuster at a project meeting on June 1, 1987. Kriegel was reporting on the various bids that were now coming in. With luck and good judgment. HRH's estimates and the subcontractors' would prove not to be too far apart— in the case of the stone, there appeared to be an uncomfortable disparity.

"We budgeted at $60 a square foot to do this work," Kriegel reminded the assembled team, and now it's coming in at $150." Meaningful looks were exchanged around the table, and Schuster put on a pained expression that was only partly simulated. "That doesn't mean I'm going to buy the 150," Kriegel added hastily, "but there is clearly a problem." There were various ways of solving the problem. If nothing could be done to persuade the subcontractor to lower his prices—and nobody at the meeting suggested this— attention had to be turned to various aspects of the design speci- fications, from the nature of the materials to the amounts that were needed and the possibility of "alternates," cheaper materials that would do a similar job. Kriegel then put before the architects some suggestions for substituting pre-cast concrete at certain points for the granite that had originally been specified. He also suggested that the stone in the arcade shouldn't go up the walls quite as high as the designers had specified.

While this discussion was continuing, Schuster was still taking in the implications of the cost estimates. Such a disparity could, of course, mean that the subcontractor was overcharging *or* that HRH's estimating department had estimated wrongly in the first place. One clue emerged when Kriegel said tentatively to the ar- chitects, "Did you ever have limestone inside the lobby?" Limestone is a much cheaper stone than the marble the architects had spec- ified. Bodnar looked at Rob Schubert, who looked at Narbutas, and they generally agreed that they had never specified limestone as a possible material for the lobby interiors. "Well, my estimate says limestone," said Kriegel. Here was clearly a place where the early estimates might be wrong, if they had been based on the use of a cheaper stone.

"Tell me," said Schuster, "how do you go from $60 stone to $150 stone in six months?"

"I don't know," said Kriegel.

"Percentage-wise, how much have you figured that you are over on all of your stone?"

"Right now, going in, I'm 100 percent over."

"Good luck to your estimating department . . ."

"I know. . . ."

"I mean, I can take that a couple of times, but I mean, if I got to listen to the same song and dance at every turn . . ."

"I know. It's where we are, and we have to work on it."

In the end, in the deal that was done, and with all the talk of alternates and lowering levels, the stone still ended up costing substantially more than HRH's estimates, with Schuster and the Zeckendorf Company gritting their teeth and putting up with it.

And that was only the first of their problems. There are several ways of losing money on a job, only one of which is paying more than you expected to a particular contractor. With such a complex project, every subcontractor's work had an impact on the other trades. The complicated multi-level schedule on the wall of Fonti's office showed a horizontal bar for each trade, with completion dates indicated. But each trade wasn't a self-contained bar, moving in stately fashion at its own pace across the months and years. Men and machines came and went on the site in response to daily calls from foremen and superintendents who depended on other trades' completing their part of the job first. The curtain-wall people— brick and stone—couldn't start till the steel had reached a certain stage, and once they moved in there would be further trades who depended on finding completed curtain walls before they could start.

There was also one other important factor, a result of the fact that there was already a tenant for part of the building. The Zeck- endorf Company was obliged to give O&M twelve months' notice of when they could occupy the building, so that they could in turn give notice to their existing landlords. In addition, they had to give six months' notice of the date that O&M could start their own interior construction work. For them to be able to do that work, the floors had to be enclosed enough for the trades to work in. Not necessarily fully air-conditioned and heated, but at least no longer open to the elements.

As part of their contract, if they weren't given enough notice to prepare their offices for their moving-in date, O&M could withhold rent until the date they were able to move in. Fonti and HRH were aiming for April 1988, as the date when O&M could start their own construction work on the floors they would eventually occupy, three to eighteen. Any postponement of that date would result in a loss to the owners of the building of about $300,000 a week. So the pressure was on all through late 1987 and early 1988 to get the interior enclosed by April 15, come what may.

A key part of O&M's space was the ground floor and the two floors above it, where they had a lot of finishing work to do in their own lobby area. After Hunts Point were given the stone contract, HRH took a keen interest in how they were getting along during the early weeks of their work. In particular, the success of the Hunts Point contract depended on a smooth, steady progress through the various stages of designing, manufacturing, and assembling the trusses that would hold the pieces of granite. Only when the exact design of the trusses was finalized could the stone be cut to the correct size in Italy. And even then there would be an inevitable delay while the pieces were packed in Italy, shipped to New Jersey, and fixed to the trusses before being driven into Manhattan.

Whatever reservations anyone had about Hunts Point, they were the lowest bidder and they *were* known to do a reasonable job with stonework. So once they were appointed, HRH and SOM sat back and awaited the first shop drawings that would show in detail how Hunts Point proposed to design the trusses for the stone. Four weeks after the contract was confirmed, the first drawings arrived at SOM. Narbutas was one of the first to see them. "The drawings were useless. Very amateurish. All we got was a sketch, just a geometric sketch of the truss."

This was very bad news so early in the relationship. There was a huge area of complex curved and articulated wall to be covered, in a way that was unique to the building. Hunts Point were first and foremost stone contractors, and they had hired an engineering firm to design and make the trusses. Although it was clearly their responsibility to supervise that firm, the longer they let poor design continue, the more the job would fall behind. In fact, it took nearly three months, punctuated by a series of late, poor-quality drawings, for HRH's and SOM's dissatisfaction to come to a head.

On November 16, 1987, the regular project meeting took place in HRH's temporary site office above the restaurant. It was one of the few such meetings attended by Jim Parker, who sat silent for most of the time, making notes about the unfolding story of the building he was meant to be managing. About half an hour into the meeting, Schuster, in the chair, reached the stone item. In a brief, clipped sentence, Fonti announced the end result of a great deal of angst that had been generated between HRH and Hunts Point over the preceding weeks—HRH had asked that the engineer who had been designing the trusses be fired. Fonti then reported that three thousand squre feet of granite was already cut and polished in Italy, simply waiting for confirmation of the truss design before being finished off and shipped. At a meeting the following day, Migliore would be asked to reassure HRH that a new engineer would be able to work at high speed to produce the accurate, detailed drawings of the trusses. No one was looking forward to the meeting.

It was a period in the building's life when everybody was beginning to show signs of edginess. So much was now at stake. Halfway through the construction period, there was, by definition, only half the time left to complete the building and to make up for lost time. There had already been concerns about the brick, and now it was clear that there were serious problems with the stone. What more would creep out of the woodwork to delay things further?

On the pavement of 50th Street, Artie Nusbaum stood with Fonti and one of the contractors. In a fine display of Nusbaumian rhetoric, Artie berated the contractor for delays in welding metal edging to the floors: "They're taking four and a half days to do a floor. It takes only two and a half days a floor up above. Obviously there's a disparagement [sic] between the two. I know how to solve that—I have a two-and-a-half-day crew here and a two-and-a-half-day crew here and another two-and-a-half-day crew here. What do you know? Next thing, you've got a whole floor." The problem seemed to be due to a shortage of generating power. "Buy two more generators!" Nusbaum shouted. "Where is it written that I'm tied to two generators?" To the contractor's murmurs of complaint about the extra expense, Nusbaum gave short shrift: "You know what— you're a hooker. You got paid; do what you got paid to do. You got paid to spread your legs; spread your legs." Fonti looked as if he wished he were somewhere else, on the moon perhaps. Nusbaum turned to him and put his arm around Fonti's shoulder. "Dominic, who are we doing all this for?" he said, indicating the building. "Who is our friend?" Like a good pupil Fonti said, "Mr. Zeckendorf." "And are we serving Mr. Zeckendorf well by letting the concrete be delayed?" "No," said Fonti.

Fonti was in a gloomy mood as he left the site office at about five-thirty that evening. Right outside the door was a reminder that even the project manager can't know everything. Parked in the street was a massive generator, still roaring an hour and a half after the last man was supposed to have left the site. "I'm supposed to know everything that's going on on the site," says Fonti, "and I haven't the slightest idea of why that thing's still running. All I do know is that it's costing $5,000 an hour."

The meeting with Migliore was scheduled for 4:00 P.M. the next day. Stan Orr would be taking part, as well as Fonti and Kriegel. Each of the participants had his own expectations about what would happen at that meeting. None of them was optimistic. Kriegel displayed a keen sense of realism:

Right now they're going to be claiming *mea culpa*: "Look, I had this designer that was supposed to be a terrific designer. He failed me and we'll do whatever overtime that we need to bring the schedule back." You know, that's what we're hoping he's going to say, and we kind of know he's going to say something like that. We still don't know exactly what the dates are going to be—when he thinks the stone will be here, when will the trusses be ready for shipment from Ross's yard in New Jersey to the site, when will erection start—we need all these dates, because he has to do something to bring this project back on track.

The trouble is, we don't really have a set plan for this meeting. No matter what he's going to say, it's going to be too long. No matter what. Absolutely too long. He's going to say two weeks, we're going to say one week. And if he says three days, we're going to want it tomorrow, right? But we have to be realistic; certain things can't be done. But that's going to be our game, to push him, to have him promise the most to bring this project back on schedule. That's the purpose of the meeting.

Orr had sat through a number of frustrating meetings with Hunts Point and he hoped that this one would be different: "It seemed the result of every meeting was. 'I will square it away, you're right, we'll correct it tomorrow, it's going to get better,' and everything was, 'Tomorrow, tomorrow,' and nothing for today. I felt it was necessary to have a showdown. We are at the end of the lead time. If we go any further without getting positive results, we're going to fail to meet the deadline that we have committed to the owner that they would be able to move a tenant in. It was our duty at that point as the construction manager to call this meeting."

There was an odd sense of tension about the HRH people whenever the meeting was discussed, some of which might have been attributable to Migliore's Mafia role. No one doubted that they were doing the right thing. Migliore had to be confronted with the increasingly appalling situation—if he didn't quickly get new engineers on the job to do the drawings, and get the stone cut to size, the lower floors would not be covered in time for the tenants to start their work. And if they didn't start their work on time, they wouldn't be finished on time and couldn't move in on time.

At four o'clock Migliore, wearing sunglasses, arrived at the

HRH offices with a female colleague and went into Nusbaum's office to meet the team. At that moment Nusbaum was hurrying back from another meeting to join the fray if he could. Orr said afterward that the meeting had not been as lively as he might have expected, although anyone passing within three feet of the office door would have heard raised voices and even the hint of an expletive. Lively or not, many of Orr's fears were confirmed, as he confided right after the meeting: "Our suspicions were well founded. We were in trouble. To be honest with you, we really don't know today, as a result of this meeting, whether we are out of trouble or not. We should know in, I would say, a week to ten days."

Orr and his colleagues had tried to convey to Migliore the depth of their concern:

> I started the meeting by saying, "I don't want you to think I'm being self-serving, that I'm trying to look like a hero saying, 'Look how fast we can build.' " I took the schedule which is on the wall, I showed him the milestones. I actually went so far as to say, "You know, either produce or tell us you're not going to and we'll go and get somebody else." As bad as it is, I would rather do that than to continue on with a loser. But that was why we didn't want to just take Mr. Migliore's word. We've done that many times before, and it seemed that things would fall through the crack. It might not have been his fault.
>
> I said, in case there was a misunderstanding on his part of the urgency, I would walk him through the twelve-month notification to the tenant and the owner, and the six-month. I showed him that we planned to have the brick in place to let the tenant do his work, but he was the cause that was affecting the lower part of the building. And he says he recognized that. And he said, "I have good news for you," and that's when he shared with me that he had gotten rid of his engineer and we went on from there.

Migliore was clearly eager to convey the message that all would now be well, according to Orr. He had already appointed a new company for the job, whose engineers were even now at the end of a phone, ready to confirm their eagerness and competence for the job:

> So we called his firm out in Long Island. I happened to know the firm and I've worked with them on occasion before and they are quite a good engineering firm. I was pleased that they selected these people. In our conversations with them, it became evident that they had about five or six engineers working on the drawings, and they would be prepared to meet with us and the architect and the engineer to satisfy us that they're doing the right thing.
>
> This of course was all a positive step. We've never had this sort of response before, and that's why I say to you it will take about a week to ten days. We also made a phone call to Italy, to Mr. Migliore's collaborator, to validate that there is a substantial amount of stone that has been slabbed and polished and is waiting for the engineering so it can be cut to the precise dimension.

It was a touching display of faith on the part of HRH to believe in the reality of their stone, slabbed and polished in an Italian stoneyard, on the basis of one long-distance phone conversation. But what else could they do? There were dangers in confrontation, as Orr was well aware: "Sometimes you have to make a business decision: do you go with the horse you're on now or do you go for another ride? To get rid of this gentleman now leads one obviously to some sort of a lawsuit for the services done, and he would inflate the cost of these things for his own benefit, which anybody else would do in that position too. Then I'd have to go out and look for another contractor. Many contractors in New York are very close-knit, very tight. I might find that, even though there're two or three others that might be able to do the job, they would say, 'Thank you, I'm too busy,' because they owe an allegiance to this guy. So then where am I? I might have to go back to this guy, and then it's a different ball game. Then I'm completely subservient."

As the meeting broke up, the group shook hands, willing themselves to believe that their problems were over. Fonti and Orr had a series of meetings planned over the next few weeks which were expected to demonstrate that the stone contractor was well and truly in control, beginning with a meeting on the following Wednesday at the engineer's to discuss the details of the trusses that would determine the exact sizes to have the stone manufactured. By the end of November the measurements would be in Italy so that they could start finishing the stone. Hunts Point had offered to air-freight an initial delivery of granite to the pre-cast concrete plant in Canada to allow them to start making their molds.

Plans had also been made to anticipate the actual installation of all this stone. Migliore had agreed to start installing the clips for the stone trusses on the columns on December 15, and arrangements were made for HRH to meet the foreman in charge of the team that would fabricate the trusses and put them in place on the building.

The whole episode—the early incompetence, the catalogue of complaints, the firing of the engineer, the summit meeting—was an object lesson in practical construction management. A knowledge of textbook management procedures, architectural design skills, engineering measurement, and logistical flowcharts was as useful as an Italian cookbook when faced with the realities of building a skyscraper in New York in 1987. What was needed were nerves of iron, an ability to hope for one thing and expect the opposite, a degree of street-level profanity, and an unflagging sense of when to tolerate the intolerable. But none of the Worldwide Plaza team accepted such situations with equanimity, least of all Schuster, custodian of the millions of dollars of money that can be unnecessarily dissipated when a project goes wrong: "You don't learn to live with it, but there's not a damn thing you can do to stop it. It's there. In my judgment it's almost cancerous. And there's not a damn thing you can do about it."

Through most of the period of the Worldwide Plaza stone contract, Neil Migliore was a co-defendant in a trial at the Federal District Court in Manhattan. He was one of twelve people accused of rigging bids on construction projects, intervening in union elections, and plotting murders. The trial had begun in April 1987, and during December 1987 and January 1988 Migliore had had the additional problem of a bad back, which meant that he was unable to do much work or attend his trial. He watched the daily proceedings on a television monitor installed in his hospital room.

On May 5, 1988, as the stone columns and slabs were finally going up on Worldwide Plaza, the *New York Times* carried a story on its front page that made interesting reading for the Worldwide Plaza team: "SALERNO AND 8 FOUND GUILTY AS RACKETEERS." After nine days of deliberations, a jury had found Anthony (Fat Tony) Salerno guilty of a range of crimes, including a multi-million-dollar scheme to rig bids in the construction industry. The story said: "Besides Mr. Salerno, who is already serving a 100-year sentence for his 1986 convictions as a member of the Mafia's ruling 'commission,' the defendants were six men identified by the authorities as mobsters and four businessmen accused of working with them. Among those convicted were Mathew (Matty the Horse) Ianniello, and two brothers, Vincent and Louis DiNapoli, of the Genovese family, and Aniello Migliore of the Lucchese crime family in New York.

12

ALL TRUSSED UP

I mean, I've been up for some thirty-odd hours now and I'm getting kind of punch-drunk, but, I mean, it's scary. Here we are playing with millions of dollars that we don't have. It's coming out of the bottom line of the project and here we are sitting here on a rainy night in Venice, and literally just pouring it down the drain.
—TERRY SODERBERG, Café Florian, Venice, January 25, 1988

In December 1987 it was clear that the Hunts Point contract was still a problem. Some of the commitments the company had given at the November meeting had still not been met. No one entirely believed the messages from Italy about the state of the marble and the stone. It was clear that a trip to Italy would have to be organized—to put pressure on Hunts Point and to reassure the Worldwide Plaza team. Once the trip was mooted, there were weeks of indecision about who would go and when. David Childs would have liked to go but was too busy, having recently been appointed to design the controversial Columbus Circle scheme, a major mid-

Manhattan project that had just lost one architect because his design did not meet with community approval. It was decided that Jim Bodnar would go in his place. This was sensible, since everybody agreed that they worked very closely together. Dominic Fonti would go on behalf of HRH, since the method of fabricating and assembling the stone would determine how smoothly things could go on site. He would be an asset on the trip for another reason: he spoke Italian, which would make it easier to get at the real situation in the event of any disagreement or incipient hoodwinking by the contractors. Ed Narbutas would go as the technical partner of the SOM team, concerned to see that decisions to do with assembly and design didn't squeeze out the million-and-one architectural details to do with the way in which each of the many design elements impinged upon the other design elements and upon the other aspects of the building.

Till now, to get a sense of what the lobbies would look like it had been necessary to go by the drawings or models and imagine the marble or granite in shades indicated by samples in SOM's stone "library." These samples were used by the architects to make up their minds about the colors and types to use. They would then specify on the drawings the name of the stone they wanted. For example, Bodnar had chosen a white streaked marble. He had then given instructions for this marble to be named on the drawings so that, when they were put out for bids, subcontractors knew what they had to supply. Of course, every piece of marble is unique— being made by God, as marble suppliers never tire of reminding architects, particularly when the latter complain about not getting what they asked for. This well-known unreliability, even deviousness, of marble suppliers was one reason that architects and construction managers needed to make a visit to the suppliers. But in late 1987 there were other reasons to plan such a trip. Even Jack Schuster, who had to sign the bill for a number of first-class round-trip tickets to Venice, agreed such trips were necessary:

Obviously, if the stone came from the United States you would visit there, no matter where it was, once a week, and you would really know what's going on, really have more control. I recall stories where stone was coming from Italy and all of a sudden we got a wire from the suppliers saying the boat broke down and turned back to Genoa. You know, that kind of thing. If you want to believe it, you believe it. If you don't want to believe it, you don't believe it. But you don't have the control of the transportation.

The product is a good product. The Italians have fine quarrying and fine fabricating facilities. But a lot has to happen from the time it comes out of the mountain until the time it arrives here and is installed. And at each stage, if a clinker shows up, you know, you lost a week. You may say, well, what's a week? A week is a great deal on a project of this nature. You can erect a lot of stone in a week—if it's here to erect.

The Italian end of the trip would be handled by Augusto Michelato, an Italian stone contractor who seemed to be acting as a consultant to Hunts Point, HRH, and SOM, as well as running one of the stone fabrication plants. He had made several trips to New York and was arranging visits to the marble yard, the fabrication plant, and the place where the granite and pre-cast columns would be assembled.

The Venice airport on Monday, January 25, 1988, was not a particularly pleasant place to be. After a weekend with hazy cloud but enough sun to see the city at its wintry best, the rains began to fall, and by the time the flight carrying the Worldwide Plaza party touched down, the tarmac was awash with driving rain. The flight had been without incident apart from a superfluity of breakfasts, which seemed to arrive every couple of hours. The group from SOM and HRH had arrived without Jim Bodnar, delayed by a family health problem. They were accompanied by Terry Soderberg, keeping an eye on things for the owner, and by Rick Mi-

gliore, representative of Hunts Point and owner of one of the factories the group was to visit. Migliore was on the trip because his father, Aniello Migliore, was in the hospital with a combination of
symptoms that included partial paralysis of the legs and a blood clot
that was threatening to find its way to the brain or the heart. Migliore's health problems came on top of the racketeering trial. As one
of the team said, "Neil Migliore could have run the whole thing from
jail, but the combination of jail and sickness was too much."

The group came through customs and were met by a driver
from the Verona factory, who was to take Migliore straight to Verona
to check on the state of readiness for the group's visit the following
day. Meanwhile, the rest headed damply for a water taxi to take
them to the hotel in Venice to rest and sightsee a little. The prospects for sightseeing did not look good. There was little to choose
between the water of the Venice lagoon and the air above it. Both
were at saturation point. As the boat sped toward the city, the group
pondered each other's feet and wondered whether smart leather
shoes were going to be the best form of footwear for a city whose
streets were known to be full of water on the best of days.

The Café Florian is on the south side of the Piazza San Marco
in Venice. In the spring and summer months, when the tables and
chairs are laid out in the Piazza, the string orchestra plays popular
classics while tourists pay enormous amounts of money for a cup
of frothy coffee. On January 25, 1988, it was a very different place.
The rain had poured all day, and by mid-afternoon it was already
getting dark. The only tables and chairs were inside the café, and
the pavement outside was coated with puddles and sodden pigeons.
In a corner near the window, Soderberg, Fonti, and Narbutas sat
around a marble-topped table damply contemplating the prospects
for the next few days of their visit to Italy. As the three of them
relaxed in the warm atmosphere of the half-empty café, they un-
wound a little from the tension of the previous few weeks. In the
stress and pressure of a work week in Manhattan, the relationships
among these three important members of the team were largely

professional, and confined to the immediate matters in hand—
across the table at meetings or down the phone from Eighth Avenue
to Madison Avenue. Now their conversation was discursive and
jokey. They had, as Soderberg pointed out, been up for thirty hours.
But the stimulus of a new country and the world's most beautiful
city was keeping them awake, with the help of a glass or two of
Italian aperitif.

As Narbutas and Fonti mused on what awaited them the following day, Soderberg picked up the fact that the granite came
from Brazil. "From Brazil?" he said, with some surprise.

"Yeah, it's a Brazilian stone," said Fonti. "It is quarried in
Brazil. . . ."

"Now, wait a minute . . . wait, wait, wait. Now we're in *Venice*,
going to look at stone from Brazil?"

Fonti explained the reason, patiently: "Yes, the salmon-pink
granite is a Brazilian stone; all the other stones are Italian stones.
The technology for cutting and dressing stone is better in this
country than it is in the United States, so that's why they're here.
It's cheaper and more efficient; that's why it's sent from all over
the world."

"We could have gone to Brazil," complained Soderberg. "The
carnival's on down in Rio."

"Well," said Fonti, "I'm sure the weather is better. If the owner
insists . . ."

They also shared a concern about the fact that, if things went
badly wrong over the next couple of days, there might not be much
they could do about it. Soderberg put it succinctly and with passion:

Right now we have no leverage at all on Hunts Point. We don't
have a signed contract. Tomorrow, if we reject what they have
put forward for either technical reasons, aesthetic reasons, veining, anything, and he says. "OK, you want this? It's a million
dollars more," we have no choice. None. No choice at all, because
we can't change contractors, we can't change suppliers, we're

already five, eight, maybe nine million dollars in the hole already. I mean, we are behind the eight ball and there's not a darn thing we can do.

Even allowing for the effects of jet lag, several breakfasts too many, and a drink or two, this was a dramatic statement and added a certain edge to the group's scrutiny of the state of the project over the next day or two.

On Tuesday morning the sun came out, briefly. Over breakfast the group discussed the various options for the day. Things were complicated by the fact that Bodnar was due in at the Venice airport. Michelato, seen as the organizer of the itinerary, seemed unaware of the benefits of making a decision and sticking to it. A thin, friendly man, he often gave the mistaken impression that nothing was too much trouble. When pressed about the day's plans, he did suggest that the first visit should be to see the interior marble at a factory near Vicenza and check that it matched the architects' expectations. But this raised a logistical problem. Bodnar's flight was due at the Venice airport sometime in the morning—no one was quite sure when—and there seemed little chance of getting a message to him to tell him where everybody had gone. He was apparently planning to rent a car and drive straight to Verona. Perhaps the group should go direct to Verona and meet Bodnar there, before going on to Vicenza. But Vicenza was halfway from Venice to Verona, so if they did that they would all be doubling back. Perhaps they should go to the airport and intercept Bodnar before he set off for Verona, and then they could all go to Vicenza together and then on to Verona.

While these various plans involving Italian towns beginning with V were being considered, Soderberg and Fonti seized the chance to see the Piazza San Marco under better conditions than the day before. When they returned, the signal was given for the group to get their bags together and check out for the trip to the airport to meet Bodnar. To move six people and their bags from the hotel to the airport was a task that would have been simple in any other city in the world. In Venice it was a major operation, masterminded in this case by Michelato. Apart from anything else, you couldn't even be sure where the water taxi would be, since there were at least three different places it could arrive, none of them on the doorstep of the hotel. It all seemed to depend on the maneuvering skills of the taxi driver and the state of the tides. Then, when the boat arrived, there was the problem of getting the many pieces of luggage to it. Venetian porters weren't always easy to find and appeared to be octogenarians when you did find them. Michelato's cars were at the Piazzale Roma, where road and railroad track arrive at the end of the causeway that now links the city to the mainland. It takes about half an hour to get there by boat, and you then have the reverse problems of porters and bags.

The consequence was that, when Bodnar's plane landed at about ten-thirty-five in the morning, the rest of the Worldwide Plaza party was still chugging along the Grand Canal. By the time they had landed, transferred their baggage to the cars, and driven the five miles to the airport, Bodnar was already on the road to Verona, where he would find a message telling him to go back to Vicenza to the marble factory. Over cups of strong espresso at the airport, Fonti, Narbutas, and Soderberg began to express minor reservations about how things were going so far. Michelato seemed unmoved, his normal placid self, while Migliore sat in the car. Since it would take Bodnar a couple of hours to get to Verona and then back to Vicenza, there was no need to hurry.

In the increasingly sunny morning, the convoy set off for the drive to the marble factory at Vicenza. The various samples of Worldwide Plaza marble were laid out in the sunlight, and the group stood looking at them, area by area, checking for color and pattern. Narbutas asked a question about the veining; Fonti about the quantities that were available now and how much more still had to be cut. Twenty minutes after they had arrived, Bodnar turned up in his rented car. He was in shirtsleeves, jacket over his shoulder, and

looked as relaxed and elegant as any man who has been on an all-
night flight from New York. For the rest of the morning, the group
moved around the large stoneyard, each paying attention to specific
points that affected his own role in the building. Bodnar took a keen
interest in the appearance of various samples. He would sometimes
take out a marker pen and put a ring around a particular blemish
or taint, initialling it "JB." He complained when he was shown a
marble that was white with black veining and saw the occasional
hint of yellow from a different mineral in the stone. Some of the
stone was in large sheets, and a stonemason would pour water over
it so that the group could see what it would look like when it was
polished.

As the sun moved behind a nearby hill, Fonti, Soderberg, and
the marble men discussed their findings. It was clear that there
was work still to be done. There were several different areas of the
interior of the building where marble would be used, and the architects weren't yet happy with what they had seen. Fonti decided
to return to the yard on Thursday instead of going back to Venice.
Meanwhile, they were due at Michelato's factory, where the marble
would be cut into floor tiles, wall panels, or vanity tops for the
washrooms. He was proud of his fully mechanized assembly line
and wanted to show it off.

It was about 7:00 P.M. when they finished the tour of the robotic
factory. The group assembled in the marble-lined conference room
for detailed discussions about the columns for the arcade. There
were to be forty-eight pink granite columns around the arcade,
framing the shops that were reached from inside the lobbies. From
the outside the columns were designed to look like solid granite
blocks on top of one another. In fact, one of the design changes
made early in 1987 in order to save money had been to opt for
granite facing attached to a pre-cast concrete column instead of
granite all the way through. It was a complicated manufacturing
process, because granite and concrete behaved differently with
changes in temperature, expanding and contracting at different

rates. If the granite slices had simply been stuck to the concrete, stress would build up at the interface, which could have led to the pieces' falling off after a few years. Each column was about eighteen feet high, the top section having a segmented circle to contain a light. The granite was in alternating bands of dark and light stone, but instead of using different stones, the architects had specified the same stone treated in two different ways: flamed and polished. Polished granite brings out the full depth of color in the stone; flamed granite has a layer burned off with a torch, so that its rough appearance presents a much lighter color. It's something like the difference between sandpapered glass and clear glass. One well-known Manhattan building where this difference is exploited most dramatically is Philip Johnson's "lipstick" building on Third Avenue, with its alternating light and dark bands all the way up the building.

The Worldwide Plaza team needed the columns to start coming on site within the next four weeks. At the moment there existed in the world one such column, at a plant in Brescia, and none of the team had even seen it. This trip would approve the details of its design and coloring and give the go-ahead for full production.

As the group sat around the table looking at the drawings, Bodnar raised the issue of the lights that were to go into the circle at the top of the column. The light fixtures had changed since the earliest designs, which had shown a light fixture that looked like a cross between a giant flashlight and the fasces symbol popularized by Mussolini. Now they were a simpler, hemispherical design which required a larger hole to be cut in the granite veneer of the column. For ten minutes or so the group discussed whether the changes would contravene the New York City code by weakening the layer of stone behind the lamp, through making it thinner. Then they decided to provide a circular hole right through to the concrete, which would be filled by the base of the lamp.

As every fine detail of the forty-eight columns was discussed, drawings were unrolled and pored over. Michelato sat at one end of the table or walked around it, puffing on a cigarette. As questions were raised, he would try and answer them, either in English to the whole group or, when that gave out, in Italian to Fonti. Migliore sat silent most of the time and occasionally rubbed his eyes.

That night, at Soderberg's request, the group had dinner at the 12 Apostles, Verona's best restaurant. During the conversation over dinner, the architects looked back on the day with mixed feelings. The session at the marble works had gone on interminably and some problems still hadn't been satisfactorily resolved. The meeting at the Verona plant had been encouraging, mainly because of the reassuring way in which Michelato spelled out the production schedule he felt he could keep to, and the ease with which he promised to carry out the changes in the lamp circle and the column joints. Nevertheless, none of them had yet seen the column, and it was crucial that they liked the colors when seen together, and that the pre-cast/granite combination didn't look somehow tacky. After dinner, although it was nearly midnight, Michelato took them for a walk around some of Verona's Roman monuments and pointed out some of the detailing on their columns, standing after eighteen hundred years. But, then, they were solid stone and not a cost-saving combination of concrete and granite slices. Tomorrow would show how Worldwide Plaza's columns would compare with the old-fashioned techniques of the Romans.

It was an early start on Wednesday—at last an element of urgency had entered the proceedings as the group realized that there was still much to do. They had to see the all-important column, visit a marble quarry, and then return to Verona to continue the meeting they had started on Tuesday night. On the road by 8:30 A.M., the two cars sped along the autostrada toward Brescia in a light mist. About halfway through the fifty-kilometer journey, the Dolomites suddenly appeared as the mist lifted. These were the mountains whose quarries, less famous than the quarries farther west at Carrara, would supply some of the marble for the building. By the time the group reached Brescia, the clouds had descended again, and the factory was rather gloomy inside. There was an assembly line where the concrete was mixed and poured into molds around steel reinforcing rods to give the beams or columns the strength in tension that the concrete lacked on its own.

The far end of the factory opened out into a yard and here, standing among piles of stacked slabs, was the column. Afterward the architects agreed that they had been very apprehensive about what it would look like. However good you are at extrapolating from marble samples and drawings an inch or two high, the impact of the real thing was bound to be considerable. And it was. There was an almost audible sigh of relief as they all stood around the foot of the column. Here at last was a piece of the real building, and it was good.

The first thing that struck them was the color. It was more vivid than they had expected. The polished granite slabs were quite a deep red, and when they were juxtaposed with the light flame-treated granite the overall impression could be slightly over-whelming—hardly surprising, perhaps, from the land that gave us Mussolini and his monumental public buildings. For the group, one of the important things was to check the appearance to decide whether it really looked as good as an all-granite column. Narbutas looked closely at the corners, where two thin slices of granite met. There wouldn't be any joins here if they had used solid blocks of granite, but he seemed satisfied that the difference didn't show.

After initial impressions, Bodnar climbed onto some concrete slabs and stood back to inspect the first fruits of his design skills. He stood apart from the rest in silent contemplation. This column was still made to the original plan, and so the framing around the lamp socket was too small for the new type of fixture. In an attempt to see how the new design would look, one of Michelato's men stuck tape around the existing hole to show its new boundaries. People seemed satisfied. Fonti dictated notes to himself into a small pocket tape recorder.

There was no concealing the elation and the relief that most of them felt at seeing one granite column. The color was uniform across the range of samples they had seen and, although it was slightly darker than expected, they felt comfortable that it would still tone in, and might even help to accent the horizontal bands that ran around the base of the building. Some of the emotional tension of the previous months of argument and worry about the stone contract had been lifted—unreasonably, perhaps. But surely someone who could make a column as attractive as this one would have no trouble making another forty-seven? And shipping them to New York? And fixing them on site in the right position? They all wanted so much to believe it.

It was time to go on to the quarry, ten minutes' drive away. Here the Worldwide Plaza team were treated to a lecture on how marble was selected and quarried. There was something unnatural about the walls of the quarry. They looked like the facets of some giant crystal. Here in the open mountainside were smooth planes of stone, some of them a hundred square yards in area, and other planes at right angles. It had the regularity and order of a man-made construction, which in a sense it was, but there was no visible purpose for these rectangular formations. The *purpose* had been removed; the smooth planes and right angles were a mirror image of the reason for the quarry's existence.

At various points in the quarry wire-saws buzzed away, cutting into the marble along predetermined planes. These saws consisted of twisted steel cables up to two thousand meters long which ran over pulleys at a speed of over forty kilometers an hour. Some of them were threaded through holes drilled into the marble. As they ran over the pulleys, a slurry of sand or tungsten carbide was poured on the wire. Because these minerals were harder than the marble, they wore it away at the point of contact, and slowly a large block would be cut out of the mountainside.

The Worldwide Plaza architects had chosen marble for only the floors and walls of the lobbies, and they had made their decision on the basis of samples. But sometimes, when a large area of marble is needed, the architect will go to a quarry and identify the part of the rock face from which he wants his marble. With luck, he will get it. But one developer has a story that illustrates the unreliability of Italian marble men. He had chosen just the marble he thought would go well on the outside of his new building, and had given the company details of the amount and the delivery date, and they had quoted him a price that he had agreed to. Some weeks later he received a call from the marble company telling him that, unfortunately, all his marble had been washed away in a flood. This seemed an unfortunate, and unusual, catastrophe to have befallen his marble, particularly in view of the well-known heaviness of the substance. Furthermore, when he went back to the quarry to choose a substitute marble, he was amazed to see how well the company had cleaned up after such a cataclysmic flood, since there were few if any signs of the disaster. Some months later the developer was invited to the opening of a shopping mall in Florida, built by a friend of his. To his surprise, consternation, and fury, the walls of this shopping mall were clad in just the marble he had chosen for his own building the previous year. Clearly the flood of money the marble men had been offered for this particular marble had washed away any desire to stick to their original contract.

As the Worldwide Plaza team drove back down the mountain, they considered the situation and discussed whether they had achieved what they came for. The stone clearly existed and was being cut in the quantities they needed. This was reassuring, for two reasons: one, of course, was that the nightmare of nonexistent stone was behind them; the second was the extra sense of security they derived from knowing that they now had some sort of hold over Hunts Point. They were still not sure whether the other important component of the stone contract, the trusses, would materialize, and they would have to turn their attention to that when they returned.

Back in New York waited the usual multitude of problems to be solved and tasks to be undertaken. Fonti was concerned about problems of access and coordination on the site now that it had reached peak activity. At this time, January 1988, almost every possible construction activity apart from excavation seemed to be taking place on the building. While the steel skeleton was at the thirty-second floor and rising, electricians and plumbers were already at work on the interior of the lower floors. Around the outside of the lower floors, pre-cast concrete contractors jostled with ornamental metalworkers and the first masons, all wanting access to the same areas and wanting to use the same area of street to unload their trucks.

The lowest six stories were fully framed and concrete floors were being poured. The arcade and the lobbies were nearly ready to receive the stone on its trusses from Hunts Point, although there wasn't a truss in sight. Felix Germano, the supervisor for the lower floors, was an outgoing Italian-American with a friendly brashness which he used to good effect as he whirled around the floors like a hurricane, looking for problems to solve: "I enjoy everything— the excitement, the people, the yelling and the screaming, the building, you know, finding out the information. I really love it. I guess the most rewarding thing is when it comes together—that's the ultimate. But I love it. Every day is different, really different."

"How're ya doin', Tony?"—with a slap on the back—was Germano's standard greeting as he weaved his way unerringly along temporary routes from one part of the structure to another: up a staircase, across a pile of steel decking, through a gap between two block walls, down a slope to the cellars, always on the lookout for things he wouldn't recognize till he saw them. A contractor trying to cut corners, metaphorically if not literally; someone putting up a wall with no electrical lines in it; a hole in the floor needing a temporary covering; a loose cable that could electrocute someone; craftsmen in search of instructions about what to do next. A foreman for one of the subcontractors: "Hey, Felix, this doesn't work; I can't make this fit." Germano had to decide whether to go back to Fonti, who would call the architect and suggest an alternative and, if need be, a sketch to redesign that particular area altogether.

Of the superintendents on the site, Germano considered that he had one of the most exciting parts of the building to look after: "The six floors with the lobbies are gonna be tremendously beautiful. It won't be loud or gauche, you know, like that type of thing. I'll tell you, it's gonna be beautiful. It's got a lot of detail, with the stone. It's something like I've never seen. I figure it will be beautiful. I'd compare it with the Basilica of Saint Peter's in Rome. Really it should be; there's a lot of different types of stone, granite, marble. The pattern itself is beautiful."

Germano's pride typified the feeling that motivated many of the men on the job. In part, it's a defensive pride. Our society doesn't always put a high premium on the physical tasks that are the main activity of many of the trades on a big construction site, and construction workers tend to romanticize their own jobs rather than accept the evaluation of others. As Germano put it: "They're here for the same purpose, the same goal—building the building. They make a good salary and they know what they have to do. I mean, a lot of the guys are not super-intelligent. We don't have college graduates working in every trade. So they know they've got to stay with what they do for the salary that they make. So they've gotta do a damn good job. They know they could be replaced immediately, on a minute's notice, so they drive a little harder than someone working in an office."

Conversely, Germano's views of what office workers do are almost as far from the truth as society's view of construction workers: "Office workers spend their time looking out the window, nice, with their little attaché cases, not worrying about anything, answering the phone, calling the butcher, calling the baker, making orders, you know. Construction workers have got to be a little more secure than they are. That's where the union comes in and gives them the security they need." But some might consider that the role of the union in giving their members the security they need sometimes errs on the side of overenthusiasm.

When developers and construction managers talk about the problems of the construction business, there will be only two main topics: the Mafia and feather-bedding. And they will often disagree on which is worse. But Artie Nusbaum claims to be in no doubt:

> We did a job in Kansas City and we said to the clients, "What do you have in your budget for temporary lighting?" and they said, "What's temporary lighting?" And we said, "Who stands by for temporary heat?" and they said, "What's temporary heat?" Now, when we're on a building in New York, our total budget will include in it numbers like 4 or 5 percent that have to do with feather-bedding, and other items of cost that have nothing to do with putting the building together. We have in this city fractionalized unions. For example, in other cities there's only one iron-workers' union; in New York there are two. In other cities there's only one steamfitter plumbers' union; in this city there are two. The steamfitters will only use a pipe threaded by a steamfitter, and it's a two-man trade. In other cities there's no such thing as a two-man trade. If you've got a job for one man you send one man to do the job, not two. And I'm not trying to pick on the steamfitters. They're just the one that came to mind.
>
> This is the only city in America that has separate elevator operators and hoist engineers. In other cities there is no such thing as an elevator operator, but if we have men working in the middle of the night, even if they could walk down, you have to keep an elevator operator up there to bring him down. Now, would you pay it out of your pocket at double time? If there's a healthy person who can walk down thirty floors, would you keep the man standing there at roughly $70 an hour to bring that one man down? I certainly wouldn't have spent that kind of money.
>
> So the biggest evil in this city that raises costs is feather-bedding, but no one wants to discuss that. And that's through every union. The people who represent the city on plumbing or electrical are all ex-plumbers or all ex-electricians, so they're never gonna change the code. Other cities permit plastic pipe. Other cities permit exposed wire. In this city you can't have

plastic pipe or exposed wire. We have an unnecessarily tough code in many ways. So of all the sins or evils that raise costs in New York, it's far more by feather-bedding than even the infamous concrete deals of the Mafia. Get rid of the feather-bedding and the Mafia can stay all day long. . . . Oh, that's not an invitation, by the way. . . .

During the winter of 1987–88 a major bone of contention arose between HRH and the Zeckendorf Company in which feather-bedding played a part. It centered on the heating of the building while construction workers were working in it, what was called "winter protection." It had become apparent in recent weeks that there was a disagreement over who should pay for certain measures that had to be taken to keep work going during the colder periods of winter. Three main areas needed winter protection: concrete pouring, fireproofing the interior, and bricklaying. The Zeckendorf people believed that winter protection was already included in the "general conditions," HRH's fee of about $12 million that was fixed at the beginning of the contract. Now it appeared that this had *not* been included and that the necessary procedures could cost a lot extra. Fonti said that it was very difficult to estimate at the beginning of the contract, when you didn't know how many days would be cold enough to justify heating. Soderberg thought that some fixed number of days between January and March could have been specified. Fonti said that this would mean overcharging the contractor in bad weather, or the developer if the weather was mild, and so he preferred to quantify the actual cost as the protection was needed, which was starting then, in January.

As Fonti started to spell out the figures involved, Soderberg and Jack Schuster became more and more appalled. The concrete winter protection worked out at about $1.05 per square foot. If they poured twenty floors at approximately thirty thousand square feet per floor, the cost of heating would come to over $600,000. Then there was the heating to protect the fireproofing operation, which used a water-based chemical that couldn't be allowed to freeze. That protection worked out at about $30,000 a week over ten weeks, another $300,000. The third element, keeping three floors of brick-laying heated for about ten weeks, would cost another $600,000.

"To make matters worse," said Fonti, in a tense discussion with Soderberg and Narbutas, "whenever you start a winter-protection program, you cannot start it at eight and finish at three; you have to pre-heat and post-heat the areas, and the amount of time you pre- and post-heat is dependent on the weather, on the temperature, all these things, so it's a decision that has to be made daily. I have estimated the overtime hours in this program by fig-uring I'd start at four o'clock in the morning to midnight, rough figures. However, for every single overtime hour that you work, by union regulations of the city of New York, you have what we call "standby people," and we have approximately fifteen individuals who are required to get paid by the union rules."

"They stand by and get paid," said Narbutas.

"Actually they're there to maintain the equipment, to ride the elevators up and down, that's their duty and function," said Fonti.

"But they don't do it, right?" said Soderberg. "Let's be honest about it."

"Do they do it? Yes, they are on the job." Fonti valiantly tried to stick up for the union.

"Yeah, but they don't do anything, right?" Soderberg pressed his point home.

"No, if there's a problem they'll do it; if there's no problem they're on the job. But the man's time is dedicated to the job. That's why it's called a 'standby.' "

Soderberg was not impressed. So far as he was concerned, standbys were just an added term in the equation Fonti had just spelled out, a term that increased an already overloaded budget: "So, in other words, you're telling me that I'm a million dollars above what I told the bank?"

What might have been surprising to an outside observer was

the matter-of-fact way in which some of these facts and figures were bandied around. What Nusbaum called "the search for the guilty," one of the six phases of construction, went on all the time, since any project as huge and uncontrollable as Worldwide Plaza would be experiencing mistakes and problems all the time. And yet the search for the guilty rarely results in any permanent action against the culprits when they're identified, perhaps because every individual knows that the innocent today might be one of the guilty tomorrow. When things went wrong, a personal reaction of anger or disgust was often as far as it went. Schuster had bureaucratized the search for the guilty, with an "FU HRH" or "FU SOM" scribbled by his signature when he had to approve such payments. He described his reaction to the winter-protection foul-up:

Hair pulling, screaming, it didn't matter. You weren't going to stop, you had to go ahead, you made the best of it. We did approach some of our subcontractors, who were gracious enough to lower their prices a wee bit, but the numbers were there. And remember something else, we're talking about basically overtime work. This is protection basically in the evening and on weekends, so that not only are you paying the subcontractor for his people to do that work but you're paying a tremendous number of people who are on your payroll who due to union requirements and otherwise must work every minute that anyone else is working.

Dominic and I are very friendly with one another. He's doing a job which I think would be a commendable one. He knows I'm doing a job. His is a little bit more difficult than mine, in that he is trying to keep the subcontractors working and he knows that most of the leverage is with them, that if you refuse to give a particular subcontractor a particular extra and he refuses to do the work, you can be in serious problems. True, our contract provides that if there's a dispute the subcontractor must work, but that very rarely is exercised, because it's frustrating to try to get the man to comply with it if he decides that he doesn't feel like doing it. What do you do? You can't carry a gun. You threaten, you cajole, you send three days' notices if you want to, but by the time all of this is over and done with, you know perhaps weeks have gone by and you may have lost very, very critical items of work.

One reason that problems seemed to spring out of the wood-work on a project like Worldwide Plaza is that a building of that size and scope is a one-shot creation. Nearly everything is being done for the first time, apart from the most basic tasks, like fitting doors in gaps and faucets to sinks. From the earliest stages, where HRH tried to estimate the final cost, to the final inspections by the city of New York, there was no exact precedent for what was being done. And every link in the chain of command was a human being—there were few predictable, reliable machines to do the routine jobs.

So, when the trusses finally began to be assembled by Hunts Point, it wasn't surprising that the work didn't go smoothly. How much of that was due to Hunts Point and how much to the novelty of the actual components being manufactured is difficult to say. But from the moment the trusses were designed too large to fit on the trucks that were meant to take them to Manhattan, it was clear that the stone problems were not over.

The work of assembling the trusses took place in a shed at the marshaling yard of A. J. Ross, where the steel had earlier been laid out to be called in day by day as the steel skeleton rose. In early 1988, as the truss manufacture started, most of the main beams and columns had long since been driven into Manhattan. In the gloom of a large hangarlike building, two large steel frameworks that had been shipped in from Texas stood upright with about a dozen men working around them. On the other side of the shed were crates of stone, still wrapped and crated after the journey from Verona or Vicenza. The pieces would be taken out and placed face down on the ground. Then, using a powerful adhesive, brackets would be attached to the back of each slab and left while the glue hardened. These slabs were meant to be fixed in a predetermined order to the trusses, leaving gaps for the windows to be installed on site.

Watching the men assemble the stone on the trusses, it was clear that doing this sort of thing at ground level, under shelter, was far safer than it would have been on site—safer for the men and safer for the passing public. What wasn't quite so clear was why, day after day, there were grumbles from the architects and the construction managers about the state of the trusses when they arrived on site. Pieces were missing from some of them, for example, meaning that fieldwork was still required on the stone. Narbutas had expected to see a fully formed panel, complete with insulation and flashing. These trusses, after all, had to do the job of an efficient curtain wall, just like the masonry higher up. Instead they turned up on site with stone panels missing and without many of these key components.

Of course, the more work that had to be done on site, the less advantage was gained from the prefabrication method. The site was frenetic enough as it was, without the inconvenience of extra people around finishing off the work they were meant to have done on the trusses.

Though it was clear to everyone that this work was slipping behind, there was a muted reaction among the people on site. Part of this was due to the resigned feeling that there was not a lot that could be done to change the situation. And *that* belief might have been linked to the character of the man in charge of the operation of assembling the trusses. His name was Al Bulis, and he was a tall, bulky man with a strong grip and a burly exterior, an employee of Hunts Point who displayed considerable loyalty to the company that employed him, and in particular to Migliore. His skills were not entirely unappreciated—Felix Germano used a military metaphor to describe him: "I guess he sees the stone and all his men as soldiers and he plans how he's got to arrange everything, where he will attack next. And he visualizes everything as a big battlefield. 'I will attack the northeast corner. I will set the columns, set the left-hand stone. Then I will attack from the left flank.' Everything is on the ground as an attack. General Patton, they call him."

But by all accounts Bulis had a fierce temper, particularly after a drink or two, and it is easy to imagine that he was not someone who would listen to complaints about Hunts Point workmanship with sympathy and understanding.

Toward the end of 1988 most of the stone trusses *were* finally all in place, integrated with the pre-cast concrete, and enclosing the lower floors of the building in time for O&M to move in. The columns *had* arrived for the arcade, later than promised, but eventually. Even so, there were odd pieces of stone, on the parapets around the lower floors, that were not finally in place until June 1989. No one looked back at that particular episode in the construction of Worldwide Plaza with pleasure or pride. Artie Nusbaum gave a wry summary of the general feeling:

> We made the decision to use that stone contractor directly with Bill Zeckendorf. It was the steel truss, which was a technology they didn't understand, that killed them. Plus the contractor carried with him certain personal problems which in the end destroyed him, and he was three to four months late, and we therefore were three to four months late. But Hunts Point was so much cheaper that it was very, very difficult not to use somebody who was that amount of money lower. It turned out to be impossible for us to recommend the second bidder, who had problems, and the third bidder—who was a good contractor—who was several millions of dollars higher. On that one we consulted directly with Mr. Zeckendorf. We took the poison pill together.

13

HIGH ON STEEL

The second half of 1987 and the first half of 1988 were memorable because of the convoluted practical and emotional problems of the brick and the stone. For the architects and the HRH team, every day had brought some new surprise or worry in connection with the color or the shape of the bricks, the truss design for the stone support, the delivery date for the bricks, the existence or not of the marble, the possible bankruptcy of the bricklaying contractor, or the imminent incarceration of the stone contractor. Often these concerns were inextricably intertwined, in job meetings, phone calls, and after-hours bar conversations.

It was therefore refreshing to observe one area of construction that seemed trouble-free. Whatever was happening at ground level—in site offices or around the lower stories—above the heads of the Worldwide Plaza team the steel rose inexorably. At about a floor a week, from sixteen floors in the late summer of 1987 to forty by March 1988, the steel erectors performed in a smooth, steady routine, in which each man knew his part. Only rain or ice stopped the work. Brave they might be, but these men were not foolhardy, and wet steel is treacherous to walk on.

When Gary Steficek put pencil to paper in the design of the steel structure of Worldwide Plaza, he had never engineered a building so tall before. His company had, of course: Sears Tower, the tallest building in the world, was designed in SOM's Chicago office. In any case, Steficek alone didn't design Worldwide; a more senior engineer, Dick Rowe, oversaw his work. Nevertheless, on a day-to-day basis, the structural engineering of the skyscraper was his, and whether the steel framework had the right design for the job would become clear only after the building had reached its full height, acquired its full weight of cladding, and opened its doors to its full complement of people, desks, and equipment.

Engineers have a habit of using the word "column" in two ways. A steel column on Worldwide could be seen as the continuous piece of steel, with an I-cross-section, running from the foundations to the top floor. Sixteen of these were arranged around a square to form the core of the building, with another fifty or so forming the support system for the outside walls. But these are not actually continuous pieces of steel: each is made up of a number of steel sections, bolted one on top of another all the way up the building. These sections are also spoken of individually as "columns." The sections themselves vary in size and weight, since the lower ones have to take much more load than the higher ones. At the base, the thickness of a typical column might be such that a foot length weighs a thousand pounds. As one section is placed upon another, the thickness reduces, and the top sections of the column might

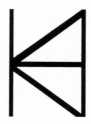

weigh only two hundred pounds a foot, reflecting the much lighter load it has to support.

Since the beams too vary in thickness and weight, each of the connections on the framework might well have to support a unique pattern of loads. This determines how the pieces of steel meeting at that connection are joined together. Some will be bolted, some bolted and welded, and some braced—that is, they will have an extra piece of metal across the corner, providing added extra resistance to bending. Provided most of the ten thousand or more connections in the building are correctly carried out in the field, the pattern of loads and stresses on the building will give it the required stability. In the case of Worldwide Plaza, the pattern of connections gave the building a source of double strength—a strongly braced core and a stiff outside tube.

The core is a useful structure to bear the wind load, because it can be braced with diagonal beams without interfering with the aesthetics of the building, since the core is walled in to hold the elevators, toilets, equipment rooms, and so on.

A building could be made really rigid by making all the connections moment connections—that is, welding the beam to the column at the point where the two surfaces meet instead of simply bolting them together. But the extra labor costs of both bolting and welding every connection would be high, and the engineers opted for moment connections mainly on the outside columns, to form the stiff tube.

During the process of steel erection you realize how very simple the building of a skyscraper can be. At the growth surface of the building, where the top floor meets the sky, it couldn't be simpler. The construction of the floor below has left the tops of all the columns poking up around the edge and at various points in the core of the building. These columns, pierced with boltholes, form the connection points for the next pair of floors.

There were five different tasks for the steel erectors, one following another in the coordinated process of erecting two floors of steel at a time. There were raising gangs, who put the steel loosely into place, making sure that all the pieces were there and fabricated in such a way that they fitted together. Then came the "plumber-ups," to check the alignments of the framework to ascertain that the verticals and the horizontals were correct, and if not to correct them. They were followed by the "bolter-ups," who bolted and welded the new framework firmly into position. As these three teams headed for the next floors, two more teams of ironmen worked on putting metal deck across the beams, and welding metal strips around the edges to make the floors into a vast shallow tray that would hold the concrete.

By the end of February 1988 the steel erectors had reached the fortieth floor. Two raising gangs were working separately to construct the next two floors of the steel skeleton. Each team performed the same tasks, but their activities were staggered so that they did not get in each other's way. Each member had a specific role, to which names were given—a foreman, two connectors, a phone man, a hooker-on, and a tagline man. As they went through their routine, the derivations of the names would become clear.

The "package" of steel for that division had been ordered up the day before, arrived on a truck at street level, and been hauled to the roof by one of the cranes. Team A had then "shaken it out," under the supervision of their foreman, Wiggy. "Shaking out" consisted of laying out the various pieces on the decking in the best position for the next stage, where each piece would be picked up and fixed into position. The next task was the actual erection, in which the team would work in a smooth, coordinated way to connect the network of columns and beams together.

While team A was involved in hauling and shaking out, team B would be erecting. They would be fed the steel by two cranes, lifting it from the trucks below. These cranes were supported on the steel framework itself. To have used cranes based in the street would have been difficult for two reasons: first, the city of New York places severe restrictions on the number of days per year a street crane may be used; second, in the cramped surroundings of Manhattan it would be very difficult to achieve the stability of a crane that would eventually have to be as tall as the building.

So a system has been devised for "jumping" cranes all the way up the building. The crane cabin and arm are supported by a tower fifty or sixty feet high which is bolted to the working floor. The steel erectors build the next few floors up around the tower of the crane until the steel framework has risen to be level with the base of the crane cabin. Then the crane is "jumped." In this process, the tower is unbolted from its original position, which is now several stories below the working level, and the crane on its tower is raised by huge jacks pushing against the steel skeleton. When the tower has been raised to its new height, above the new working floor, the jack pistons are retracted and bolted with the tower base, to the new level of steel. In this process of leap-frogging, the two tower cranes have been jumped over five hundred feet to reach the fortieth floor. The actual movement of the pistons is just perceptible as the team of ironworkers cluster around the crane in a smooth routine of unbolting the frame, moving support pegs, and checking the jacks. The regular interruption to the day-to-day steel erection seems to inject a new excitement into the ironworkers as they stand around watching the almost imperceptible ascent of the tower at about a foot a minute. In the words of one of the HRH project managers, crane jumping is "super-sexy."

On a freezing-cold but sunny day at the end of February, the cranes were in their lower position, level with the top floor, the fortieth. The steel for the forty-first and forty-second floors was waiting on trucks below. While the crane on the west side of the building lifted the steel, some of the ironworkers jumped the crane on the east side. Each of the two tower cranes would work for a specific team, and in some miraculous way they managed to keep their long arms from colliding as one swung out over 49th Street while the other lifted a thirty-foot beam from the decking to its final position between two columns. The floor was divided into seven areas, and the teams worked their way around in an order decided by Wiggy until, in a couple of days, the ironworkers would have assembled most of the next layer of steel to a stage where all the right pieces were connected together.

At about 8:00 A.M. a crowd of construction workers gathered on the ground floor, by the two passenger elevators. As the elevator rose, about half the workers had got off by the time it reached its current limit on the thirty-seventh floor. The rest swarmed out and made their way across the steel decking. "Always look down" was the rule when walking across the higher floors, since there would often be gaps in the decking where some work needed to be done between floors. On the other hand, danger could also arrive from above, as one of the teams of bolter-ups dropped the occasional bolt, or the ironworkers laying the steel decking let fall an offcut. The advent of hardhats, now worn by all construction workers, minimizes cranial damage, although it was interesting to see that the favored headgear of one of the quality inspectors on Worldwide Plaza was a wide-brimmed Stetson.

To get to the forty-second floor, the ironworkers had to clamber another fifty feet or so up wooden ladders poking through the steel decking. On top that morning it was sunny but chilly. There was a good all-around view, although New Jersey to the west disappeared into a layer of yellowish haze. Wiggy took out the rolled-up plan of the floor and decided on the order of assembly. He was older than the rest of the team, short and slim, wearing glasses, and with a pencil permanently stuck firmly behind his ear. Al-

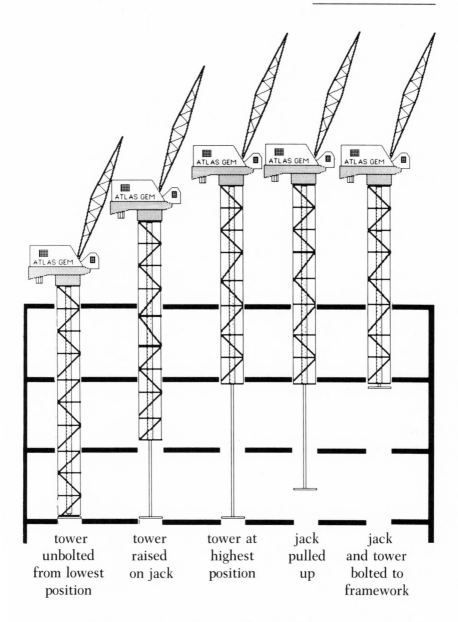

tower	tower	tower at	jack	jack
unbolted	raised	highest	pulled	and tower
from lowest	on jack	position	up	bolted to
position				framework

though from the same tribe, the Mohawks were all very different in appearance. Pete Marquis was of medium height and had the most characteristic Native American face—broad and strong. Kevin, the tagline, was small and agile, a suitable physique for bounding across the uneven, steel-strewn decking in pursuit of a beam being moved by the crane across the sky. Greg, the phone man, was tall and had a Native American handsomeness but less pronounced features. They worked quietly and well together, each knowing his place and not afraid to point out to the others when they weren't doing their bit.

The team would erect the steel on the northeast corner of the floor. Several outside columns had already been erected the day before, but two more had to be erected across the corner itself. At this level, the cross-section of the building changed shape from a square to an octagon. This meant that at each corner there was to be a triangle of flat roof. When the triangles were concreted and waterproofed, they would then support the davits for raising and lowering window-washing equipment.

Once Wiggy had decided to raise a specific column he told Greg, the phone man, who used a walkie-talkie, to speak to the operator of the crane on the east side of the roof, the nearest crane to that corner. Within less than ten minutes the column was up, after the following demonstration of teamwork: John, the hooker-on, looped a steel cable near the top end of the column; Greg phoned to the crane to lift it; Kevin steadied the column with another line as it hovered over toward the corner of the building; when the lower end of the column was over the top of the column poking up from the floor below, Pete and Wally, the two connectors, moved it into position over the connecting point. With a little heaving they lined up the holes in the new column with the holes in the connecting plate, and Pete and Wally each slipped a bolt through one of the holes and gave the nuts a few turns with a wrench. Finally, Kevin unlooped the steadying cable from the top of the column, sending it crashing down onto the steel decking.

One column was up, and it was only nine o'clock, about half an hour since they had arrived on the roof. Having erected fifty such columns for every two floors all the way up the building, the team had no trouble with this one. The bolts that held it in place were a temporary measure, awaiting the plumber-ups and bolter-ups, who would arrive when the whole framework was in place. As the wind blew across the roof, the column could be seen to sway from time to time, and an observer could be forgiven for wondering if a few bolts were enough to prevent the heavy column from bending right over with a strong gust. But the strengths of bolts and the gravity forces of columns are very familiar to steel erectors and the engineers who design the buildings, and even this temporary support was enough to keep the column upright.

Another column was erected nearby in exactly the same way, and the team then turned their attention to the rest of the structure. Moving across the north side of the roof, they started on the beams. The side arms of each of the tree columns had to be linked by beams.

Each of the tree columns along the edge had a connection for a beam in the middle and one at the top. John hooked up the first beam, Greg called to the crane, and Pete and Wally shinnied up the columns that were to be joined by the beam while Kevin steadied it with the line. At one end, Pete eased the beam in so that its holes lined up with the holes in the column. When the holes were roughly aligned, he used the indispensable tool of steel erectors: the spud wrench, a tool with a wrench at one end and a long steel point at the other. Slung in a leather holster from the ironworker's workbelt, the spud wrench usually has a sheen and a dented exterior that show years of personal use. Pete positioned the pointed end of his wrench through the two holes that had to be lined up, as the beam was heaved into position. When the holes overlapped only a little, he pushed the tapered end through the overlap, which helped to ease the beam sideways until the holes were properly aligned. Then he put a bolt through one of the other holes and used the wrench end to tighten it. Wally had clambered up the column at his end of the beam and was starting to line the holes up in the same way when he discovered a snag. He called Pete over and they looked at the end of the beam. Something was stopping the holes from lining up.

One of the beams had turned up at the end of its long journey from Texas without a half-inch cutback that was supposed to have been made in the shop. Such a small error, and it was small, had escaped everybody's attention until this point. It was the sort of mistake that Gene Miller of Mosher had pondered back in April:

> Steel doesn't always fit, and there are many reasons for it. A detailer can goof. The shop can goof. Even worse, Murphy can cause us to goof, and when I say Murphy, I mean an accumulation of tolerances, all added, like eighty-six basic steel tolerances, plus shop tolerances, plus the field tolerances. When they all add up to a misfit, then we have to address it. But we have troubleshooters on each job and they resolve them. The steel goes out. It goes out in place and somehow we fix it. It doesn't

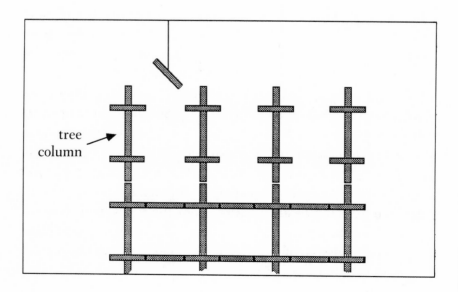

go back down on the ground again. Once it goes up on the hook, it goes up there and it stays up there.

When such errors are discovered on site, there are a couple of ways of dealing with them. If it's a very big mistake, and a new piece has to be fabricated and shipped, the supervisor will look at the plans and see if there is another piece of steel, perhaps intended for another part of the structure, that is nearer to the correct shape. If there is, and if it can be adapted on the spot, he will call off that piece of steel and use it in place of the misfabricated piece. The problem is postponed rather than solved, because the piece he has used must be replaced before it is needed on site. But if the error can be corrected on the spot—say, by drilling or cutting—that will be the best solution. Today's problem was easy to solve. Pete called Wiggy, who climbed the column to look at the problem. He brought up a cutting torch and on the spot cut through the flange to shorten it by about an inch. Pete and Wally then wrenched the beam end into position and bolted it in place.

One thing remained to be done. This beam was one of a supposedly identical pair. Wiggy checked the other one and, sure enough, it too had not been cut back. So while the team got on with erecting another beam, he wielded his torch to correct the error on this one too.

By eleven o'clock the columns and beams that made up the northeast corner of the forty-second floor were loosely linked together. While the raising gang moved off to shake out their next pile of steel, the plumber-ups moved in to carry out the next important task, making sure that the building continued to rise vertically.

It may seem surprising that attention needs to be paid to the verticality of the building by the time it's reached five hundred feet. You might think that if the foundations were level and the first columns were erected vertically the rest of the structure would follow automatically. But it would take only a small discrepancy from the vertical on each floor to produce an alarming lean to one side higher up the building, if it were not corrected. If each floor was an inch out of true, the building could be leaning four feet at the top. It's the job of the plumber-ups to check as each floor goes up, to correct any discrepancy. This is not simply a matter of preventing desks from rolling across the floor or pictures from hanging away from the wall. Even minor deviations can significantly change the forces within the steel skeleton.

The columns are designed to take vertical loads. By the time

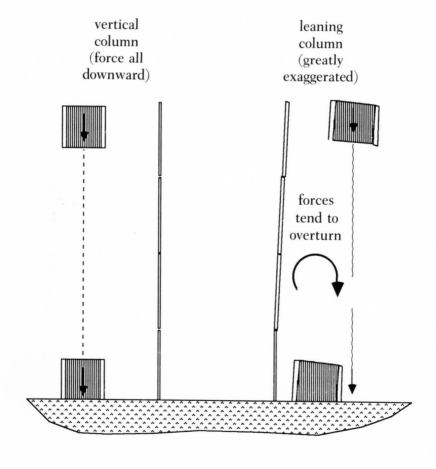

vertical
column
(force all
downward)

leaning
column
(greatly
exaggerated)

forces
tend to
overturn

the gravity loads from each floor have been channeled into the nearest column and carried down to the ground, the base of the column could be under a load of one million pounds or more. This is a purely vertical load. If the sections of a column were to lean slightly as they rose, the twenty-five or so joints could be subjected to forces trying to pull them apart because of a tendency to lean out. Overall, the column could experience what is called a "torque," a force tending to turn it over, and one for which the building has not been designed. Even a few inches out of true at the top produce a large torque at the bottom, and it's for this reason that the steel erectors are followed all the way up the building by the plumber-ups.

When the raising gang erected the steel, they had secured each component with enough loosely fastened bolts to hold the connections together. The boltholes between beam and column

ruler held against column

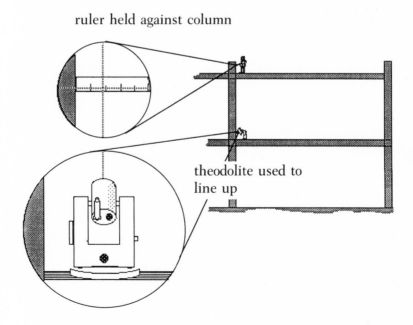

theodolite used to
line up

were about an inch in diameter, slightly larger than the bolts, to allow for the final easing into position of the whole framework by the plumber-ups before it was firmly bolted and welded.

On Wednesday, March 2, on the forty-second floor, the plumbers set to work on the framework that team A had erected the day before.

A plumber-up named George was on a lower floor with his theodolite, a telescope with a very accurate means of leveling its base. On the next level up, standing on a beam next to a column, George's colleague held a ruler horizontally out from the column. With the theodolite base positioned exactly six inches out from the lower column, George looked at the ruler on the level above and saw that the crosshairs of the theodolite were half an inch away from the six-inch mark, showing that the column was half an inch out of the vertical.

How do you straighten up a steel framework that's half an inch out of true? Well, unsurprisingly, you do it by pulling it back into shape. Another member of the plumbing-up team tied a steel cable between the errant column and a fixed point on a lower floor that had already been bolted firmly in place. He then used a device called a "turnbuckle" that twists the cable and shortens it, pulling the column back toward the vertical. While this was being done, George watched through the theodolite until the six-inch mark on the ruler coincided with the crosshairs. A building is allowed to deviate by an inch or so in every hundred feet, so as long as the twenty-foot column wasn't more than a fifth of an inch out of true, it would be acceptable. George signaled to his colleague to stop turning, and the team moved on to the next column to carry out the same procedure.

When the plumber-ups had finished, a third team moved in to complete the steel erection on the forty-second floor. Now that the beams and columns had been plumbed up, they could be bolted firmly into position. Most of the important connections had half a dozen boltholes, each secured loosely with one or two bolts. The

detailed drawings of the connections, prepared twelve months before by Haskell Ray and his colleagues in Houston, showed the size
and strength of bolt needed for each hole and how tightly it had to
be turned. Ordinary bolts need only to support a load at right angles
to the shaft, like a horizontal bolt holding one piece of steel against
another. But there are sometimes connections that work by squeezing two pieces of steel against each other with very tightly turned
bolts, using high-strength steel that is under great tension along
its length—twenty tons or more per square inch. With a device
called a "torque wrench," a lot of the hit and miss is taken out of
the bolting process. It looks like a power drill without a bit. The
head is put over the nut and with a deafening rat-a-tat-tat the nut
is turned several times until it reaches a predetermined tightness.
With a plastic bucket of bolts in one hand and a wrench in the
other, the bolter-up moved along the beams from connection to
connection. Sometimes the team works in pairs, one using his spud
wrench to hold the bolt while the man with the torque wrench
tightens the nut.

Much of this work looks dangerous. It's not just the erection
team who perform daredevil deeds, leaping from column top to
swinging beam. The plumber-ups also have to adopt tricky posi-

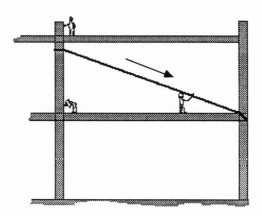

tions. One of them will lean out from a beam at the edge of the building on the fortieth floor to look down to the floor below, where a marker has been set to enable him to judge whether the building is out of true or not. The topmost floors, where these ironworkers work, are the most dangerous floors anyway, because they don't necessarily have their full complement of steel decking: there may be holes to fall through. Also the staircase, temporary or permanent, that follows the building as it rises travels more slowly than the steel erectors can work, so even to get to their workplace involves some rickety climbing for the final few feet.

Safety on a construction site is one of the responsibilities of the construction management company. The construction industry has always been near the top of the industrial-accidents list. Early on in the construction of Worldwide Plaza, Dominic Fonti was sanguine about the possibilities ahead:

> We have six hundred feet to go up in the air. It's a masonry building. We anticipate a certain amount of mortar, of chips from bricks, to fly off the building and fall into the streets. We take reasonable precautions. We have catchalls below the mason; we're going to have several bridges over the pedestrians; we'll have all other protection that we feel is necessary and that is required by law. We just hope for the best, that nothing will happen, but we cannot foresee most of the accidents. What happens is that people get overconfident and that's when accidents happen. Most of the accidents that have occurred on projects I've been on have been due to carelessness.

There was one safety officer on the Worldwide site, Harry Weidmyer, for both the skyscraper and the residential buildings. He did not have an easy job. There is a close relationship between safety levels and money. To make a particular procedure safe means spending more money or taking more time. The temptation for any subcontractor was to neglect safety in order to save time and money.

If he was caught by Weidmyer in breach of the regulations, he could be fined. Weidmyer also had the power to arrange for a hazard to be removed and send the bill for the work, and his own time, to the contractor.

But Weidmyer has the best type of personality for a safety inspector. He seemed easygoing, cheerful, and casual as he patrolled the building, day after day, on the lookout for anything that might have led to the injury of a worker or a member of the public:

> My idea of controlling safety on any job in New York City is to be involved. You cannot control safety from sitting in the office. People respect you the more they see you. If it's the cold weather and you're out there with them they respect you. If it's hot and you're not sitting in an air-conditioned office but you're up on the building with them, they respect you. There are approximately twelve hundred people on this job and I deal with a thousand of them on a regular basis. I will stop or talk. I will ask them how they're doing. If there is a problem and I can resolve it, I will get it done right there. If not, I'll go to their shop steward.

Weidmyer has a fistful of certificates for emergency medical training, first aid, and cardiopulmonary resuscitation, and was usually the first on the spot in the event of serious injury. People in the construction business admit that most accidents arise from drinking on the job. Every lunchtime on every floor groups of men gather to eat their packed lunch and, sometimes, to drink beer. Other groups go off the site to bars for a drink or a bite to eat. Often among the debris nestling in the grooves of steel decking or the corners of the stairwells are the familiar red-and-blue crushed Budweiser cans. In any thousand men there are bound to be some with a drinking problem, and those are often the ones who miss their step on a ladder, drop a wrench while they are working on a beam, or don't look down as they put their foot into a hole in the floor.

Although the ironworkers have the most visibly dangerous

jobs, they don't suffer the most accidents, perhaps for the obvious reason that anyone doing something so clearly hazardous will take a great deal more care than when walking on firm ground. Most accidents on construction sites happen in the vicinity of elevator shafts.

"With an open shaft at the forty-ninth story, if somebody accidentally falls into it, death comes very quickly," said Harry. "Elevator installation is a high-pressured job. My biggest problem with the elevator constructors is to have them tie up the shafts, by protecting them with a steel cable rail." There are very specific regulations about temporary safety protection wherever there are gaps in the sides of a building or in a floor. Before the core of the building is walled in, the elevator shafts are just gaping holes from top to bottom. Every opening on each floor should be wired off, with cable strong enough to take the weight of a man. This also applies to the perimeter of the building. As soon as the steelworkers have reached a new level, they are followed closely by men with strong steel cable and welding equipment, who fix a series of metal loops on the inside of each column at waist height and thread the cable through.

However much protection the regulations impose, the individual worker can never be entirely protected from his own foolishness. And Artie Nusbaum, looking at it from HRH's point of view, didn't really see why he should be: "In the end the individual has to protect himself. I know the law says *I'm* supposed to do it, but that's unreal. I can't have four or five hundred men working in a building and watch each man or woman as he goes into a shaft or works near the edge of the building. Anyway, you don't have to fall down a shaft or from any great height to die. On one job I was working on, a man fell from a four-foot-high scaffold and died, so it can happen anywhere at any time."

When workers do suffer injury, it is in their best interests to maintain that it's HRH's fault rather than their own negligence. This is where Weidmyer's evidence can save his employers—or their insurance company—many times his own salary: "I've been through a case recently of an ironworker that slipped on the spray that's used for fireproofing. He was suing for $1.5 million. I had gone to court with several pieces of evidence stating how negligent the general contractor was, and the employee. The examination before trial ended right there. There was an out-of-court settlement for $3,500, from $1.5 million. That is a feather in my cap."

Protecting the workers is only part of Weidmyer's job. He also has to protect the general public from falling windows, pieces of wood and steel, and bricks. Debris of this type has caused the most horrifying incidents of recent years, particularly distressing because of the random nature of the incidents and the blamelessness of the victims. Early in 1987, on an HRH site downtown, an eight-foot-long piece of wood fell off the top of the building and decapitated a pedestrian. That's one of the reasons why Harry visited the higher floors of the building every day, looking out for loose timber and steel dangerously near the edge of the building. These inspections were not, of course, the only means of preventing such accidents. HRH were obliged to suspend a series of protective nets around the building to prevent anything that did fall off from reaching the ground. Because of the large areas of bricklaying on Worldwide Plaza, Weidmyer and HRH between them devised a system to catch any bricks that fell off the walls, before reaching the street below. The graphic name for the system is "diapering." The level at which the bricklayers were working was clad in protective material to seal off every chink through which a brick might slip. The system was linked to the moving scaffolding so that, as the scaffold rose with the bricklayers, the "diaper" moved with it. But even this system didn't prevent the odd incident.

One Friday at about 8:00 A.M., just outside the north entrance to the building, a black Lincoln sedan was driving beneath the office tower when the driver heard a clunk on the rear bodywork. He stopped and got out, looked up and around, and saw a dent made by a brick fragment that had fallen from the thirtieth floor. Fortunately for HRH, the brick hit the car rather than one of the many passers-by heading for the subway or the local school at that time of the morning.

Within a few minutes Weidmyer was on the scene, calm, placatory, understanding. He started taking down the driver's details and was joined by the passenger in the car, who revealed that he was a litigation specialist. Weidmyer cast his eyes to heaven. But everyone was good-natured, and the incident was over in ten minutes. Fortunately, it could be dealt with informally rather than developing into an official investigation into a violation of safety procedures. Nevertheless, Weidmyer took the hoist to the thirtieth floor in search of a leaky diaper.

Artie Nusbaum was used to incidents like this, and accepted them as an almost inevitable accompaniment to construction in the cramped spaces of Manhattan. "Fortunately, cars are made of steel—if you do hurt a car, I don't want to say I don't care, but I *don't* care."

Rules and regulations are Weidmyer's daily newspaper. He has to know the details of every obligation the city of New York places upon a developer and his construction team. A small slip can lead to a summons and a large fine. One incident from his crowded daily life shows how easy it is for things to go wrong. On May 10, 1988, the Worldwide Plaza construction site received a visit from a group of city occupational-safety officials called informally the "BEST squad"—Bureau of Enforcement and Safety Testing. They turned up on site three or four times a week to check that Weidmyer and HRH were doing their job. As part of a routine inspection of the paperwork in Weidmyer's office they discovered on this visit that a crane being used by Hunts Point to set stone on 49th Street had a different number from that shown in the operating permit.

If any crane comes to any job site in New York City, the owner must organize a number of different pieces of paper to allow the crane to be used. The first is a submission to the Department of Transportation, describing the working area and showing that it is strong enough to support the crane. The department sends an engineer to inspect the site and stamp his approval on the certificate. This achieved, the submission is sent on to another department called Cranes and Derricks. They look more closely at the type of crane and also approve that it is on a surface strong enough to hold it safely. Finally, they send the submission to the Department of Buildings, who operate the BEST squad, and they look at what everyone else has said and decide whether to give final approval.

During the BEST squad's regular inspection, Weidmyer was summoned on his personal intercom from the top floor, where he was at the time. The papers he had been given by Hunts Point actually referred to a crane on another construction site. A member of the BEST squad rang Cranes and Derricks and discovered that this particular crane had never been approved for work on this site. The order was issued to stop work until the right papers could be filed to allow it to resume. Weidmyer told the masons to stop work on the lobby stone, which didn't please Felix Germano, who was cracking the whip to keep up the pace. Weidmyer described Germano's reaction: "Felix at that time was yelling, 'What's wrong? What can you do to resolve the problem? Take care of the problem! Please let's get the machine going!' That's when I started to deal with the city. We had to make several phone calls and they lifted the stop-work order within forty-five minutes."

But the incident didn't stop there. Although the problem was sorted out fairly quickly, the following day HRH and Hunts Point received summonses. Fines of $1,000 to $5,000 can be imposed for a first offense, $5,000 to $10,000 for the second offense, and on a third offense the job can be shut down. If fines were to be levied, HRH would try to make Hunts Point pay their fine, since it was entirely their fault that the paperwork was not in order.

No one took the incident as anything other than an occupational hazard. Fonti kept a sheaf of such summonses, which marked an uneasy compromise between workers' freedom to cut corners and the city's desire to make construction as safe as possible. But cranes *did* fall and injure or kill passers-by from time to time, and frustration over having the job delayed was not a serious indication of Fonti's feelings about safety.

14

FINDING THE GUILTY

Architects deal in all sorts of magical materials and models and mirrors and two-dimensional drawings that are made to look three-dimensional. We can never work in the final medium of our art, as painters or sculptors usually do, so it's frightening to see the final thing come together being crafted by other hands than your own. And not everything is right; things change constantly. Many of the materials that we specified are now different. Shop drawings came in showing that something could not be fabricated or was too expensive to fabricate the way we wanted, and so we're constantly losing pieces of the project. There's a constant fight to keep what you can, but you recognize right in the beginning that you're not going to be able to keep 100 percent of it. I've never been in a project in which you can. It's a frustrating and slightly scary process to go through.

—DAVID CHILDS, November 17, 1987

E ach member of the skyscraper team felt differently as he looked at the bulky edifice that neared its full height during the winter of 1987–88. Childs looked at the rising building and worried about the compromises in his design that might be lurking behind the brick-clad steel framework; Dominic Fonti saw more than a thousand people at work every day, yet still there were gaps in the façade, and in his schedule, that made the building less advanced than it should have been. Terry Soderberg and Jack Schuster viewed the building as one overspend piled up on another.

299

For mechanical engineer Marvin Mass there was little evidence from the street of how his contribution to the skyscraper was progressing. The mechanical engineering of Worldwide Plaza was carried out by small groups of men in distant corners of the interior of the building and would be almost entirely invisible in the completed skyscraper. Mass and the company he had founded, Cosentini Associates, were responsible for designing the heating, cooling, lighting, plumbing, sewage, and elevators of the building—the heart, lungs, waste disposal, and nervous system, to adopt his anatomical analogy—and to achieve the task in such a way that the eventual occupants of the building would be entirely unaware of his methods. All they would know was that the building was warm or cool enough, supplied with enough water and power, and equipped with elevators that didn't keep them waiting more than half a minute.

Mass sometimes felt that he was expected to achieve this without using a square foot of valuable, rentable floor space in the building, that—like mechanical engineers in general—he was the least understood member of the team:

> People don't understand what I do for a living—I don't drive a railroad train, for example. My dad really never knew what I did for a living, because he couldn't understand I didn't build anything and I wasn't manufacturing anything, I was just drawing lines, and I wasn't even drawing art. He said, "People pay you to do that?" The fact is, it takes a while to explain my role to people. If you're an architect, people understand you design a building that has shape and color and form. I tell people that I do everything to make the building work. Without me the building is useless, because you can't flush the toilet.

Mass is a bulky man, with a deep voice and slightly formal way of speaking. He gives the impression that a mechanical-engineering consultant has an easy, even routine job, but this is misleading. He has been doing it for so many years that the right decisions are made, most of the time, on the basis of a seat-of-the-pants intuition that actually represents the accumulated experience of dozens of complex construction projects around Manhattan over the previous thirty-five years. His offices are lined with pictures of each of the buildings whose toilets flush thanks to Cosentini Associates. And if, years after the completion of a building, they don't, he still feels a responsibility for putting things right.

He was appointed the mechanical-engineering consultant for Worldwide Plaza on Bill Zeckendorf's personal insistence, although, since he was a popular and extremely experienced member of the small circle of New York consultants, HRH and SOM had no qualms about working with him. Mass is a member of a small group of development and construction people who meet every year to commemorate the death of Bill Zeckendorf Sr., and his connection with the family goes back to the early 1950s, when Zeckendorf Senior was Mass's first client. One of his earliest jobs was to design Zeckendorf Senior a round elevator with an exotic lighting system for his office. The work for Zeckendorf increased, although it was not particularly well paid: "We never made a lot of money on his fees, but we were able to survive. As a result of doing work for him, we got an enormous number of other clients, who said, 'If you're doing Bill Zeckendorf's work, you've got to be a pretty good engineer,' and that's how we grew. To this day I'm still doing quite a bit of the family's work, and it's quite exciting. And the son pays considerably better than the father."

In November and December 1987, as the concrete was poured on the floors up to the twenty-fifth, the ducting contractors could follow and install the vertical and horizontal channels for the various pipes, cables, and tubes. As was clear in November, the mix-up over the coordination of concrete pouring and risers had meant that this work was about four weeks behind schedule. But gradually the separate parts of the system crept toward one another, ready for the day when they would all link up and start to function. At certain points in the building, the largest pieces of equipment, such as elevator motors, transformers, and pumps, had been hoisted into position weeks before, when the building was open enough for the cranes to lower them into place. Certain areas of the building were entirely given over to the mechanicals—north and south machine rooms, east and west electrical closets—and at the eighteenth floor a significant division took place that effectively divided the building. The stale air and exhausts from the first eighteen floors were collected and expelled just above ground level; the remainder would be expelled through the roof. The hollow, pyramidal roof itself had an important function as a giant mechanical room to house some of the elevator motors and the cooling towers. These are large boxes, twenty or thirty feet across, where the warm exhaust air from the building flows through a fine spray of water. The air causes the water to evaporate, and this produces a cooling effect, similar to the way perspiration cools hot skin as it evaporates. The cooled water then circulates in a network of pipes forming part of the refrigeration system of the building and produces cold air for the air conditioning.

Over the last fifty years air conditioning in office buildings has been transformed from a luxury to a necessity as buildings have grown larger. Before World War II even the most famous skyscrapers, such as the Woolworth Building and the Empire State Building, did not have central air conditioning. The only way to stay cool in your office on a hot summer day was to open the window—always assuming you were close enough to a window to obtain the benefit. This was fine in, say, the Empire State Building, where no office was farther than twenty or thirty feet from a window, but as ambitions became grander and buildings became wider, this was impossible. Worldwide Plaza, for example, was designed for people to work fifty or sixty feet from the nearest window. Air conditioning made it possible to put more people in an office building provided you had a large enough site. In New York itself, a further development accelerated the introduction of air conditioning in office buildings. When most buildings were not air-conditioned, there was a union rule for some office workers that if the temperature exceeded ninety degrees Fahrenheit everyone could go home. With the introduction of air conditioning, an outside temperature of ninety degrees produced no discomfort inside—but everyone was still allowed to go home. The only way to get rid of the rule and its cost to companies in lost work was to fit all buildings with air conditioning, so that the problem no longer existed. The 1950s produced many millionaires as the older office buildings were "retrofitted" with central air conditioning.

As mechanical-engineering consultants, Cosentini had to design the main systems in the building and play a role in deciding which subcontractors carried out the work. The company was brought in at the earliest stages of the project, in 1985, when barely the shape of the building had been decided, let alone the detailed design. At that stage a decision about the mechanical engineering could simplify or complicate the tasks of the structural engineer or the design architect. Even in its earliest phases enough was known about the characteristics of the building for some important decisions to be made. Questions such as the overall power needs of the building, the amount of air conditioning, the volume of sewage to be disposed of, the number of sprinklers in the fire protection systems, how many elevators the building would need—all could be roughly determined from the facts and figures laid down by the developer for the amount of floor space and the approximate number of people who would work in the building. It was the job of Cosentini Associates to play around with different combinations of systems and different locations for the necessary equipment, in order to produce the most economical and effective method of fulfilling the building's needs.

Each of the building's systems depended in some way on connections outside the building, to a city-wide network that had existed for decades beneath the streets of New York. Mass put this down to the vision of the original New Yorkers: "A hundred years ago the city fathers of New York dreamed of a city that had all these buildings. And today we have a complete network of sewage pipes, storm drainage, gas, electricity, and steam in practically every street in midtown Manhattan."

Cosentini had a number of alternatives when it came to deciding how and where to design the connections for the facilities the building would need. Electricity was available on all four streets. To bring it into the building, they had to design transformer vaults beneath the street, so they chose the street that involved least interference with the rest of the construction work. There were also sewers on all four streets, and the building was connected to all of them, so that one particular sewer would not be overloaded. Clinton was mainly a residential area, and homes produce far more sewage than an office building of equivalent size. The same applies to water consumption. Another underground system is the storm-drainage network, which carries away the huge volume of water that descends on the city during a rainstorm. Although the storm sewers around Worldwide Plaza are big enough to accommodate 99 percent of all the rainwater, on occasions there is so much rain in a short space of time that the drains can fill up. Because of this, the city asked that there be some provision in Worldwide Plaza for what is known as "roof retention." The architects designed the roof so that it could hold up to three inches of water during a rainstorm, which would then be allowed to dribble slowly down into the storm sewers, avoiding overloading the system during the storm.

One other utility was available to the building. Wisps of steam arising from manholes are a familiar sight in Manhattan's potholed streets. From the tip of Manhattan up to 96th Street there is a 106-mile-long network of hot steam pipes under the streets. This system started as a way of using steam produced in the power stations of Consolidated Edison. Water is heated, by coal or gas or oil, to produce steam to turn power generators, but after the steam has done its job it is still very hot. It soon became clear that it was a valuable resource in its own right, to be used for heating buildings, and nowadays Con Edison produces twenty-eight billion pounds of steam a year and pipes it around the city at a pressure of 150 pounds a square inch and a temperature of nearly two hundred degrees centigrade.

Each of the skyscraper's systems needed to be connected to one or more of the city's utilities. Heating and ventilation—HVAC for short—needed water, steam, and electricity; the building's plumbing had to be connected to the water main and the sewage system; the elevators needed power for their motors.

One of the most important factors in working out the cost of the mechanical systems was the amount of space that they would take up. Some of the necessary pieces of equipment were the size of a small house, and these had to be fitted into the building so that they would not take up too much prime space. Mass described the problem:

> Nobody wants us to take up space. Every square inch of space I take is lost rent because they can't rent the space, or it's a volume they've got to build which costs money. I'm always asking for a little more than I really need. The architect knows I'm asking for more, so he squeezes me down to what he thinks I really need; then along comes the operating engineer, the man who's got to really run that building, and he looks at that space and says, "Oh, my God, it's not big enough, and I should have had more." So I have to prove to him he can work in tight spaces, but space is money. Space is time. It's sometimes very difficult to explain to a developer or a builder or even an architect why I need certain things. All he can see is that it's taking more space up and it's costing more money.
>
> For instance, the heating system for the lobbies of the building is critical, because the lobby is used before the building is finished, with the top still open to the air, and many of the windows not yet installed. The designed heating system can't possibly heat that lobby if the building is still open. So we try to provide enough extra heating for the lobby. The minute I provide more

heat, I need more space; there are more grilles, more architectural implications. But in the long run I know I'm going to win, because if the building was to open up and be too cold they'd come back at me, so I have to fight that battle from day one. And it goes on. I can go through hundreds of different items the same as this in the building. I'm constantly fighting for my space and making claim to my territory, like the territorial prerogative.

Mass has fought enough battles with enough architects less experienced than he is to know that he is right: "The whole magic of our industry is twofold. One is to build a beautiful building but, more important, it's got to be successful. The only way it becomes successful is if you start collecting rent. The sooner you start collecting rent, the sooner the building becomes more successful. The minute you start collecting rent, all the sins of the fathers are forgiven. Everything that we've done wrong they forget about— we're all friends again."

Asking for more space than necessary is sometimes more than a game. The need for power and air and cooling has multiplied in a very short time, as the technology of work has changed. Computers, faxes, and the increased use of telephone lines for data transmission have meant that tenants find that buildings designed for the office environment of even ten years ago cannot cope with the increased demands for electricity to power the equipment, and air conditioning to carry away the heat generated by the increased electronic activity. There is nowhere to put it all without lowering ceilings or raising floors. Today's new office building will have much more space designed between the floors, to take the increased amount of cabling and ducting that is required. Because he doesn't want his buildings to be caught in a similar trap in the future, Mass pushes for every extra inch of space for the mechanical equipment, now or in the future: "More and more of the tenants that are coming into the buildings are not so much asking, 'What color is the marble?' or 'How many toilet seats do you have?' They're now asking, 'What provisions do you have for me to expand my office functions?' If you build a building that can be expandable in the future without tearing it apart, that makes the building successful."

A measure of Mass's claim to be the least understood member of the team is the overall cost of the mechanical engineering in the skyscraper. The materials and labor costs of the various mechanical and electrical systems take up about 30 percent of the total construction cost of the building. Then there is the cost of the floor area occupied by the equipment, 6 or 8 percent of the total. If you add to that the volume of space that is occupied—between the floors, through the ducts and pipes, in the various machine rooms—Mass estimates that the mechanical and electrical systems account for 60 percent of the cost of the whole building.

Like HRH, Mass and his colleagues must take into account the special requirements of New York's unions and of the city regulations when planning what to put in the building and how to install it. One or two examples show the minefield the Worldwide Plaza team operated in. If Mass decided that the building needed a fan capable of moving air at less than twenty-nine thousand cubic feet per minute, he could order one from any manufacturer in the world, who would assemble it and deliver it complete to the site. If he needed a fan with a throughput *greater* than twenty-nine thousand cubic feet per minute, the components of the fan would have to be brought to New York and assembled with local labor. A refrigerator cannot be installed by a member of the electricians' union, even though he can deal with the cabling and the plug: it must be fitted by a member of the steamfitters' union, because it is classified as a heating device. Every wrinkle like this affects the cost of the job, because each union member is paid at a different rate. Even such a mundane matter as delivering a piece of equipment to the right part of the site and opening its box is fraught with complexity: a lighting fixture, for example, can't be delivered to the floor; it has to be delivered to the street, where an electrician picks it up and brings it to the floor. Laborers on the site may carry the boxes away but are not allowed to open them.

The winter of 1987–88 was a peak time for many of these events to take place at the Worldwide site. Each subcontractor was delivering pieces of equipment and installing them, as soon as the necessary piping, ducting, or cabling reached the appropriate floor. It was a worrying time for Cosentini as they tried to achieve the impossible task of simultaneously supervising a dozen different subcontractors and ensuring that their work was done properly. And because it was winter, there was an extra problem, as Mass explained:

> There's a tendency on the part of the tradesmen that when they are putting a pipe in or a duct in or a piece of wire in in very cold conditions, they want to get out of there as fast as they can, and we find that that's when we get sloppy installations. We don't get pipes properly supported, for example, and the equipment isn't installed the way it's supposed to be. It's just put in so that the man can get his job done and get out as fast as possible. We go around the building and draw up "punch lists" to pick up all those items before any damage occurs.

With the chain of command that can operate in a complex subcontracting job, it is not always easy to allot blame for poor work. If a contractor employs a trade that buys materials or other skills as part of *its* contract, mistakes can occur at any point in the chain. But for HRH and the Zeckendorf group, provided the design was not at fault and there were no last-minute changes, they would require any errors to be corrected at the expense of the contractor they were paying. It would then be up to him to sort out where blame really lay. On Worldwide Plaza, as on any complex project, there were daily examples of things going wrong. Most of them were easy to correct on the spot, like the steel misfabrication on the forty-second floor; a few needed minor or major compromises in the design or construction, so that they didn't make any differ-ence to the overall design or cost of the building; and one or two might linger on as lawsuits long after the building was occupied.

While Mass and his team were compiling their punch lists, HRH and SOM were also coming to terms with the huge number of details that had to be attended to as the whole building began to develop a finished look to it. For the first time since the exca-vators, the end was in sight for some of the large subcontractors. But before any job "signed off," someone from HRH had to certify that the work had been done satisfactorily. If it hadn't, the sub-contractors would not get paid the final installment of their fee, the "retention." Unfortunately, there was to be no signing off yet for those working on the task of enclosing the lower floors of the build-ing. On April 15, 1988, the day when O&M were to have been officially allowed to move their subcontractors in to start work on their premises, the lower floors still showed huge gaps where they were meant to be enclosed and weatherproofed. It looked as though about three-quarters of the work still had to be done. The longer the delay in enclosing the floors, the more penalties O&M could exact from Zeckendorf for late occupancy. In fact, O&M people had already started preliminary work on their floors, allowed as a favor by the owner, and part of a game that would have to be played quite carefully by each side. One side would make a point of legal obligations that had not been met by the other, while the other would look for any contributory factor that mitigated the offense. During the next year, the issue of when O&M would start to pay rent to the owners became a source of endless argument and po-sitioning by the two parties, even though O&M were themselves an equity partner in the building.

For the steel erectors, the end really was in sight, as the teams of ironworkers reached the forty-sixth floor at the end of April, nearly completing the entire steel structure up to the point at which the copper roof would be erected. This symbolic achievement would be traditionally marked by the "topping-out" ceremony and party, which Dominic Fonti would have to organize for a budget of $18,000, along with other, more pressing tasks.

Friday, May 6, 1988, was a day of rain. New York had experienced a wet six weeks or so, and Friday was no exception. The mood throughout the project seemed damp and confused. Fonti looked and felt as though he had been twelve rounds in a boxing ring, as problem after problem piled on his head from all sides:

> I have some bad days and some worse days. Lately it's been very difficult—everything's coming together. But the only way to remain sane is that if I have twenty problems I try not to grasp all twenty at the same time, because if I did I'd lose my senses. I try to look at which problem is most pressing, to resolve that, and try to sort of push that along. I try to give secondary problems to my other associates in the office, try to give them some concept of how to do it and what result to expect, and, hopefully, they're good enough to be able to push it. I mean, I can't make it happen all by myself—there's a lot of people involved with this project.

Information flow, never particularly good on this project in spite of the flood of memos, bulletins, advisory notices, and letters, had dwindled to an all-time low, partly because the site telephones were out of order. Ed Narbutas had tried fruitlessly to call the site and in desperation sent a fax to ask anyone to ring him. But of course the fax, being transmitted by telephone lines, got no farther than SOM's fax machine. Rumors abounded in this "infofog." One in particular—and one source of Fonti's headaches—was that the steel erectors had walked out. Some said that Mosher Steel themselves had walked out in the wake of a disagreement over who paid for the lintels and other changes. Hurried meetings were called from HRH to Zeckendorf's, and Fonti trudged across Manhattan in the rain to find out what was happening. It was a week when everyone was discussing cost overruns that were more than the usual, everyday few percentage points that people accepted. Some of these were laid at Mosher's door by HRH, who were in turn being gotten at by Zeckendorf. It could well be that Mosher, sensing the possibility that their bills might seriously be challenged—and payment refused—were threatening to pull out, or at least stop work temporarily until the matter was sorted out. Any stoppage now would only add to the schedule problems Fonti already faced, now that the April 15 deadline had passed. And in the midst of all this he had to organize the printing of the peaked caps, T-shirts, and balloons that were an obligatory feature of the topping-out party.

Much of life has rituals, conscious or unconscious, and the construction industry is no exception. The practical significance of topping out is virtually nil. There was certainly no longer any specific significance in the date chosen, May 20. A building like Worldwide Plaza is built by such a series of parallel and superimposed activities that there are very few clearly distinguishable key moments in its life. Topping out is meant to mark the emplacement of the final piece of the steel in the steel structure, but—with a schedule that was continually changing by a day here and a day there, an erection crew that were to stay on to put up the metal framework of the roof, and the need to set a date for the ceremony several weeks ahead—the actual date had very little to do with the stage the building had reached. The original date had been May 6, until one final factor intervened. Because of the old Madison Square Garden's links to basketball, someone had suggested that a suitable celebrity to invite to the ceremony would be Willis Reed, the basketball star. However, Reed was not free on May 6, but would be on May 20. The ceremony had to be on a Friday, because the general conviviality of the topping-out party would render many construction workers unfit for further work, particularly at height, and they could be sent home for the rest of the day and the weekend.

If there were two individuals for whom the day would be expected to have particular significance, they probably would be the developer and a steelworker. But for Bill Zeckendorf the ceremony seemed little more than an irritant:

If I had my way I wouldn't even have one. It really is for the workers—that's where it started. It used to start with the steelworkers. They'd have it on Friday and then they'd take the day off and drink beer. Now they're making a PR event out of it, but from my standpoint it's really a nonevent. I have to show up, of course. It's all part of the public relations thing, but I will be surprised if it even gets in the newspapers. You know, they have to use a basketball player putting a ball in a basket as a reminder of the Madison Square Garden site to get enough interest. It seems pretty farfetched to me.

He was not in any case a man who was at his best at parties, and he had a few other things to think about on that day anyway.

On Friday mornings, at about eight-thirty, Zeckendorf would meet Terry Soderberg and Jack Schuster, and sometimes someone from HRH, to discuss how the project was going. On this particular Friday, there was no one from HRH, which was perhaps just as well, since Zeckendorf came away from the meeting seriously considering whether to use HRH on any of his future projects, on the basis of what he was told by Soderberg and Schuster about the delays on the project.

The meeting started innocuously enough, as the three men sat around in the armchairs in Zeckendorf's office. Soderberg described the plans for the topping-out ceremony and, in particular, the ceremonial signing of the last beam to go on the building, by all the main participants in the project: "They didn't want to use spray paint, which is more appropriate for New York, so they're using Magic Marker and painting a section of the beam white." They discussed the need to find ways of preventing the prospective tenants from seeing too much of the exterior of the building and realizing how incomplete it was: "I'm kind of hoping that a lot of them will just leave the site around two-fifteen or two-thirty. It might make it easier, but it's going to come up eventually, so if they see it they see it. We can't hide it."

Then came the bad news. Soderberg prefaced it with a crumb of comfort: "There will be no problem at all with enclosing the sixth to the eighteenth floors for the tenants, none at all. But two to five is going to be a major problem, no matter what we do. We're working weekends, we've got two twelve-hour shifts for setting of pre-cast and granite in the trusses. Jack said we had one option, which was to shut the subway down and work for a couple of weeks, but if we shut them down we'll just be dead. There's not enough money or hours or anything we can throw at it to get two to five totally enclosed per the lease."

Zeckendorf looked stunned. In a more than usually clipped tone he said: "That's just terrible, that's terrible—how much will this delay the opening?"

Soderberg thought for a moment. "Let's say it's the third, fourth, and fifth floors; optimistically it's three weeks; pessimistically or realistically, as Jack looks at it, it's more like five or six weeks. When the granite trusses are hung we could work around the clock with the Sheetrock, but there is no way to make a July 1 date physically."

The implication was clear: the delay in enclosing the floors could give O&M the excuse to delay paying rent, and also allow them to claim a penalty payment based on the amount of time they would have to stay on in their existing premises. Zeckendorf asked Soderberg what the cost of the delay would be.

"You're looking at $1.8 million."

Schuster chipped in with the suggestion that they activate a *force-majeure* clause in the contract, to avoid paying the penalty.

"Jack, it's not going to work," said Zeckendorf, and then he added with some exasperation, "How did we ever fall so far behind?"

"Bill," said Soderberg, "I think we were overly optimistic. We can control everything that we can control here in the United States. The drywall, the electrician, all of those trades were controllable. But we couldn't control the Italian stone and we couldn't control the Canadian pre-cast, and they're massive jobs, they're very difficult, complicated jobs, and we lost control of it, and once the die was cast there was no way that we could throw the contractor out and bring somebody else in without compounding the problem. We bought a problem and we're now suffering for it."

"And the other problem," added Soderberg, "was with the control problems of the US Granite Company. We had no one running the job for them. I mean, the stone's been there in slabs since January, but no one's given them the information."

"But isn't that really our fault for not having supervised them?" Zeckendorf asked.

"It's HRH's fault, yes," Schuster said, making sure there was no ambiguity about who was to blame. Soderberg didn't entirely agree on this point:

"I'm not sure of that, because HRH did everything they could. But how do you force a company to put somebody on if they say they're adequate to do the job? They were thrashing around and blaming everybody in sight. I don't know whether I'd be in a position to say it was HRH's fault. They tried their damnedest, we all tried our damnedest."

He then referred to the fact that Hunts Point were by far the lowest bidder for the stone contract, by at least $1.5 million: "I'm not convinced, Bill, that, had we not given it to them, had we given it to, let's say, the second bidder and given that $1.5-million premium or whatever it was, that we would have been any better off than we are now."

There was no mistaking Zeckendorf's thoughtful mood as he returned to his desk. This delay, with its potential cost implications, was the latest factor in a steadily rising cost overrun for the building. For Zeckendorf, normally protected from the day-to-day vicissitudes of the project, these costs were more of a surprise than they were to the others. The estimating process carried out by HRH on the basis of SOM's drawings had produced a construction budget of about $145 million and a general-conditions figure—paid to HRH— of about $12.5 million. Now the totals were looking more like $154

million and $16.8 million, and everyone had different reasons for
the overspend. But one thing couldn't be denied: for whatever reason, HRH's estimate was wrong. Within HRH, people were already
worrying that the magnitude of the underestimate would jeopardize
any future relationship with Zeckendorf; they were right. There
was even discussion of whether O&M might sue Zeckendorf over
the delay, and Zeckendorf in turn sue HRH.

Looking back on the meeting later and on Zeckendorf's reaction, Soderberg explained the dilemma that he and Schuster
faced:

> It's a question of when you really run a red flag up. There were
> some very heated battles, is, I guess, the polite way to say it,
> between HRH and Jack and I, and between Jack and I and Bill
> about what happened and the causes of it. We told him what we
> felt at the end of the day the cost would be. The unfortunate
> thing with HRH is that there was a period of time when no one
> was watching the hen house and things got a little bit out of
> hand and no one knew how out of hand they were until some
> time really in January, February, when it all sort of mushroomed.

While Zeckendorf spent his morning on calls, correspondence,
and meetings in connection with a dozen other projects, the activity
on Worldwide Plaza was concentrated on the party preparations at
the bottom of the building, and routine steel erection at the top.
Wiggy's team had been chosen to install the "final" beam, to be
hoisted from the ground level after it had been signed by partners,
managers, and representatives of the various crafts. Pete Marquis,
working in the warm spring sun 650 feet up in the air, was almost
as blasé about the celebration as Zeckendorf had been: "I guess
it's really a big deal for the owners of the company, but for me it
gives me a good chance to finish early on Friday so I can get home.
The work ain't over yet for us. We still have a derrick to put up,
we got this big monster crane to take down, and maybe we're talking

another few weeks, a month left to go." He looked across the street to a hole that was being excavated two blocks away. "That's where I'm going next," he said. "A couple of my buddies from home are already starting to put up a kangaroo crane there, and I'll be joining them soon." For someone who had had such an intimate relationship with Worldwide Plaza he seemed remarkably unaware of some important facts about the building. "I guess I'm just hired to come put up this building—I know it's supposed to be a big famous building, but that's all I really know. What's the owner's name? Zeckendorf? I never in my whole life heard of him, but, then, I don't suppose he's heard of Pete Marquis."

Across the street from the site was a small building that was being used as a sales office. On the first floor a table had been set for a lunch that had been arranged for the partners. It would be a chance to catch up on the financing of the building before they joined the topping-out ceremony. At about twelve-thirty the group assembled. Soderberg and Zeckendorf were there from the Zeckendorf Company, Arthur Cohen from Arthur G. Cohen Properties, Victor Elmaleh and Frank Stanton from World Wide, and two representatives of Kumagai Gumi.

It was more of a social occasion than a formal partners' meeting, but the group used the opportunity to explore some of the options for future financing of the project. A project as big and expensive as Worldwide Plaza is financed in two phases. There is a construction loan, from banks and financial institutions, which is short-term and covers the costs incurred during the period of construction. This money is usually lent at high rates of interest because of the general uncertainty inherent in an unleased building. Then, as the leasing picture becomes clearer, the partners would want to seek a longer-term loan at more favorable interest rates from different sources, which were less interested in profit than in long-term security. This second loan could be used partly to pay off the first loan and partly to cover the continuing costs of running the project until the rents reached a level where the whole thing became self-financing and, everyone hoped, profit-making.

Some of the preliminary possibilities for the longer-term loan were laid before the partners by Arthur Cohen, from whose lips tripped the complex terminology of finance as if it were a grocery shopping list: ". . . straight debt financing . . . convertible mortgage . . . commercial paper . . . $500-million credit enhancement . . . sixty-day remarketable paper . . . seventy-five basis point savings . . . protect your upside . . . a little bit of a zero coupon . . ." In a final, dramatic flourish to a five-minute monologue Cohen finished with: "What'll happen is we'll catch a low in the market, get a right rate, and lock it into the ten-year fixed rate. Sooner or later we'll catch something." The partners all nodded wisely in agreement.

At one o'clock 49th Street at the Eighth Avenue end was filling up with knots of people. A trolleyload of Budweisers was wheeled across the pavement and into the hoist. Three cans per man had been ordered, twenty-four hundred in all. Fonti was fussing over a small dais with microphone, where speeches would be made. A video crew from O&M were filming Bob McGarry talking about the forthcoming ceremony. A large white-painted beam had been placed on stands in front of the south-side lobby, and two men were now fixing a basketball net to it. The ceremony displayed a certain randomness in the order in which things happened and didn't quite seem to know when to start. The partners had drifted over in ones and twos after their lunch, and they stood under the canopy of the nightclub called Better Days. Soderberg and Fonti were chatting to Willis Reed about historic moments in basketball; either of them might have been expected to give the signal to start the proceedings, but neither of them did. The sun was breaking through after a week of solid rain, lighting up the areas of brick that stretched up to the twentieth story on the south side.

At one-thirty Soderberg started handing out felt-tipped markers for the important figures among the assembled people to write their names on the beam. Rob Schubert, with his new angle on the building, stepped forward to sign the beam. Fonti, of course, and each of the partners, and someone from O&M took turns. The individual workers were represented by the names of each of the main craft unions.

Up on the forty-sixth floor, Wiggy, Pete, and the rest of team A were waiting for the signal to lift the last beam. Zeckendorf stepped forward with a few prepared words to mark the occasion. Unfortunately, the dais and microphone had been put in the wrong position, and so he spoke without them. With unerring accuracy, Willis Reed put the basketball into the net attached to the beam. This was less of a challenge than it might have been, since he was nearly seven feet tall and the net was within reach of his hand. He did it again for the cameras, and again, and then handed the ball to other important bystanders to throw, including a surprised Bill Zeckendorf.

It was time for the party. Bankers, accountants, architects, and advertising men and women stepped their way through the rubble toward the outside hoists that carried them to the sixth floor. Some of them found their way through the mazelike interior of the building to the spanking-new elevators, some of which were now working. In the bare surroundings of the south side of the sixth floor, blue balloons relieved the grayness and temporary lights showed the way to trestle tables with ham and salad rolls, hot dogs, hamburgers, and cakes. A Little Richard lookalike sang rock hits with a deafening backing and, in a gathering where the ratio of men to women was about a hundred to one, burly bejeaned male construction workers danced energetically with one another to the music. Fonti suggested that the party was a good test of the strength of Gary Steficek's structure. On the whole, office floors were not designed for the weight of eight hundred people, particularly when some of them were dancing.

There was little or no mingling of social groups. The construction workers in their working clothes were clearly distinguishable from the suited architects, construction managers, and eminent guests. In the midst of the hubbub, Zeckendorf could be seen in a huddle with Schuster. They were discussing whom they should choose to manage the construction of the next Zeckendorf project. Various well-known New York construction managers were mentioned, but not HRH. The morning's news had clearly had a major impact on Zeckendorf's views of HRH's competence.

When it was decent to do so, Zeckendorf sloped off across the concrete floor to the southwest hoist, and took it down to the ground floor, sharing it with another member of the project team, a laborer who clearly didn't know whom he was traveling with. He got into his chauffeur-driven car and headed back to the Zeckendorf offices on East 59th Street, to develop more buildings.

By about 4:00 P.M. the party was winding down. The men in suits had left, and many of the workers had taken the opportunity, like Pete Marquis, of going home early, although few of them were driving to Montreal. Fonti was tired but happy, happier than for weeks. "It's one of the fringe benefits for all the tension and pressures that you feel throughout—throughout the eighteen months that it takes to put up a fifty-story office. This is where you can let your hair down and relax and, as you can see, a lot of workers are doing the same. A lot of planning went into this to make this successful, and I'm happy that everyone is enjoying themselves, including me." As he walked back to his office on the second floor, he was carrying the basketball under his arm, autographed by Willis Reed. But unfortunately it was not his to keep: "It has already been claimed by Terry Soderberg. Since he's the real owner's representative on the project, he's the one who controls the dollars. He said, 'Dominic, it's my ball, I've paid for it, I want it.' So he's getting it."

In the following weeks Zeckendorf's unhappiness with HRH became more widely known. Artie Nusbaum put a brave face on the situation, but his habitual joviality was tempered by a "more-in-sorrow-than-in-anger" mood. As happens sooner or later with anyone who is good at delegating, things had gone too far. The way Nusbaum saw it, it wasn't HRH's fault that Zeckendorf suddenly found out about the problems. Every cost overrun had been reported to, and approved by, Soderberg and Schuster. It wasn't Nusbaum's job to go to Zeckendorf and say, "You do realize that the costs are going up, don't you?" He felt he had a right to assume that the information was getting back to source and duly being noted. But this was not the case, or hadn't been until May:

> My main problem is the feeling of the owner that we deserted him. I find that an unbelievable position on his part, because we broke our ass and I really feel we did a good job. I take it very personally that he does not understand who are the guys with the white hats and who are the guys with the black hats, and I think I'm a white-hatter. I don't think that he's going to give HRH any more work, and that's unfortunate, because we did a good job. I think it's easier to blame them than to look at his own staff. I feel it's a failure that I didn't go up and talk to him personally. But Mr. Zeckendorf is a fairly private person. If it had happened with some of the other owners I would have no problem picking up the phone and telling him, "Hey, what you're doing is stupid. Do you understand where your money's going?" But Mr. Zeckendorf puts a whole line of people between himself and the construction manager, and it was my assumption that those people were telling him the news, good or bad. But evidently they were not. Shame on me.

15

COPPER AND DIAMOND

You can't tell an architect not to draw something. If he wants architecture and the owner's willing to pay for it, hey, it's our job to execute it.

—ARTIE NUSBAUM, HRH

The peak is up forty-seven stories. To build that kind of a peak of copper on top of which you're planting a glass crown, with all of the difficulties that go with it which we haven't even seen yet, is scary. To me it's scary. I think it's going to be the toughest part of the job.

—JACK SCHUSTER

At the beginning of 1988, once the steel was two-thirds up, the project switched into a higher gear, with many of the operations taking place simultaneously. At this stage many of the inevitable problems were ones that could not be solved by time—there wasn't enough to go around. The intertwined momenta of the stone, the bricks, the pre-cast meant that at times Schuster had no alternative but to agree to a change order or a quick and dirty solution to a problem that might have been sorted out more cheaply had Dominic

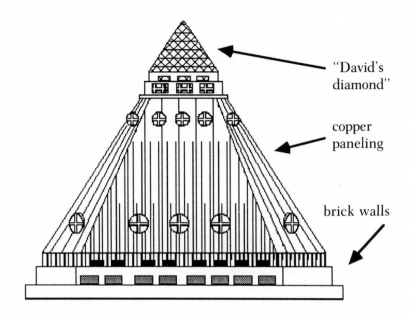

"David's diamond"

copper paneling

brick walls

Fonti, Ed Narbutas, and the rest had the time to give it care and attention.

One other component of the building contributed to the pressure: the roof. Although the last major element to be installed, it had been a constant preoccupation since way back in 1985 and 1986, during the design stage. But it became a major cause of timetable pressure only in 1988, when the pieces started to be brought to the site.

Ever since the first sketches were made of the tower, the roof was to be an important visual feature of Worldwide Plaza. In fact, from the earliest days it was clear that this was not to be a *roof* in the true sense of the word. The real roof would be the concreted and waterproofed surface of the forty-eighth floor. The architects considered putting a spire on top, like the one on the Chrysler Building, but discovered that the city approval process would take too long, and they settled for a kind of eight-sided pyramid. This would be, to all intents and purposes, a sloping curtain wall with holes in it.

Why Worldwide Plaza has a fancy roof was purely for architectural reasons. It formed the third element of a three-layer concept, with stone at the bottom and brick in the middle. In David Childs's words, it embodied "the energy of the building," and Jim Bodnar saw it as bringing "a piece of color to that portion of the skyline which is lacking now." In some ways, as Artie Nusbaum pointed out, the roof was a throwback to the recent past:

> If you look at the buildings around the city built in the thirties and forties—the Chrysler Building, the Empire State Building— all of them had a lot of architecture on their roofs. I find the roofs of most buildings more interesting than the lobbies. But from World War II on architects just ignored the roofs completely. Now architects are going back up onto the roof, influenced to a large extent by the Citicorp building, where the architect was the first one to say, "Hey, the roof's got to look as good as the lobby and floor level do." I don't know if I have any feelings about the look. I like the roof. I'm interested to see if we can execute it as good as the architect would like to see it. Notice how I change right away into thinking about how to build it more than what it looks like. I think the taste is in my mouth.

Nusbaum's appetite for construction challenges was to be more than satisfied by the task that faced HRH in carrying out SOM's wishes. As a construction manager, Nusbaum saw his role as more interventionist than if he had been a general contractor, expected to make the roof by whatever method SOM first suggested. A construction manager's job is to look at the cost implications of construction methods and to come up with better or cheaper ideas if he can.

Four main aspects of the roof provided opportunities for such intervention, and Nusbaum made the most of them: the issue of color—the architects suggested a copper roof because they wanted green; the question of how to construct the roof, which didn't have to be done the way Childs's and Bodnar's initial design drawings suggested; the issue of what to do with the space under the roof; and the technicalities of dealing with the interface between the roof and the rest of the building. Some of these topics led to complex and sometimes expensive remedies' being adopted to solve problems that nobody anticipated, although they might have been expected to.

Color was an issue because of the specific qualities of copper, the material chosen by SOM for the roof's exterior coating. New copper coming out of the mill in thin sheets is a familiar shiny brown. But Childs decided to use it because of the green patina it acquires after fifteen or twenty years of weathering. And he seemed quite happy to live with the fact that for the first two decades of its life the roof of his building would not have the final color he had chosen for it.

In 1986, as HRH began to cost the plans, it became clear that an all-copper roof would be expensive. Quite appropriately, HRH made some suggestions to save money, including reconsidering the materials for the roof. They didn't see why the desired green color couldn't be achieved by painting some other, cheaper surface material. But they picked on a topic the architects regarded as nonnegotiable. Furthermore, SOM didn't even want the issue to be raised, in case it actually seemed a good idea to the owner. Rob Schubert took every opportunity at every meeting and in every piece of paperwork to make sure that whenever the word "roof" came up it was invariably accompanied by the word "copper": "I would be reminded every once in a while when I didn't correct them, by Jim or David or whoever, 'This is a copper roof, guys, just keep that in the budget.' I told everyone at HRH, 'There are a few buttons you can push with us that will make us explode. One of them is copper. Don't mess with the copper. Keep it copper, don't paint it green. These are the places where you don't fool around.' "

So the color issue was resolved without difficulty. In the early days, when pressure on costs was not as great as it later became, it was easy for HRH and the owners to give in gracefully and accept the luxury of an expensive material because the architects wanted it.

Next in the planning stage for the roof was the matter of how to build it. This was where Nusbaum's combination of great experience and desire to innovate came to the fore:

> The architect had drawn a traditional copper roof—he did it the way it had been done hundreds, mabye thousands, of years, using new materials, but doing it as everyone else has done it. While we were working on the design and development, it occurred to me we could build this whole top of the building differently than anybody has ever done it. We suggested this method to the architect. He said, "Fine, if you can make it work." He pretty much left it up to us to make it work. What are we doing that's unique? Traditionally you'd build a copper roof by building a whole substructure. Modern technology says you use metal deck, you apply plywood to the metal deck, you apply waterproofing to the plywood, and then on top of that you put your roll-out copper. To do all this you need to erect scaffolding all around the outside of the top of the building, and it would probably take six to eight months to build the roof this way. We felt that we could do it better using the technology of building a curtain wall. Now, a curtain wall gets built from the floor, without outside scaffolding. So we felt we could make these copper panels up in a factory and then hoist them to the top of the building with a derrick, and leave them on the floor and have the contractor who made the panels install them on the steel, which had already been prepared to receive these panels. By doing that, we would have only one trade working from the floor, instead of four trades and the big scaffolding.

Now, if you think about what the cost of the land is, and the cost of the building, the interest alone on this building at the time we reach there will be $2.5 or $3 million a month. So every month we can cut off the top of this building and open it is money in the owner's pocket. In addition, the method we're doing is probably half the price, mainly because of the money saved by getting rid of all the field labor and the scaffolding.

Nusbaum was very proud of this solution and pointed out how it was one consequence of the owner's employing a construction manager rather than a general contractor: "If we were a general contractor instead of a construction manager, we would never have had an opportunity to have this input. The architect would have drawn his plans. It would have been in a traditional way, all built from outside scaffolding, and it would get done. It is not in a general contractor's best interest to suggest cheaper alternatives. There's no point. Maybe, after he got the job, he would suggest this method and put the money saved in his pocket, but he certainly wouldn't be there during the design development to even suggest it. So it just wouldn't occur."

So the plan was to find a company that would prefabricate the copper panels and dormer windows away from the site, and bring them when they were needed to be hoisted up to the pyramid-shaped skeleton framework to be built above the forty-eighth floor. The panels would then be stored and installed from the inside.

The broad outlines of this construction method were explored very early on in the design process, during 1985 and 1986. A working group including design and construction people looked at the early designs and tried to find ways in which the roof could be divided into panels that would be easy to prefabricate. Bodnar also looked at the purely decorative elements, to see if they could be simplified in some way. There was a series of "standing seams" on the roof: vertical ridges of copper which in a traditional copper roof indicated where the copper panels meet and are folded over to seal

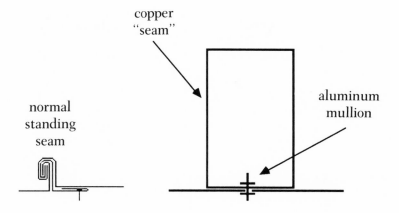

the joint. To be functional, the seams need to be only an inch or two above the surface.

With the Worldwide Plaza roof, there was no need for the copper to be linked via such seams since it was being prefabricated in panels, but Childs and Bodnar had felt that it would provide an interesting texture to the roof to incorporate "false" standing seams that were large enough to be visible from the ground and to create shadows on the copper roof. These seams would have to be seven or eight inches high and specially manufactured as separate roof elements. Since their sole purpose was decoration, they could theoretically be placed on the roof in whatever pattern the designers liked, and their first designs were based on what seemed the most pleasing proportions. But it turned out that the copper paneling could be fabricated only in certain widths, which were not an even multiple of the space between the steel members of the framework that SOM had designed and ordered from Mosher. As a final constraint, the architects had to pay some attention to the costs. The narrower the copper, the more seams there would have to be, and that would involve expensive fabrication.

As soon as the SOM architects started to draw the three-dimensional layout of these seams, they came across one irritating design problem. There were four wide faces on the roof, separated

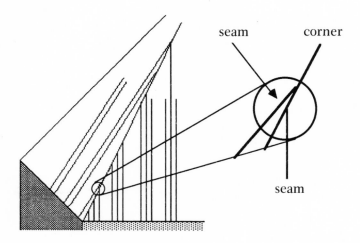

by four narrow faces. Because of the tapered nature of each of the eight sides of the roof, the vertical seams on a face would meet the sloping edge at a certain point. But there was no easy way to make the seams on adjacent sides meet at the same point on the corner. If the seams were regularly spaced across a face, they intersected the corners at different places from the seams on the adjacent face.

If the seams were designed to meet at the corners, they could not be regularly spaced across the face. Various models were made and placed around the main drawing floor of SOM, and small knots of architects would cluster around and argue the merits of various arrangements of seams. In the end, the architects decided to live with the fact that the standing seams didn't meet at the corners and hope that nobody would notice or worry about it.

During this design period, Nusbaum had another bright idea to save the developer money. In the original plans, the roof space was to be largely empty. Then Marvin Mass, the mechanical engineer, commandeered some of it, as a useful place to put his cooling towers: "Until about 1981 every building built in the United States, especially in New York, had a flat roof, so I was able to put my cooling tower there. Then suddenly along came the 'nouvelle cui-

sine' with roofs that had characteristic shapes, and it was almost
impossible for us to take this piece of equipment and just plop it
on top of the roof. With Worldwide Plaza we had to integrate the
cooling tower with what the roof looked like, and David Childs and
I found a way to use the empty space under the copper panels."

Looking at the early designs, Nusbaum realized that even with
the cooling towers in the roof a lot of free space was still available.
The plans also had most of the forty-seventh floor occupied by more
mechanical equipment—elevator motors, pump rooms, electrical
machine rooms, and so on:

"When we first saw the 'tepee' on top, it was all hollow except
for a cooling tower in it. What we did, with Skidmore's cooperation,
was to push everything up into the tepee. So, whereas originally it
was all hollow, now if you go up in it you'll find all the elevator-
machine rooms up in there, the pump rooms, and even a floor of
tenants. And we were able to release one whole floor of the building
by pushing it up in there."

What's more, the floor space that was now available would be
a highly desirable penthouse floor able to generate another ten
thousand square feet of rental income for the owner.

With these two decisions—building the roof from the inside
and moving the mechanical equipment into the roof—Nusbaum
felt he had more than justified his reputation as New York's leading construction manager. The savings that would accrue to the
Zeckendorf group would have paid his salary many times over. In
the light of Zeckendorf's subsequent disillusionment with HRH,
Nusbaum was perhaps entitled to feel aggrieved that all this good
work was forgotten: "We lowered the budget, saved a lot of money.
But I don't think they wish to recognize that. They assume anybody would have done the same thing, you know, so I feel a little
bitterness."

But one of the things that made it difficult for Zeckendorf and
Schuster, in particular, to see these early decisions as entirely ben-
eficial was the fact that in the months after HRH had made these

suggestions and begun to act on them a good deal of the financial benefit was dissipated by a series of blunders.

One of the subsequent problems was the fact that costly changes had to be made to the support system for the roof. As a purely decorative element, albeit a huge one, the roof and its steel frame had been designed to be comparatively light. It still had to be structurally sound, but the main loads that had to be considered were wind loads rather than gravity loads. As with the rest of the building, the roof design was tested early on in the Western Ontario wind tunnel. As a hollow "tent" with holes in it, the surface would get wind loads of up to fifty pounds a square foot applied to the inside and the outside at the same time. The surface weighed only about three pounds a square foot, and so these tests were necessary, as Rob Schubert put it, "to prevent the roof from ending up on Tenth Avenue."

Nusbaum pointed out at early meetings with SOM that the changes in function for the roof space must be accompanied by changes in structural strength. The poles of the "tent" now had to support intermediate floors carrying some of the heavy mechanical equipment, and that would also be used to store the copper panels to be installed from the inside. So Gary Steficek had to calculate how to reinforce the steel so that in combination with the strength of the concrete floors it would do the new job required of it, and he then had to issue change bulletins to Mosher—which resulted in late and expensive refabrication.

In making the supporting aluminum framework and the copper panels, SOM and HRH would have to pay special attention to a corrosion problem that arose because they were using different metals. If different metals make contact in the presence of rainwater, a weak electricity can flow between them. Essentially, the metal-rainwater-metal combination acts like a battery, because rainwater is acidic. The normal advice to builders about to build sheet-metal roofs with different metals is "Don't." There is a list of

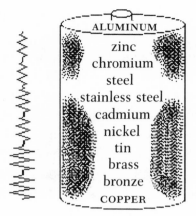

metals that corrode when used together on roofs, arranged in a hierarchy. The wider apart the metals in the list, the more severe the corrosion. Aluminum is at the top of the list and copper is at the bottom. HRH could not have picked a worse combination. By putting cooling towers in the roof space, they were also adding to the general moistness of the environment. And the situation was made even more interesting by the use of stainless-steel screws to link the copper to the aluminum so that there were actually three metals that could come in contact.

If a solution to the problem wasn't found, the steady contact between screw and metals over years of New York rain would have eaten away at the aluminum until the screw holes became too large to hold the screws. At this point the copper panels could fly away in the next breeze. There was a series of meetings during 1987, with HRH and SOM, particularly Ed Narbutas, trying to come up with a satisfactory way of prefabricating the roof and minimizing corrosion. At times the situation threatened to jeopardize Nusbaum's whole new concept for the prefabrication, since there would have been no corrosion with the traditional method of assembly, using wood underlay and wood mullions, or with some other types of material like "terne" roofing, made of a coated steel sheet. Having managed to hold on to the expensive copper in the face of HRH's cost-saving suggestions to the contrary, SOM really didn't want to have to give it up now because of the corrosion problem.

In June 1986 Schuster suggested that SOM take some expert advice on how to solve the corrosion problem, and they consulted an engineer who worked on the oil rigs in the Gulf of Mexico. The solution consisted of making sure that, at every point of contact over the entire roof, the different metals were kept apart, by a gasket or washer or some protective coating. This added to the complications of the fabrication process, because the coatings and gaskets sometimes had to be put in at the plant. It also meant that a 100 percent absence of corrosion wouldn't be guaranteed, since, with thousands of possible points of contact, it would be very unlikely that the installation would go so smoothly that not a single gasket or washer would be out of place. The belief was that, statistically, it was likely that the roof could be held in place even if a scattering of screws eventually worked themselves loose.

While some of these design details of the frame and copper were still being sorted out, HRH was putting the job out for bids. It sometimes happens in the construction business that only one contractor bids for a particular contract. It's clearly important in such a situation for the construction manager not to reveal that there is no competition for the contract; otherwise the contractor will set his prices at a luxuriously high level. In this instance, it transpired that the only company that could even attempt the job of making the copper roof was a firm called Wernher Dahnz in Canada. Their main plant and copper mill were in Toronto, and they had a local factory in New Jersey where some of the smaller elements of the roof could be made.

During the contract discussions, in February and March 1987, Dahnz had no idea whom else HRH were talking to, as Nusbaum explained:

They don't know, because the material they use is generic. You can get it anywhere. When you're bidding mechanical systems where there are certain specified materials—say, fans or motors of different sizes—the manufacturers soon learn who's bidding. They get calls from a local contractor saying, "I'm interested in bidding this job," and very soon the manufacturer of the material knows everybody who's bidding. But with this kind of work, they have no way of knowing. You can buy copper in any one of a thousand places. You can buy aluminum in thousands of places. So they have no ability to tell if they're competitive or not competitive.

Dahnz in Toronto would have to make several hundred copper panels two feet wide by twenty-six feet long, and an aluminum framework to which the panels would be bolted. The ribs of aluminum would then be covered by the standing seams, to be made separately at the Dahnz plant in New Jersey. Dahnz would supply 250,000 pounds of copper, at an agreed price of about $3.5 million. It was generally agreed that it would be the largest copper roof ever made, and the only copper roof that was to be self-supporting, instead of being laid on top of a wooden substrate.

One other element in the roof challenged Nusbaum's pioneering instincts: the small glazed pyramid right on top of the copper roof—what became known to everyone as "David's diamond." At least it was small in comparison with the rest of the building, although it was still forty-three feet high. Childs wanted a beacon to shine out from the very top of the building and pierce the night sky of Manhattan, and he and Bodnar had designed a triangular "space frame," as it was called, a tubular steel pyramid with panes of frosted glass in a diamond pattern around its four sides. Nusbaum was inspired to suggest a rather daring way for the diamond to be constructed and installed: "We were going to build the whole thing on the ground and then pick it up with a crane in one pick-up to the top. But the contractor felt he couldn't build in enough structural strength to handle the strain of the pick. That lost the fun, but I'm not sure I would have been in New York the day we were going to make the pick. I think I would have gone home."

Because of the difficulties, and the dangers, the diamond ended up being constructed like the roof, *in situ*, by taking all the elements, piece by piece, to the very top of the building.

It took the best part of a year to wrestle with the complex details of design and construction implicit in the simple and elegant roof drawings the architects produced in mid-1986. When the fabrication drawings were ready and Dahnz had had their input into how the pieces would fit together, SOM decided to carry out a "wind-and-weather" test on several panels of the roof. Since it was constructed like a curtain wall, it might as well be tested like one, in the same place—Miami, Florida.

The roof test was originally scheduled for the first week in November 1987, but as Dahnz started to put the components together they realized that it was much more complex than they had anticipated. Steel framework, aluminum and copper mullions, copper panels, screws, bolts—some made in Toronto, others in New Jersey—all had to fit together in three dimensions. There was the feeling in SOM that Dahnz might not be putting every last ounce of effort into making the structure as strong and stable as it should be. The architects felt that HRH and the roof contractors should recognize the need for people to walk on the support framework for repairs and maintenance, and they weren't at all sure whether that safety factor had been built in. The test date slipped from November toward January as it became apparent that the mockup for the test had been built at the wrong angle, eight degrees out of true.

In the second week of January 1988 New York shivered under snow and temperatures of twenty degrees Fahrenheit, and little was happening on site. It was too cold to pour concrete and too slippery to erect steel. But in the warmer Miami climate, the section of the copper roof was subjected to the buffeting of mock winds and rain. In a not-too-subtle prediction of how the test would go, one of the testing team turned up at the test site wearing a raincoat and carrying an umbrella. His prediction was fulfilled. The test was disastrous. Not only did the roof leak, because of some missing sealant, but it also showed signs of coming apart under the shaking it received from the wind test. It appeared that the vibrating of the panels and the mullions under the wind forced out the screws that were supposed to hold everything together.

On the one hand, it was another indication of the cussedness of complex structures that no one has ever made before, and the difficulties of predicting three-dimensional behavior from two-dimensional drawings. On the other, it did demonstrate the value of the mock-up tests carried out on the curtain wall and the roof. To use one of Nusbaum's favorite maxims: "Pioneers take the arrows." The roof section was taken apart after the first test and inspected for lessons about how to put it together again, and three months later, in April, a revised structure passed the test.

While the roof was being planned and tested, all the other work was continuing apace. The first copper was expected to arrive in September or October. Once the fabrication drawings were out of the way, SOM and HRH left Dahnz to it, keeping an eye on progress by sending an assistant superintendent, Peter Chorman, to Toronto from time to time. Other matters, large and small, needed Fonti's attention on site, and he just trusted that the roof would arrive in the fullness of time.

By September 1988 the project meetings had reached the stage where the main issues had long ago been resolved, and for a while the temperature was lower. The topic that generated the keenest discussion on Tuesday, September 6, concerned a little matter of about sixty light fixtures to be installed outside on the fortieth floor. With a flourish, Fonti plonked down one of the lights on the table before Schuster and the other participants and explained that, after installation, the lights needed to be aimed so as to pick out the parapet above them. This could not be done right away, and there was no means of access other than through the adjacent windows. Since those windows were theoretically unopenable, how was he to provide access? He was asking permission to leave the glass out of most of the windows on the fortieth floor until the lights could be aimed. This raised the whole issue of how access could be gained to the lights once the building was completed. Ed Narbutas tentatively suggested that the electricians use the window-washing platform, and Schuster left him in no doubt as to the likelihood that electricians would be found who would be happy to work their way around the fortieth floor of Worldwide Plaza on a swinging gantry. Fonti considered installing the windows and then smashing them in order to get at the lights, but this dramatic suggestion was rejected. In the end he was given permission to leave out some of the windows for the time being, until it was appropriate to aim the lights, but how the lights were to be maintained was left unresolved.

Also that week a guided tour of the building was organized for some Cravath employees, as part of the process of letting everyone in the company see where they would be moving. It was a sunny morning as a small knot of lawyers, secretaries, and accountants stood outside the oddly named La Femme Gaté snack bar on the corner of 49th Street and clustered around Ira Schuman, from the brokerage company that had drawn Cravath's attention to Worldwide. The group proceeded in a straggly line to the site office to acquire hardhats and a briefing about how to behave on a construction site, and then went to the hoist on the north side of the building. Construction hoists can be fairly hostile environments when you are not used to them. A rackety wire cage that shoots up several hundred feet with scrawled obscenities on the plywood walls is unfamiliar territory for prestigious Wall Street lawyers and their staff. The incongruity was heightened by high-heeled shoes and smart suits topped with uncomfortable hard hats as the group wandered around the cavernous innards of the office tower, trying to imagine where their offices would be and what they would look like. Fortunately, this particular group seemed fascinated by the experience—no one was at all put out by the seediness of the area they were moving to.

As the steel rose toward the forty-eighth floor, Fonti and Tony Raffiniello started to look in more detail at Nusbaum's method of installing the roof. Because of the decision to erect the copper panels from the inside, there would be no need to erect scaffolding all around the building at a height of seven hundred feet. They would use a crane to hoist the copper panels up to the framework for the roof—the tepee without its covering—and store them there. Then the roof contractor's men could attach the panels, one by one, to the framework.

It sounded simple and ingenious. It turned out to be neither.

As with several of the other technical problems in the building of Worldwide Plaza, it was difficult to unravel the complex weave of wrong decisions and miscommunication that contributed to the roof-assembly problem. But the problem can be stated fairly clearly. When it came time to assemble the roof, HRH discovered that the support structure did not provide a strong enough base to store the copper panels. Nor could it take the weight of a derrick to raise the panels from below. At this point the stories of the participants diverge. Dominic said:

> Artie has lived through other buildings where the roof area has been smaller and there's a lot of equipment that needed to go up there. Knowing this, he early on made a recommendation to Skidmore to design the roof level above the cooling towers—the 731-foot level—and the very top, just below the glass pyramid, so that we'd be able to bring up the copper. But what finally happened was that either someone forgot or someone ignored Artie's comments, and now we're faced with a structural-steel framing so light in capacity that I'm even told now that I have to reinforce the steel framing to land my cooling towers on top. I cannot even support plants and men working and walking. This has removed all kinds of flexibility for construction of the roof

and has added a lot of cost to the subcontractor. Now he has to hoist material by hand from the lower floor and install the pieces one by one as he's hoisting. You can't even store material up on that level.

The only way around the problem at this late stage, with the roof framework already fixed, was to reinforce the various floors with extra steel. Fonti was unable to persuade Schuster to agree to the extra cost: "We're talking about easily over $100,000 to reinforce something up there which could have been bought for nothing at the time of the contract. Artie's ideas and concepts were excellent, but unfortunately we do not have the structural system to make it work. So we're improvising now on the forty-seventh floor. I did get back to SOM and express very vividly my feelings. But at that time it was a question of whether to spend the $100,000 or trying to make the best of it, and obviously Jack Schuster and the owner are sick enough with the dollars on all the other changes. We don't want to aggravate the bad feelings even further."

As Ed Narbutas saw it, this problem was HRH's own fault:

As architects and engineers we designed the building for the finally built condition. But during the course of construction there are going to be times when you need to load things from the structure or bring in concrete trucks and so forth. Now, HRH sometimes came back and told us about where they planned to have heavier loads, where they're planning to have hoists, how they're going to tie back the crane to the structure, and so on. But they didn't think about the top of the building. Then all of a sudden they say, "Oh, my God, where do we put this stuff until we erect it?" Well, it's a fine time to tell us now.

Nusbaum was clearly disappointed that some of the savings that would have resulted from his scheme would now be dissipated: "The steel up there proved to be too weak to take it, and instead the copper will have to be hoisted by hand. That doesn't delay us. It just—I don't want to use the word 'just'—it will cost more money to raise them by hand than it might otherwise have cost if we raised them with a derrick, but it won't delay the project. But we won't be able to save the money that we could have saved if we had been able to put the panels on the roof framework."

As diplomatically as he could, Nusbaum made it clear that he felt the mistake lay with Fonti and Raffiniello. "Why wasn't the roof steel upgraded to take the weight? It should have been upgraded. I don't feel our guys input enough to the engineer to tell him how we intended to use it, and because of the failure to tell him how we intended to use it there was no rationale for the engineer to make the steel stronger. Why should he spend the extra money? Sometimes you have the miscommunication between the idea and the actual performance of the idea."

One of the things that strike you about a skyscraper under construction is the strange contrast between hectic activity in one area and total silence in others. In September 1988, at street level it was pandemonium: interior-stone contractors mingled with exterior-stone contractors, frantically trying to recapture time lost by the problem with the trusses; trucks arrived with the copper-roof components, to be lifted to the top of the building. On the O&M floors above the lobbies, concrete was being noisily chipped away from the floor—concrete that had been laid carefully a year before in the space that O&M now decided they wanted to use for an interior staircase. This highlighted a disadvantage of fast track—if the whole building had been designed before construction started, including O&M's interiors, the staircase could have been designed in, including the stronger steel beams and columns needed to support the weight and divert the loads from the rest of the building away from this weak spot. Above these floors all was silent. In the enclosed floors between twenty and thirty, those that would be occupied by Cravath and Polygram, it was possible to get a sense of what the building would be like inside when it was completed.

Here you could walk from a real elevator away from the core area toward glazed windows and imagine carpets, walls, water coolers, computers, and all in place as they would be in six months. But now you could hear a pin drop, with only the muffled roar of traffic six hundred feet below to remind you where you were.

Farther up the building, the bricklayers laid bricks on the fortieth floor, working their way around the building followed by caulkers and flashers. Transistor radios played, and there was the swish and clunk of brick and mortar. Then again silence on the six floors above the bricklayers. Large concreted floors spread out to the edges, where there was just sky and the New York skyline visible between the columns. Here there was no activity at all, and no noise apart from muffled sounds from the core of the building, where the elevator installers were working. The floors above forty-six were more active, under the light silver-colored "tepee." Teams of men were supervising the hoisting of the copper mullions and arranging them in piles. The larger components, like the huge circular dormer windows, had not yet arrived from Toronto, and so the roof construction proper could not start.

On the very top of the skyscraper, a dozen men were working on a platform that was to be the base of "David's diamond." For these men, the daily journey to work took them through several stages. Only one hoist remained that went to the highest floors: that on the southwest corner. The two hoists on the north side were being taken down, in preparation for tenants to move in without the irritation of construction workers whizzing past their windows every few minutes. The southwest hoist went up to the forty-eighth floor, where the bricks stopped. From there on up, as the roof sloped inward, there were no proper floors, just large spaces filled with machinery—cooling towers, elevator-lifting equipment, pipework for ventilation and steam. Buried in the center of this equipment was a staircase, surrounded by a block wall. The stairs rose to a height equivalent to a ten-story building, often in darkness and usually littered with rubble, cables, ladders, and blocks of concrete.

The top of the staircase opened onto the final concrete floor, which formed the base of the skylight.

After one of the hottest summers in years, early September 1988 was blessedly cool. On the first Tuesday in the month, the first members of the white space frame for "David's diamond" were being assembled on the very top of the building by workers from a company called Fisher Skylights. A strong white tubular pyramid with wide spacing between the members would form the support for a much lighter framework of aluminum and glass. The support framework was as near as you can get to a giant child's construction kit—four-meter-long poles with threaded ends and a collection of heavy white spheres with threaded holes, forming the nodes of the whole network.

There was a classical beauty about these components, particularly in the bright morning sunlight. In fact, so attractive were the nodes that several had gotten lost between the shipment's arrival on site and the pieces' arrival at the top of the building. It's difficult to think what they might be used for, since as paperweights they would make it very difficult to remove the paper from underneath.

As the men assembled the framework, they would from time to time consult a set of diagrams that showed which poles had to be screwed into which node. The starting point for the whole pyramid was a square base made up of horizontal tubes linked by nodes. It was important that this *should* be horizontal, since the connection angles and lengths of all the other members depended on it. Any slight irregularity in the base could be magnified as the rest of the structure was attached to it. The horizontality of the base depended in turn on the steel columns coming up from the floor below, on which each of the nodes rested.

Unfortunately, while the Fisher team was putting together the south edge of the square, they discovered that the top of the second column in from the east was half an inch lower than the tops of all the others. Even half an inch would have imparted an unac-

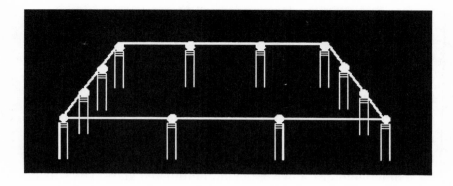

ceptable kink to the base and to the rest of the frame. This was one of those problems that could easily be solved in the field. They prepared a half-inch slice of aluminum, called a "shim," and covered it with plastic to avoid the problem of contact between two different metals. This was then placed in the gap to bring the base of the node up half an inch and enable the base to be accurately horizontal.

Between September and November the men worked their way up to the pinnacle of the white tubular pyramid and then began to

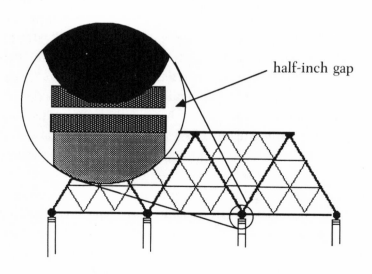

half-inch gap

install the aluminum framework with triangular apertures for the frosted glass that would eventually enclose the pyramid and diffuse the light from the beacon. From this viewpoint, the very highest point of the building, the views were spectacular. The workers could look right down on the residential tower, diminished to the size of a house from this near-vertical viewpoint, and the whole of Manhattan was the center of a bowl whose edges stretched to the horizon. A line-of-sight juxtaposition made the Empire State Building poke out of the top of the Marriott Hotel. From up here, on a day as clear as this, it was possible to see evidence all around of the frenetic pace of construction that still continued in New York. Within three or four blocks of Worldwide Plaza were seven or eight sites showing the familiar signs of rising steel festooned with orange safety netting, their highest floors swarming with concrete-pouring men who looked tiny from this height, hundreds of feet below the Worldwide Plaza roof but hundreds of feet above street level. Even over in the borough of Queens, the other side of the East River, a new Citicorp building was rising, as if the skyscrapers of Manhattan had begun to seed themselves across the water. And the sounds were a symphony that was characteristically New York. Pile-driving thumps and the rat-tat-tat of riveting hammers from other sites around produced multiple echoes off the many walls around them. The whoops of ambulances and police cars pierced the low, rumbling background from time to time. And there was the regular flutter of a helicopter going down the Hudson River or crossing Manhattan a few hundred feet directly above the building.

The four sides of the glass-and-aluminum frame were to be attached with brackets to the more solid white tubular frame that had gone up in September. In the Fisher plant on Long Island the frameworks had been laid out on the floor to check that all the pieces were the right length and in the right configuration. But the pyramid hadn't been erected at ground level, so the first real test of whether it would fit together in the size and configuration required was to take place seven hundred feet up. And it turned out that it *didn't* fit together as required, to the annoyance of Sylvan Phillips, leading the assembly team. Sylvan—or Butch, as he was called by his colleagues ("If you've got a name like Sylvan in the construction industry, you better change it fast")—was a short sturdy man swathed in several layers of jacket, sweater, and padded waistcoat. As he spoke, he worked away with a penknife at a small piece of metal needed to widen a joint by a quarter of an inch or so. He had covered the metal with plastic and was now cutting holes in the plastic to correspond with the holes in the aluminum. "Never get involved with a space frame," he said, as he described the problems they'd faced once they started to fit the pieces of the frame together. Back in September, when they had leveled the base of the pyramid with the half-inch shim, they expected the glass-and-aluminum frame to fit easily into place in the spaces between the white tubular struts. But it didn't. Putting it together according to the instructions led to the base sides' being three inches too short. "I *knew* they should have put it all up first at the plant," said Butch. "That way we wouldn't have discovered the mistake up here and had to deal with it on the spot." Although the individual sides of the frame had been laid out on the factory floor, Fisher had decided not to spend time and money on assembling the whole forty-three-foot-high structure to see if it worked in three dimensions.

It is reassuring to find that even highly trained craftsmen can make the mistakes that come naturally to home do-it-yourself unenthusiasts. And it is comforting to know that they use the same fudging to get it right. There was no question of sending the whole thing back to the factory to be made correctly. It had taken enough to get the pieces up there, and anyway what the eye doesn't see . . . So Butch and his colleagues fashioned some three-inch-long pieces of aluminum to splice into the middle of each of the base sides, making them the right length. With the virtue of consistency, the people who had gotten the length wrong had also gotten the height wrong. It was only by a fraction of an inch, but that was enough to make it impossible to fix the outer frame to the tubular support, and more patching had to be done.

Like the steel erectors, the roofmen had a knack of passing tools to each other across several meters of thin air without once dropping them. When a man threw a wrench from the floor of the space frame to his colleague halfway up, it followed a trajectory that slowed and brought it to a halt within inches of his colleague's hand.

A minor fracas occurred in mid-morning, when one of the HRH superintendents made his way to the roof to tell them that some scaffolding they were using had to be down that night because it was obstructing the area around the top of the stairs where a block wall was to be built tomorrow. No one in the roof team knew anything about it, nor did their immediate superior, a man from Fisher who had come to the top with a roll of plans. "Nobody talks to anybody" was the familiar grumble. The HRH man didn't care who took down the scaffolding so long as it was done. The roof team didn't care who did it so long as it wasn't they who had to work through the night to move it. The Fisher man went off grumbling and scratching his head to decide who would actually take it down.

But this news made them change the order of the tasks they were planning to perform. Butch decided to put up the metal cap to the whole building, a four-sided aluminum pyramid with a square door in each side. The four sides were propped up together and would have to be manhandled one by one up the scaffolding to the five-foot-square platform. Each side would eventually be fitted with a red aircraft light, fixed to the little square door. If any of the bulbs went, someone would have to climb up the inside of the building, open the door, and unscrew the bulb. Where the points of the four sides met there would be a lightning conductor. This would be the highest point of the building.

As the very top point was installed, the copper roof below was woefully spattered with gaps and holes. Deliveries were behind schedule, and the complications of getting the material up to the top were also slowing things down. From the skylight platform there was a vertiginous view at an angle down one side of the copper pyramid. Slowly a man was winching a huge copper circle, inch by inch, up the roof. Another man followed the circle up, freeing it from any projection that obstructed it.

By December 1988 the roof was still way behind schedule. Fonti had pretty much given up on it: there seemed little he could do to speed up the installation process, and he knew that the delays didn't really affect the habitability of the building: "Whether it's completed in the next two months or in 1990, it doesn't really matter, from that point of view." Then, sometime around Christmas, while work continued on the forty-sixth and forty-seventh floors, a problem was revealed that seemed to have nothing to do with Dahnz or with the men installing the roof, a problem that led to endless bickering among HRH, SOM, and the owners and added yet another unnecessary amount to the costs of the building.

As part of the rethinking of the top of the building in the early design phase, when equipment was being moved up into the roof space and releasing more floor area for tenants, Childs had suggested bringing the copper of the roof cascading down over the forty-sixth and forty-seventh floors. The idea was to achieve a kind of sawtooth effect, whereby copper from the roof above was interspersed with brick coming up from the floors below, creating a surrounding for the windows. This meant that some of the block backing for the walls would be covered with copper panels instead of brick. This led Narbutas and his team to issue one set of drawings to the masons to plan and execute the masonry work, and another set to Dahnz to make the copper panels.

In December, when the copper panels arrived to be fitted on top of the block walls, it became apparent that there was a mismatch. For some reason, on the forty-sixth floor some masonry piers that separated pairs of windows had been built four inches farther out than they should have been. There were four such piers on each side of the building, all of which were in the wrong position.

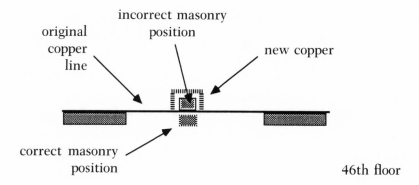

incorrect masonry
position

original
copper
line

new copper

correct masonry
position

46th floor

If they were left as they were, new copper would have to be fabricated to project out of the wall where it was meant to be flush.

As if that wasn't bad enough, on the forty-seventh floor there was another error. This time, instead of a mistake in the outward direction, there was an error in the lateral position of the block walls. Each of a series of wall sections between the windows had been built about two inches to the left of where it should have been. This meant that some of the fabricated panels were too narrow and others too wide.

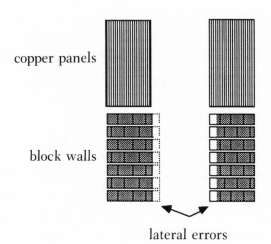

copper panels

block walls

lateral errors

47th floor

Peter Chorman had spent a great deal of time batting back and forth between New York and Toronto, making sure that the copper was being made according to the shop drawings. He had also kept an eye on the progress of the masonry on the top floors. But the possibility that the copper was being fabricated to one set of drawings and the masonry laid to another had never crossed his mind. Ironically, it was the need for enclosing the tenant space in a hurry that had led to laying the blocks some time before the copper came up to the roof, as Chorman explained: "We adjusted the system to put the copper in last because we decided that we would want enclosure first. Especially with the winter coming on, we decided that we'd deal with the block windows and then put the copper in last. So that's how the system was designed."

Chorman is tall, bearded, and soft-spoken. Even in the extreme provocation of this situation, his natural reserve made it seem as if somebody had stuck a stamp on a letter upside down rather than totally fouled up the construction of large areas of wall all around two floors of the building: "Well, you handle dozens and dozens of problems every day. And this is just more costly than some others. There are other mistakes that do occur that run into much more dollars, and there are many that happen all day long that don't run into dollars at all. What's the cost of modifying the two floors? A ball-park figure is about $100,000, somewhere in that region."

Chorman would spend a lot of time during the early weeks of 1989 helping to sort out how the mistake had happened. There was fertile scope for the inquiries: "It could be anybody involved from SOM in the design to HRH as construction managers, to the masonry people, to the copper people, to the window people. And any of the staff in between. So you have many, many hands." It could, of course, even be Chorman's mistake.

Once again Schuster was faced with the unpleasant task of approving a huge unnecessary bill, and he didn't even have the satisfaction of writing "FU SOM, FU HRH, FU Dahnz"—or FU anyone else. Fonti, a wry observer of the events, had a lot of sympathy for him. Whoever turned out to be to blame, it certainly wasn't Schuster or Zeckendorf who had built the masonry walls in the wrong position.

Understandably, it was the steel, the walls, and the roof that provided the challenges in the construction of Worldwide Plaza. The interior work was just like an endlessly repeated version of the office space in smaller commercial buildings, and, in any case, of little concern to the partnership, whose task was over when they delivered a shell to the tenants, a hollow space for them to dress up in their own image with their own team of architects, construction managers, and subcontractors. The air conditioning, power supplies, heating, and other piped-in facilities were just more powerful versions of standard technology. But there was one aspect of the interior of the building that was a major consequence of the skyscraper's size and bulk—the elevators. Indeed, the invention of the passenger elevator, with its safety features to prevent death by plummeting, was in part responsible for the development of buildings above six or seven stories in height.

The world of elevatoring has its own terminology and preoccupations. "Vertical transportation" is a major industry, with Westinghouse and Otis in the United States currently being overtaken by Japanese companies. And since Mr. Otis invented the safety passenger elevator in 1853, the art of elevatoring a building has come a long way. Worldwide Plaza would have elevators that would be able to make decisions about the most efficient way to get as many people as possible to their floors, based on the number and location of the button presses. It would have elevators that would behave differently in the mornings from how they behaved at lunchtime, and differently again in the evening, taking account of people's likely destinations, in and out of the building during morning and evening, up and down to the cafeteria at lunchtime.

Kevin Huntington is a partner in Jenkins and Huntington, a firm of elevator consultants who advised SOM and the Zeckendorf group on how the building should be "elevatored." He is a man of irrepressible good humor and an unflagging tendency to crack jokes: "I think everyone would agree that the ultimate elevator system would be if each tenant in the building had his own private elevator. He would take it up in the morning, and whenever he wanted to go anyplace it would be waiting for him where he last left it. That turns out to be impractical just because of the cost and the effect on the building—there wouldn't be much building left, just a few windows and a bunch of elevators, which sounds good

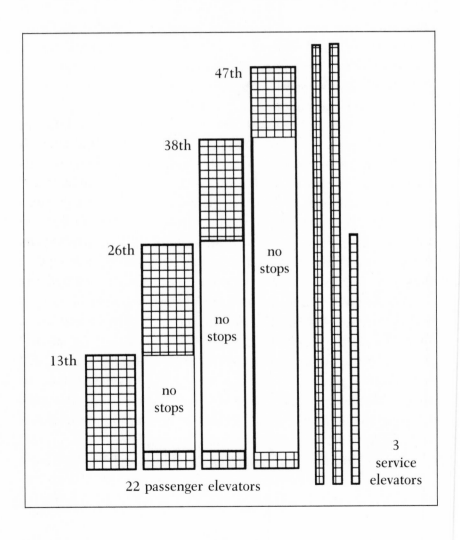

to an elevator consultant but probably somewhat distasteful to an owner."

Elevator consultants come between the owner of the building and the manufacturer of the equipment. They are paid to design the best system for the building and then help to find the company to make the equipment. Huntington's company uses computer models of the likely behavior of people in a building, based on what sort of people they are, what hours they will be working, when they take their lunch break, and so on. In seeking the best system for dealing with the several thousand people who would work in World-wide Plaza, they decided to treat the skyscraper as two separate buildings, with a top half and a bottom half, because the main tenants occupied those spaces and would have no need to visit each other.

But Huntington also had to accommodate the fact that the use of the elevators would change over a period. O&M and Cravath both had options on floors of the building that they would not occupy right away. Those ten- or fifteen-year-option floors would be leased to other tenants until the period was up, so there had to be a built-in capacity for the elevators to serve a different pattern of floors in ten or fifteen years. Armed with a number of characteristics of the building and the people in it, Huntington devised the computer program to analyze their needs: "The average person in a building like this will occupy about two hundred average net usable square feet. We also know that somewhere between 9 and 15 percent of the total number of people in the building will lock up the elevator transportation during the peak five-minute periods in the morning and at lunchtime. So we build this in the computer model and then we try different elevator systems. We try the effect of different-sized cars, large cars, small cars, fast cars. We try different numbers of cars, a lot of them or fewer."

Textbooks of elevatoring provide helpful advice about how many people should be accommodated in an elevator of a certain size. "An average person will require about 3 square feet of floor area to be comfortable . . . [although] at office building quitting time, and if passengers know each other, densities of 1.5 square feet have been observed."*

In discussions with HRH, Huntington also had to decide on an appropriate maximum waiting time to build in. If there were too few elevators, or if they were too small, waiting times in the rush hours could become a major source of irritation to the occupants. And people have gotten so used to fast and efficient elevators that they become irritated after seconds, in Huntington's experience:

> We think that in the morning in a good building you should have to wait an average time of less than twenty-five seconds for an elevator to come. This is a good-class building. If other buildings had a waiting time of fifty seconds, then you'd look great at forty, but in midtown Manhattan a twenty-five-second waiting time puts you right up in the very top. At lunch people are slightly more tolerant—perhaps 10 or 20 percent more tolerant—and then maybe we're looking at a thirty-second waiting time. We're also looking for a low total trip time. Maybe it takes you a minute or less from the time you walk into the elevator lobby until you get to your destination. If we satisfy these requirements you're going to be a pretty happy tenant, and the owner will get a return on his investment that makes it all worthwhile.

By the time Huntington had arrived at the correct configuration, he had tried forty or fifty different arrangements. When he had some clear ideas about the number of elevators, how many banks, which elevators would stop at which floors, and so on, he drew up the bidding documents for Arnie Kriegel at HRH to send out to the various companies that might be interested in bidding for the job.

Although a Japanese company was interested in the contract,

---

* George Strakosch, *Vertical Transportation*, 2nd edition. Wiley-Interscience, 1983.

the American company, Westinghouse, managed to get the job, with a budget of about $11 million. They dealt with all the "vertical-transportation" needs of the building, including twenty-two passenger elevators, three service elevators, several escalators to take people from the ground floor to elevator lobbies on the second floor, and even a huge truck elevator, to carry delivery trucks from 50th Street to the basement.

Work on the elevators started as soon as the core of the building was completed to the top. For a year or more, elevator technicians installed the rails that would guide the cars up and down the building, making sure that they were smooth and vertical. The elevator motors were lifted in by crane at the various levels where they were needed, and lay there, wrapped up to protect them from the elements, until the building enclosed them. The actual traction of the elevators is achieved very simply. Steel cables attached at one end to the elevator car and at the other to a counterweight are wound around grooves in a three-to-four-foot-diameter drum. The grooves grip the cable, which is under high tension from the weight of the elevator and the counterweight, and a motor provides enough turning force to raise or lower the elevator. Since the counterweight weighs about the same as the elevator, and pulls on the cable in the opposite direction, a comparatively small amount of force from the motor will turn the drum and raise or lower the elevator.

People often worry about the safety aspects of this particular method of travel, and elevators have to undergo a stringent series of safety tests before the building can be licensed for occupation, although Huntington believes that nowadays little can go seriously wrong. "Traveling by elevator is ten times safer than climbing the stairs," he says.

On Worldwide Plaza, each of the twenty-five elevators was put through its paces in front of safety inspectors. One test simulates a situation where the elevator accelerates down the shaft until it is traveling faster than its permitted speed. When this happens, a braking device consisting of jaws underneath the elevator reaches out and grabs the guide rails, bringing the elevator to a halt. If this device should fail, there are buffers at the base of the shaft that are meant to take the brunt of the falling elevator and slow it down at a deceleration of not more than one G, a bearable force for a group of terrified passengers. The buffers are tested with a full load (of weights rather than passengers) and with a simulated failure of the braking device. Huntington is reassuring about the likelihood, and consequences, of such a dramatic failure of the safety system. "In fact," he says, "if something like that *did* happen, far from crashing to the ground the elevator would probably go up, because the counterweight is heavier than the car." On Worldwide Plaza, all the elevators in each section of the building—low-rise, mid-rise, and high-rise—had to pass the tests before anyone was allowed to occupy the premises.

What with the delays in delivery and installation and the mistakes on the forty-sixth and forty-seventh floors, the final piece of the copper roof wasn't installed until June 1989, by which time offices twenty floors below were already occupied. But from the outside, by February of that year it was possible to get a reasonable impression of what Childs and Bodnar had intended. The two of them took a trip up the building on a bitingly cold day, clambering their way up to the "diamond" and stepping out through a gap in the aluminum frame to look at the view. "You know," said Childs, "there's a whole other scale to the the city from up here—it's a kind of reverse image. The dirt goes away and you don't see the mess." They looked down at the copper and up at the skylight. "What's remarkable," said Childs, "is that people are always surprised that it looks exactly like what we thought it was going to be. There really are no surprises. I mean, the techniques of drawings are so well defined that it turns out right on the mark."

There seemed a need for some kind of gesture and, silently, David Childs and Jim Bodnar shook hands.

The roof was the glory of the Worldwide Plaza tower. And yet, of the whole building, it was the most difficult part to see close up.

As a pedestrian on Eighth Avenue, you could see the granite and pre-cast façades, the intricate brick shapes and the recessed windows all the way up. But if you looked straight up, your eye stopped at the white brick parapets six hundred feet above street level; beyond appeared the sky. Only by walking backward a block or two could you begin to see the roof. And its full height, and the balance between the several different elements that gave it its character, assumed their correct proportions only when you could see the building as a whole, somewhere about Fifth Avenue or the Avenue of the Americas (Sixth Avenue), half a mile away. And from that distance even the largest decorative elements of the copper roof seemed to lose their impact.

"You have to exaggerate what's on the top in order for it to look proportionately correct from down below," Childs explained, but he admitted that maybe he hadn't exaggerated things enough. "We spent a lot of time in our nice warm drafting room designing the details of the battens, the strips that come down in the wall, and the reveals around the dormers. And those are largely lost when you get down below. The proportion changes." He thought for a moment. "Maybe if we thought about it again we would make those round dormers three inches larger. . . ." Then he pulled himself up: "But it's—no, it's—it's 99.9 percent on the mark. It looks like what we thought it was going to."

16

FINISHING OFF

I n the first schedule drawn up for Worldwide Plaza, the skyscraper was due to be completed in November 1988, with O&M moving in comfortably by Christmas. But November came and went with the roof unfinished, gaps in the stone, and the fire-alarm system still incomplete. A December date, a January date, and a February date also disappeared. The successive postponements, caused by the O&M changes, the steel delays, the lintel-setting problem, the later delivery of brick, the Hunts Point setbacks, added up to a four- or five-month delay in the schedule and about $15 million over the original budget.

In spite of the litany of problems, however, the project was not in bad shape. Four months late on a two-year construction job was not outrageous. A 10 percent overspend was undesirable but not disastrous. As in any complex project, everyone keeps something up his sleeve for a rainy day. The developer would *like* the ground floors to be enclosed by the date promised to the tenant but doesn't believe they will be; the construction manager would *like* the stonework to be finished on time but doesn't believe it will be; the stone contractor may even believe he can install the stone on time, although he too is aware of the possibility of delay. Sometimes, as with the bricks, the construction manager will ask for an earlier date than he needs, to allow for the expected delay; sometimes the developer gives one date to the construction manager and talks in terms of a later one with tenants or banks.

So when, toward the end of 1988, there was a general tone of depression among most of the major participants in Worldwide Plaza, it wasn't necessary to take this at face value. Each of them had been under daily pressure, and in that situation it is difficult to see beyond the pile of immediate, still-unachieved tasks to a vision of a breathing, living, working building standing on the site as an accepted part of Manhattan's new West Side.

Unlike a bridge or a tunnel, or even a book or a television series, there was no one date when the whole project would be completed. The building's "rite of passage" into maturity would be long and drawn-out. Some tenants would move into the lower half while the higher floors were still incomplete. The southwest hoist tower would still be there while people were working in their offices. Even the roof could be unfinished while the rest of the building was functioning. The construction of Worldwide Plaza had been a series of deadlines for individual contractors without any true deadline for the building as a whole. But in November the HRH team were working flat out to achieve two targets.

Dominic Fonti still seemed to bear the world's burdens on his shoulders, squeezed in the nutcracker between all the contractors he was trying to orchestrate and cajole and his bosses at HRH, who were in turn under pressure from the owners. In September Artie Nusbaum left HRH and, in Fonti's words, "a big chunk of HRH left with him." Nusbaum had hired Fonti in the first place, and had always had a high opinion of him.

During 1988 Nusbaum had been doing less and less "hands-on" work with existing projects and was expected to become more and more involved with selling the company's services to developers with new projects. He didn't see himself as a salesman and wasn't even sure if he was any good at it. "I guess selling is like hunting big game, which I never did, but to take an owner you've never met before and convince him that you're the best of the best and the organization you have is the greatest thing since sliced bread is a real ego trip, but unfortunately it's not like design development, something you do all day long."

It was also likely that Zeckendorf's dissatisfaction with HRH's handling of Worldwide Plaza had some effect on Nusbaum's standing within the company. When things started to go wrong with the stone and other aspects of the schedule, a new HRH manager was assigned to the project over Nusbaum's protégé, Fonti. Nusbaum wanted to be his own boss for a few years and had no time for company politics—he wanted to build buildings, and the further he moved from that, the less happy he was. And it was happiness he was after. Things had to be fun to keep his interest. He had tried teaching for a while, as a possible post-retirement activity, since he enjoyed training construction engineers on the job. But teaching in a college was no fun: "It seemed barren because you never saw the rewards. Most of the students are there because it's a required course. And I couldn't handle them walking in and falling asleep before I spoke. If they were to fall asleep *after* I spoke I could have said, 'Well, shame on me—it was my fault.' "

Nusbaum moved to a small construction management company that managed projects costing tens of millions of dollars rather than hundreds of millions. His work on Worldwide Plaza had dwindled by that stage and he was out of touch with most of the current issues. But every morning, from his apartment in New Jersey, he could look out over a magnificent view of the Manhattan skyline and see among the familiar outlines the pointed top of Worldwide Plaza as the finishing touches were put to "David's diamond." His feelings at leaving were mixed: he could still almost taste the excitement lingering from the time when he and the architects had sat down with pristine drawings and worked out how they would build the skyscraper; but there was also his unshakable feeling that HRH had been treated unfairly by the Zeckendorf Company over problems that were not HRH's fault.

In the early years of a project like Worldwide Plaza, the most important triangular relationship is among developer, architect, and construction manager. As the project grows, the architect's role diminishes and the tenants come into the picture. By late 1988 most of the construction hold-ups and overruns were a pain in the neck because of the effect they might have on the tenants—their moving-in dates, their ability to carry out their own interior work, the terms of their leases. Two targets had to be met and the Zeckendorf Company was under continual pressure from the tenants to meet them.

The first target was the enclosure of all the floors that O&M would occupy. In the early days of the project, first April and then July were the target dates for handing over the O&M floors so they could get on with their own interior construction work. But it was clear that the complexities of the design and the uncertainties of Hunts Point were combining to slow appreciably the enclosure of the lower floors. There seemed to be little anyone could do to control or accelerate the work. The stone contractors were the worst offenders: pieces were being set by hand in the field that should have been fixed to the trusses in New Jersey; there were still gaps in odd places, with no one being very sure why; the masons had problems with the interface between the steel columns and the steel-and-stone trusses. There was one incident in which the Hunts

Point masons made what might have seemed to them to be a minor adjustment to the building that had the architects and construction managers almost apoplectic with rage. While the masons were trying to install the granite-faced columns that had been fabricated in Italy, they had cut a piece out of one of the steel beams that seemed to be in the way. Dick Rowe and Gary Steficek had made careful calculations of all the forces at that point in the building, and had no desire to see the steel structure weakened by being mutilated to make the decorative granite column fit. Fortunately, one of HRH's managers noticed it in time to consult SOM about it, and Rowe was able to devise an adjustment to the steel that reinforced the weakened section. By that stage in the job, there was an air of resignation about the whole stone contract, and such incidents seemed hardly worth making a fuss about. Hunts Point were clearly doing the work in their own way and at their own pace.

The day eventually arrived when enough of the lower floors had been completed to hand them over to O&M. On November 20, Fonti was visibly relieved when he was able to announce that HRH had just completed floors three to fifteen. But he was still anxious. He had had some problems in persuading O&M that the floors were in a fit state for them to take over. At a point when Fonti was happy with them, O&M kept finding details that they felt needed further work before they would take over the floors. As Fonti pointed out, O&M could well have had other motives than just a desire to see the floors in tip-top condition. They might, for example, have needed more rent-free time to complete their own interior work:

> The tenant is using whatever way he has to try to avoid paying rent. Obviously I would do the same thing if I was in his shoes. So he looks at his lease with a fine-tooth comb and he says, "OK, if this is not ready I don't have to pay rent," so he writes a nasty letter to Zeckendorf saying, "I'm not paying rent if this is not done." Even though we may overcome the first obstacle and the

second obstacle, there will always be obstacles until the tenant sees that there's no more loopholes in the lease, and then he'll have to start paying rent. But the tenant's intent is to delay paying rent as much as possible, no matter what, until he's ready to move in. And so this is a game that's being played, not only at our level here in construction, but it's being played also in the lease negotiations between Zeckendorf and O&M, and this filters down to us and it causes a lot of aggravation.

In addition to worries about O&M, Fonti was starting to have to deal with extra work generated by the other major tenant, Cravath, Swaine and Moore. Because they had come in much later than O&M, they had less scope for making changes in the building to suit their own needs, since the design was completed and construction of their floors well advanced. But that didn't prevent them from wanting to make some important changes which, at some inconvenience, Zeckendorf and HRH had to accommodate. Every tenant has needs peculiar to itself. As a law firm, Cravath used a vast amount of paper, which they would need to store in a fully mechanized filing system ten or twelve feet high. The combined weight of the filing system and the paper it would eventually contain was so great that Cravath's architects had decided they wanted to make a major modification to the building to keep the filing floor and its contents from putting an unnecessary strain on the floors below it. To Fonti the proposed changes threatened to play havoc with the rest of the work going on at the time, and the design seemed to provide more strengthening than was necessary:

> Essentially Cravath is making substantial changes to the mechanical systems and to the structure, which, fortunately or unfortunately—depending on which side of the coin you look at— they're doing themselves. The columns have enough "overdesign" capacity to be able to sustain these additional loadings, but the concrete floor, which is only five and a half inches thick at its maximum, and the beams are not designed for any of that at

all. So they are doubling up on beams, they are adding cover plates on the bottom, and they're changing connections. All this will increase the capacity of the floor loading from fifty pounds a square foot to two hundred pounds a square foot. You could build a garage up there—you could park buses and trucks on that floor. By the time they finish, it will cost them a million dollars.

The second target to be reached before the tenants could move in was to satisfy the necessary conditions for a permit from the city of New York called a TCO, a Temporary Certificate of Occupancy. This certified that the building complied with certain safety standards required for occupancy, and in particular that it had a suitable fire-alarm system. The skyscraper would need three TCOs—one for the core and shell of the building, certifying that the elevators and main safety systems worked, and two more for the low-rise and high-rise office areas of the building, corresponding roughly to the floors to be occupied by O&M and Cravath. Before the TCO could be issued, the building had to undergo a series of inspections by the Fire Department and other authorities. In November HRH thought they would be ready for the low-rise TCO inspection sometime in December. It would make a nice Christmas present for everyone.

The core and shell passed most of their tests by the third week in December, and the one remaining inspection, by the Fire Department, was scheduled for December 22. Fonti was quietly confident about passing the test, but to make sure, the system was thoroughly checked the day before. The test was in two stages: a civilian inspector would approve all the appropriate devices—sprinkler, alarm, systems, and so on—and then a uniformed officer would make the final inspection to give his stamp of approval.

Early on the morning of December 22, a knot of HRH people stood disconsolately around the computer console at the concierge's desk in the O&M lobby. This was the nerve center for the fire-alarm system. The unbelievable had happened: during the night, due to a thaw in the weather, a burst water pipe higher up in the building had released a torrent of water cascading down through various electrical systems, including the wiring for the fire alarms. Now there were huge gaps on the monitor screen, showing areas of the building where the alarms were out of action.

The inspection was clearly off. It would be weeks before the system could be fixed and a new inspection arranged, unless someone could plead with the Fire Department for special treatment. In a state of incredulity at their bad luck, HRH cleared up the effects of the burst pipe and managed to fix a further series of fire-safety inspections, but not until late January or early February.

The delays in the TCO dominated Fonti's life. He was under continual pressure from Jack Schuster to sort it out. And the reason Schuster was worried was that it promised to complicate even further the already complex discussions over when O&M should start paying rent—$300,000 a week.

At meeting after meeting Schuster seemed obsessed with every nuance of the TCO question and desperate for the certificate to be issued, because it would be one less stick for O&M to beat *him* with at the meetings where they discussed when rent should start. Fonti had seen the identical situation before: "In every building in the city of New York the landlord thinks he is going to get rent on an empty floor, and it has never happened." It was clear that what was going on was, in the elegant terminology that several people used to describe it, "a pissing contest." And no quarter was being given by either side.

At last the TCO inspector turned up for the retest, on the last weekend in January. All the devices passed, but as the inspector left he said there were four or five points he would put in his letter that needed seeing to. The "letter of defect," as it is called, actually listed thirty-two. The inspector was being very rigid, Fonti said, but it was clearly within his rights to do so. Calls to the Fire Department succeeded only in bringing forward another date for inspection, mid-February, by which time HRH had to have corrected most of the faults. They wrung a concession that, if there were only four or five minor matters still to be attended to after that inspection, they would be given a conditional TCO without having to undergo a full inspection yet again.

Wearily, the HRH people went through the hoops once more for the civilian inspector in mid-February, keeping their fingers crossed. The complex fire-alarm and sprinkler systems of the first seventeen floors of the building still had four things wrong with them, but this was few enough to pass the test, provided they were fixed quickly. The inspector returned to his office and wrote his letter of approval. HRH sent a messenger around to the office to collect it and take it to the uniformed division of the New York Fire Department. Calls were made to pressure the Fire Department to send an officer as soon as possible—in days, not weeks—and he arrived on February 20. He wrote his letter confirming the civilian inspector's verdict, and someone from HRH took this by hand to the Building Department and sat there all day, nursing the process through in an attempt to achieve in a day what usually takes a week or more. Late on the afternoon of February 27 Fonti held in his hand a three-page document headed "The City of New York: Certificate of Occupancy (Temporary) No. 93708." The building was described by its address, the unfamiliar-sounding "825 Eighth Avenue," and the document certified that the core and mechanical-equipment rooms from the subcellar to the seventeenth floor "conformed substantially to the requirements of all applicable laws, rules and regulations."

Meanwhile, Fonti's attention was taken up with the fact that five different construction companies were now working on the site, where before there had been only one, HRH. By March 1989 the entire building was sufficiently complete for each of the tenants to be carrying out interior work, and each tenant had chosen a different construction company. Nevertheless, Fonti still had to supervise the whole building in certain ways—cleaning, for example, and facilities for the workers. "In terms of volume of dollars and numbers of men," he said, "HRH is the smallest, and yet I'm carrying the entire job!"

In early March parts of the O&M space were at last beginning to look like the mock-up that had been built downtown. The ninth, tenth, and eleventh floors were nearest completion. Most rooms had doors—tall, of light varnished wood, with frames containing the Ogilvy red stripe made of enameled aluminum. Some rooms already had carpets, marked by the dusty footprints of the plasterers, joiners, and electricians, who were still working. The office carpets were a desaturated browny-maroon color with the characteristic thin red stripe across the threshold, where they met the bright blood-red corridor carpets.

There was an unexpected air of desertion about the place. Clearly much remained to be done, yet the only signs of activity were the odd knot of men clustering around plans, a solitary joiner working on a door, and two electricians up ladders, wiring a light fixture. José Lambert descended his staircase, accompanied by an O&M photographer, taking some in-house stills. They arrived at the O&M lobby and Lambert surveyed this all-important space, pleased that it was now stripped of its "post-modern garbage." "If it's too bare, I can at least add to it, but if it had been as palatial as it was originally designed, there would have been nothing I could have done about it." At that moment it looked like the interior of an Egyptian tomb that had been robbed of all its contents: smooth stone walls rising to a plaster strip five or six feet deep running around beneath the ceiling. Lambert mused about the possibility of painting a fresco on the white plaster, like a similar element in the Palio restaurant in New York, an SOM project. It would probably need something to create a more welcoming impression. Even the stone had little pattern or texture, although the marble floor might change the overall feel when its protective covering was peeled off.

However, on the whole, Lambert was reasonably pleased with

what he saw and hazarded a guess that O&M would start moving in in the first week of May. But for offices that were meant to be six weeks away from occupation, the floors were in a remarkably unprepared state. What was striking at this stage were the inevitable blemishes that had occurred as the work progressed, blemishes that became more noticeable as the work moved nearer completion. In just one corner of one floor there were dents and gashes in the plasterboard, incomplete woodwork, dirty carpets, and other entirely inevitable results of that kind of building work that was still going on. If you think of that multiplied over the rest of that floor, and again over seventeen floors, it was difficult to see how even that one task of "making good" would be completed in time. But this was typical of the whole building. Looking back over two years, there had been times when it just "seemed to happen" without major human intervention, other than these knots of men who stood around in far corners of the floors. Clearly part of this impression was due to the inability of an observer to see more than one small corner of the building at any one time.

For some time now the HRH site office had been inside the skyscraper. The noise level and the comings and goings were now noticeably less than in previous months. With no steelwork, no bricklaying, no concrete pouring, and only a little stonework going on, there were far fewer trades on the job for Fonti and his team to worry about. Not that that meant there weren't problems: one of the foremen, called Scotty, poked his head around Fonti's door and said, "I don't know if you know this—I don't know if you *want* to know this—but both hoists are stuck. The cable broke. There's a hundred guys standing on the pavement waiting to go up." Fonti's face showed disbelief. "How can one broken cable stop both hoists?" "I don't know," said Scotty. "I think I'll go home now," said Fonti.

Although the tenants' contractors were there in greater numbers than HRH and their subcontractors, HRH work was still going on at the top and bottom of the building. On the north side the hoists that had lifted men and materials up the building had now gone. The Hunts Point masons were filling in the gaps in the arcade that could not be filled while the hoists were still in place, and also laying stone on the floor. They were occasionally supervised by their foreman through the window of the bar of the Seeda II restaurant, which conveniently overlooked the area of operations.

At the other extreme, the roof, work was clearly not going very well. There were still large gaps in the copper cladding, whose installation had been painfully slow over the preceding months. For a combination of reasons, the job was now four months behind schedule: the aftereffects of the mistake over the positioning of the masonry on the forty-sixth and forty-seventh floors; the need to refabricate the pieces of copper back at the Dahnz plant in Toronto, which delayed the enclosure of those floors. There was still no sign of a resolution of the dispute over whose fault it was. Here Nusbaum's "search for the guilty" was slightly more justifiable than the frequently aimless attempts of the various parties to prove themselves whiter than white. A clear mistake *had* been made by someone, and the cost had to be paid by someone. What's more, as Fonti was charitable enough to point out emphatically, "The owner *didn't do anything at all* to cause this to happen." Schuster was therefore quite entitled to say, "We're not paying for this—sort it out between yourselves, HRH and SOM." As far as SOM were concerned, they had done all that was required of them to produce clear, coordinated drawings which HRH should have been able to act on in the field. As far as HRH were concerned, there were enough ambiguities in the drawings to make it understandable why the various components had been built four inches out of position on one floor and two inches too wide on another. It seemed as though the issue might end up being left to the courts to decide, unless one of the parties eventually decided to accept responsibility.

Fonti was at pains to point out that none of these delays on the roof was affecting the rest of the building. The copper was strictly ornamental. Until it was completed, however, HRH had to comply with a set of overhead working regulations, designed to protect the public from falling debris: protective netting had to be kept in place, and sidewalk bridging had to stay in place over the heads of pedestrians. All this meant continuing expense.

It was four or five months since the brick had been completed up to the forty-fifth floor, and the building was clearly a part of the community even before it had been occupied. You couldn't miss it as you walked around Clinton; you couldn't miss it anywhere in New York if you were a reader of the *New York Times*, since regular full-page ads showed Worldwide Plaza from the air and exhorted companies and individuals to rent office space or buy apartments.

The building was now at the stage where it was possible to see the results of the architects' intentions. It was big—no doubt about it. In fact, it was huge. It was so big that by standing near the building you could appreciate little of the overall design. Foreshortening, parallax, and perspective had conspired to emphasize less significant aspects of the building and minimize the impact of important design features. The building as experienced bore only a tenuous relationship with the shapes and lines that had become familiar to all those in the project from the drawings and renderings and models.

What dominated Eighth Avenue was the brick, acres and acres of it, so it seemed. The sharp points on the brick ridges that ran all the way up the building emphasized any slight deviation from the vertical, at least for an architect who stood directly beneath the ridge and looked straight up, a method of appreciating the design that few members of the public are likely to have adopted. David Childs was privately unhappy about the workmanship, although other members of the team found it perfectly acceptable. Indeed, Schuster felt that it was "the best brick job done in years in New York." He had already made it clear, however, that he felt the amount of detailed brickwork in the building—the number of different shapes, and how they were combined—was an unnecessary addition to the cost and, as far as the corbeling, the ridges, was concerned, "as useless as tits on a bull."

At ground level, Mary Dunn peered at the daily bustle on site. Her opposition to the building remained implacable, and had been given concrete, or ceramic, expression by four rather fearsome clay masks that appeared on the exterior wall of her apartment during the previous summer: a collective work of art called *Gargoyles to Scare Developers*. She had spotted them at a local craft fair and remarked on how appropriate they would be on 49th Street. The artist had overheard her and donated them to the cause. Now the four faces stared balefully across the street at the granite and pre-cast façade of the lower floors, trying their hardest to scare developers—and obviously failing.

Around the corner on Ninth Avenue, the first apartments to be renovated as part of the Zeckendorf gift to the community had been completed. They consisted of a one- and a two-bedroom unit on each floor. The one-bedroom apartment comprised a living room entered through the front door, a small kitchen off the living room, a bathroom, and a bedroom. Strangely, the living room had eleven electrical outlets. The living room and bedroom had windows overlooking Ninth Avenue, and the white-painted walls reflected the daylight into the interior of the apartment. At the back of the building was a two-bedroom apartment. It was like entering a tomb. Because the apartment itself was long and thin, most of it stretched into the interior of the building, so that very little light reached the kitchen and living room. Even the bedrooms at the back, with windows facing the rear of another building, seemed gloomy, and it was clear that these apartments would need the lights on all day.

The question was how to judge the merit of these apartments. They were hardly in the same class as the residential accommodations rising on the Worldwide Plaza site, although the room sizes weren't too bad. Compared, however, with the sort of accommodations that had been in these houses before they were converted, the renovations were a major improvement. Even so, for people like the three ladies of 49th Street, secure for decades in their railroad flats, with fading wallpaper and layers of memories, it could seem a sacrifice to move to these white, soulless tombs on Ninth Avenue.

In fact, as Worldwide Plaza loomed over the brownstones on 49th Street, two of the ladies who had been so suspicious of Zeckendorf's attempts to shift them accepted the terms of the contract that was "only a piece of paper" and agreed to move out of their apartments so that the renovation could begin. Together with two or three other tenants, however, Bella—the third member of the group of friends—decided not to change her mind. The lady who had had a new bathroom put in fifty years ago decided to remain where she was.

Schuster felt that there was not much else he could do. Tenants staying put would make it impossible to renovate the apartments as promised to the city as part of the overall package for the project. This in turn could mean that the city would not allow the developers to sell a dozen or so of the apartments on the Worldwide Plaza site. He spoke about his frustration with the situation:

> The tenants know that—they think they're sitting in a catbird seat because no one can throw them out, no city agency will dispossess them. We're trying to use the carrot and the stick, but it hasn't worked. The word I hear is that they're looking for a substantial sum of money to make them move, and it'll never happen. I think we're going to end up by going back to the city and throwing up our hands and saying we'll do a lot of things, including giving them the dollar value of the work we were going to do, and they can use it any way you like, just don't hold us hostage on something that we had no control over and you, New York City, can't help us with.

In early 1989 it looked as though O&M would move into Worldwide Plaza in February; then March; then April looked more likely. Finally, Monday, May 15, was set for the first of four weekly moving dates, department by department. The first to move in were those with offices on the eighth floor. At least that was the designation on the elevator buttons and the floor indicator in the lobby. But the eighth floor was nine stories above street level. The steel erectors, the concrete pourers, and the interior decorators had all called it the ninth during the previous two years. Rumors abounded about this oddity. When Fonti was asked to explain, he revealed a further anomaly: the building had forty-seven occupiable floors but the top floor was number forty-nine. This is how he explained it:

> Physically you've got forty-seven floors. Ogilvy and Mather decided that they don't like the number three for some reason, and they don't like the number thirteen for another reason. So they decided that the third floor will become the fourth floor and the thirteenth floor will become the fourteenth floor. So, when you go into the elevator cab and you push the button, if you want to go to the thirteenth floor you push fourteen. OK? And for the past couple of weeks, when we switched from the exterior hoist to the interior hoist, it caused a lot of confusion. You tell someone, "I'll meet you on the thirty-ninth floor, and they go to the thirty-ninth floor. In reality the thirty-ninth floor is the forty-first floor in the elevator cab. And if you just happen to be below the thirteenth floor and you say, "I'll meet you on the eighth floor," it's not the tenth floor, but it's the ninth floor, because there's only one number added to it. So that has caused a little bit of confusion to all the workers.

Over the weekend, moving vans lined up outside the O&M lobby, with its floor and concierge desk still shrouded in cardboard. Boxes of files, chairs, and tables labeled with room numbers, favorite pictures, all were unloaded and carted up to an eighth floor that seemed unprepared for the influx. Windows were dirty, some walls were still covered with protective paper, some of the low dividing walls lacked their distinctive wood-and-metal coping. Dozens of moving men and maintenance men mingled and crossed paths as the belongings of each office occupant were delivered to offices that were believed to be the right ones.

Most of the untidiness on the O&M floors was actually cosmetic. The offices were remarkably well organized, considering the general state of affairs in the rest of the building. If there had ever been a vision of entering a pristine building, scoured of any evidence of construction, that vision had long disappeared in the face of a hoist still climbing halfway up one corner and large gaps in the stonework around the base. The O&M people did hope, however, that at least their side of the building, including the lobby, would have the polish and dignity expected of a major advertising agency. But everywhere they looked, there was evidence of delay and poor or nonexistent finishes.

This long-awaited move should have been the major preoccupation of the company: moving into a building that they partly owned, and bringing together departments and teams that had had to work separately in the past. The O&M newsletter had prepared people for the move with every possible type of assistance. Senior executives came to the new offices for lessons in how to use the telephone. However, that weekend the management of the company suddenly found themselves with something else to think about. A takeover bid had been launched by the British advertising and public-relations group WPP. They had offered more than $890 million for the Ogilvy Group, and there was a serious possibility that the shareholders might accept it. In spite of the characterization of WPP's chairman as a megalomaniac by David Ogilvy, the seventy-eight-year-old founder of O&M, on that May weekend it looked as though the company might find itself part of an even larger combine, which would be the world's largest after Saatchi and Saatchi.

So the expected euphoria of the Monday move-in was muted, as red trestle tables were laid out in the lobby and senior figures in the company mingled to greet the first arrivals to work in the new offices. An O&M tradition marked the occasion: a kilted bagpiper skirling traditional Scottish melodies in honor of David Ogilvy. But this tradition only emphasized some of the doubts in the minds of the O&M managers in the lobby. How much longer would the company be an Ogilvy company, with all that that meant? Jules Fein, one of the directors, standing with other senior managers in the lobby, expressed his anxieties:

> There's a stockholders' meeting tomorrow and a board meeting this afternoon, and it's taken away quite a bit of the euphoria about a new beginning. Because that takes on different connotations in today's circumstances. We don't even know the terms of the takeover, but in the worst case the symbolism of moving here to someone else's company is very unsettling. It sets up a different kind of environment for this move, because everyone has other distractions on their mind—coming into a new building when you don't know whether you have a new company or not.

At about 8:00 A.M. the first O&M employees arrived to inhabit their new offices. Advertising people are traditionally divided into two groups: "creatives" and "suits." The suits arrived first, account executives with the job of dealing with relations between O&M and their many clients. They always arrived earlier than the creatives, who were allowed to drift in when the mood took them, clearly unable to give much thought to punctuality while their minds were busy creating jingles, slogans, and logos. Managers and secretaries stepped hesitantly over crouching stonemasons and around slabs of granite still in the crates in which they had been shipped from Italy. They eased their way through a swinging door jammed half open and went up to the tables to give their names and receive a pass to their offices and a red Ogilvy and Mather canvas bag. O&M had a tradition of giving presents to staff. One recent Christmas every employee had been given a unisex nightshirt, emblazoned with the O&M logo.

At nine-forty-five one of the creatives, Alice Henry Whitmore, a bubbly New Yorker, crossed Eighth Avenue toward the entrance of the building. A senior copywriter for O&M, Alice had missed out on the guided tour of the premises and was about to see her new office for the first time, if she could find it. She was wearing a studded black leather jacket—she claimed it was protective coloration for the new and terrifying district of Clinton, and quoted with mock horror film titles on the Adonis Theater that she had passed on her way to work. There was some confusion about whether her magnetic security ID card would be found under "Henry" or "Whitmore," but once it was found, she went into one of the two operating copper-doored elevators and pressed the button marked "8" to go to the ninth floor.

Her new office was near the southwest corner of the building, overlooking the roofs of the brownstones on 49th Street. When Alice eventually found it she seemed reasonably happy, on first impression:

> Well, it's very clean. And it has a nice big window. I'm real happy about that. I hadn't seen it before, and it's like when people tell you that a movie's really funny and then you go and see the movie and it wasn't as funny as you thought. Well, everybody said the offices were really little, so I thought they were going to be even littler. So I'm surprised it's not as little as I thought. And everything's here. Except I have an ugly wastebasket. Oh well, do something about that. It looks like a hospital wastebasket, doesn't it? I hope it's not, like, one David Ogilvy picked out or something.

As the morning wore on, the eighth floor became remarkably like any working advertising agency, as phones rang, meetings were held, and creatively dressed people strolled from office to office seeing where their friends and bosses had settled in. Even the growing "punch list" of nonilluminating lights, nonfunctioning computers, and other irritating teething problems didn't dampen the general enthusiasm for being at last in Worldwide Plaza.

But, however happy the staff were with their offices, O&M senior management lost no time in telling the Zeckendorf Company what they thought of the state of the exterior of the building. Bill Zeckendorf was provoked to make a rare visit to the site, where he discovered for himself how bad things were:

> I was very surprised that the sidewalk was not in on 49th Street, and I found out really for the first time the severity of the problem on the West Lobby. The question is, what can I really do? We've got the construction manager and all these people looking after it. In a case like that, had I known about the interior stonework I would have started worrying about it much earlier and pushing much earlier. But there are always a couple of trades that do fall behind. As you know, the person doing the stone on the outside of the building is now residing in the penitentiary down in Atlanta. I got hold of the president of HRH and the chairman of HRH, and it was a problem that had been festering for a long time, and I think people tend to feel they can solve those problems without me getting too deeply involved in it. But, having seen it for myself, I got very concerned and started pushing the panic buttons.

One of those buttons rang the phone on Schuster's desk, and Schuster had an uncomfortable few minutes:

> Did Bill raise hell? Yes, he was very unhappy. I'm not making excuses. The fact is, the top of the house is not 100 percent complete, but it will be shortly. The sidewalk on Eighth Avenue is an eyesore, but it wasn't poured before this because we had some leaks in the subway. The reason? A combination. A little bit of poor workmanship, a little bit of poor design. It's been corrected and we're getting ready to pour that sidewalk out. And once you start pouring sidewalk, it dresses up the site a little bit. Right now it looks very raw. The stone that's to be used on the coping and on the north face is sitting on the street. This coming weekend we should be planting trees, which will help a little bit on the Plaza.

Shortly before midnight on the same day, the Ogilvy Group agreed to be acquired by the British WPP Group, for $864 million, and as a minor consequence seventeen floors of Worldwide Plaza were set to pass into British hands.

Within two weeks of O&M's move into Worldwide Plaza, the most important financial event in the life of the building occurred: the permanent mortgage was signed. Until then the construction costs of the building had been covered by loans from a group of banks and financial institutions, at a high rate of interest and for a short period, reflecting the risk being taken. Now that the leasing had gone well and the building was to all intents and purposes complete, the partners could refinance on far better terms. A permanent mortgage was arranged with the Deutscher Bank Capital Corporation for $533 million dollars. The owners would use this to pay back the high-interest construction loan, thus reducing their interest payments for the next ten or fifteen years. As rental income rose year by year, the burden of the loan would fall, relatively speaking, to a point where it could be converted into an equity share in the building for the lender, or a new loan arranged.

Looking back at the project, it was clear that the experience had taught each of the main participants a lot about how he would do things differently in the future. Fonti made an understandable plea for more people on the job: "So what if somebody sits there for half a day doing nothing? I think it's a worthwhile investment, because when the opportunity comes to follow something through and you haven't got enough people, that particular item may cost the developer $50,000, $100,000—much more than the guy's salary, who makes $35,000 or $40,000."

Ed Narbutas had learned a lot about the job of technical coordinator: "You have to be more of a gadfly. You have to demand things early enough and keep repeating it and repeating it and repeating it. It's like the squeaky wheel gets oiled. I think I should have done that more. It was gone so fast and so many things were happening and you think that at least the other side was paying attention, but they've got their own point of view."

Jack Schuster had no doubt that many of the problems had their roots in the very early events of design and pre-construction:

> If I had the authority from a developer I would be more realistic on the budget and more selective on the contractors, and I would be tougher on the design team, particularly in some of their aesthetic treatments, only so that the developer knew what he was getting into before we went into construction. Too often, construction managers and contractors, in order not to antagonize architects, from whom they get their bread and their butter, will not budget the folderol on a building properly. And then, when the time comes to build the blasted thing, you find that not only the costs have gone out of sight, but you get hurt very badly with the time. I would hope that when I saw a budget that was presented to Bill by a construction manager that I believed was unrealistic, I would have the backbone to tell him that I believe that the budget was not correct. During the course of construction I then would find myself with less wear and tear on my ulcer, without having to try to justify numbers that weren't realistic from day one.

Each of these people and thousands of others gave a significant slice of their lives to Worldwide Plaza. Looking back at the project in May 1989, Terry Soderberg put those lives into a context that the others might not have shared, but that had the ring of truth about it:

> What it comes down to is pieces of paper, numbers, internal rate of return, the net present value, discounted cash flows—that's what it's all about. It's not about whether or not the construction manager has gone from here to there or vice versa. It's not about the architect becoming the rock star of architecture in New York, as they're calling David Childs. What it's about is dollars and

cents. Sure, we want to build quality and we want to build something that is going to be a statement, but if you can't do that and still have it financed well and make a return, then why are we doing it? I'm not doing it for the fun of it, I don't think Bill is, I don't think the other partners are. And I don't think the lenders who are lending are doing it for the fun of it, so we can cut through all the philosophical stuff of the architects, the planners, the sociological statements that some of the partners have made about we're saving or we're enhancing the community life and all sorts of stuff. That's all true, but what it boils down to is whether it's financeable and whether there is a return to the partnership.

With that wordy epitaph for Worldwide Plaza, Terry Soderberg hit on the one objective criterion that can be used to judge a building—financial success. By that criterion it was a major success right away. Whether it *would* transform the neighborhood, confirm David Childs's superstar status, give O&M and Cravath employees the perfect working environment, and shine out as a beacon of New York construction would take years, if not decades, to confirm.

INDEX